T0248108

How to Survive the School Year

How to Survive the School Year

An essential guide for stressed-out grown-ups

LEE PARKINSON
AND ADAM PARKINSON
Illustrated by Tim Sadler

HarperCollins*Publishers*

HarperCollins*Publishers*
1 London Bridge Street
London SE1 9GF

www.harpercollins.co.uk

HarperCollins*Publishers*
Macken House, 39/40 Mayor Street Upper
Dublin 1, D01 C9W8, Ireland

First published by HarperCollins*Publishers* 2024

10 9 8 7 6 5 4 3 2 1

A catalogue record of this book is available from the British Library

ISBN 978-0-00-865767-3

Printed and bound in the UK using 100% renewable electricity at CPI Group (UK) Ltd

This book contains FSC™ certified paper and other controlled sources to ensure responsible forest management.

For more information visit: www.harpercollins.co.uk/green

To Nana Maureen, we miss you every single day; your legendary appearances on the podcast will live on forever, and we hope we've done you proud once again.

Not too bad!

Contents

Welcome everyone to the [illegible] from the two of us. For new readers [illegible] from Manchester who work [illegible] you're joining us on our [illegible] sometimes not-so-typical) [illegible]

If you're someone that has read [illegible] our [illegible] then it's down to [illegible] complete our trilogy!

I like to think of this book as [illegible] other classic movie series, like [illegible] Grease, The Lord of the Rings [illegible] Toy Story 3.

I'm [illegible] I'm welling up just [illegible]

Welcome everyone to the third literary instalment from the Two Mr Ps. For new readers, we're two podcasting brothers from Manchester who work in education, and we're so glad you are joining us on our jovial journey through a typical (and sometimes not-so-typical) school year.

If you are someone that has read our previous books or listened to our podcast, then it's down to you that we have managed to complete our trilogy!

I like to think of this book as the triumphant third instalment of a classic movie series, like *Indiana Jones and the Last Crusade*, *The Lord of the Rings: The Return of the King* and *Toy Story 3*.

Toy Story 3**... I'm welling up just thinking about them holding hands before they enter the incinerator...**

Erm... Spoiler alert!

Sorry.

Definitely like those (well, hopefully), and a lot less like *Jurassic Park III*, *Blade: Trinity* and *Home Alone 3*. I mean, how the hell can you make a *Home Alone* film without Macaulay Culkin?

Let's be honest, we're more likely to be bringing something closer to *Jackass 3* to the table, but it's all the readers' fault for making our first two books *Sunday Times* bestsellers. (I still have to pinch myself when I type that.)

Seriously, though, thank you so much to everyone who has supported us through listening to the podcast, joining us for our live tour and buying our books. We are so grateful for all your support. And what better way to thank everyone than by producing another book of silly classroom observations, crazy tales and a few more fart jokes – even though I think we exhausted pretty much every euphemism for guffing in the last book. If you think we could have possibly run out of the ridiculously humorous tales from primary school life already, think again! You'll be delighted to hear that we are still receiving literally hundreds of crazy anecdotes submitted for our podcast, every week. Many of the best ones will feature in the next 300+ pages of this book. We love the stories we receive and many of those included will have been reworded to protect the innocent (and not so innocent). As with both previous books, we have definitely used some artistic licence to make them as entertaining as we can and certainly embellished certain aspects in order to hopefully make you laugh (and sometimes cringe) as much as possible.

For new readers, I promise that you don't need to have read our previous two books (please feel free to check them out, though) to hopefully enjoy this one. For those already accustomed to our brand of humour, there'll be plenty of what people enjoyed before, but with this one we'd like to take you on a little journey; a voyage through the school year that can be appreciated by teachers AND parents alike. We like to think that with *Put a Wet Paper Towel on It* we pulled back the curtain on primary teaching and *This Is Your Own Time You're Wasting* was a cavalcade of confessions, calamities and clangers. However, this new book aims to be a silly school-year survival companion, in which we'll give insights on how NOT to get overwhelmed by the demands of primary school life – that come from both sides of the school gates. There are only so many hours in a day, and remembering that next Thursday has swimming, spellings, singing club and a PTA-sponsored bounce can be quite a challenge for anyone.

Make no mistake, **this is not a parenting guide**.

Neither Adam nor I would dream of telling others how to bring up their younglings. I'm far from a perfect parent (ask my kids). It doesn't matter how many likes I have on social media, how much engagement a video I've made receives or, indeed, the number of podcast listens we get, Lily, Charlie and Harry think I'm a knobhead. It brings you down to Earth with a huge bang when your now-secondary-school-aged triplets won't follow you on TikTok through embarrassment. It was all fun and games in primary, but as soon as they started secondary school, the difference in them – the self-awareness – has been an eye-opener. Having my children tell me to stop making videos online because their peers follow me and wind them up about it certainly hits deep. I decide to fight fire with fire and say I don't make videos for 13-year-old kids and what 13-year-old follows a teacher on social media? Losers! And the less said about Adam's parenting skills, the better.

Harsh but fair!

We have tried to make this book as universal as possible because school life is such a universal topic. We want teachers, school staff and parents to be able to pick up this book and immediately find something they can relate to. We're both parents ourselves so we have the perspective of seeing when things go right (which is less fun to write about), but we share way more in this book about things going comically wrong, as you will soon find out.

If you are a parent reading this book because you genuinely want to know how to survive the school year, then we hope there'll be plenty in here that helps, but there's no denying that the majority of the content will be funny observations and anecdotes about what to avoid during school life, and certainly how not to make the same mistakes twice. We totally get that teachers and parents have legitimate anxieties about all manner of school-related things, and while this book won't solve every problem, we aim to humanise the process and let you know that it's not just you feeling a certain way. Our fantastic readers and listeners will always send us plenty of hilarious stories they'd like us to share, but we are increasingly being contacted by nervous parents and school staff asking for advice as well. I even did a phone-in for parents on *This Morning* about their back-to-school worries and general concerns. One example being where some of my friends have asked me in the past, how do I know if the school is the right one for my child? Should I be reading the Ofsted reports?

Uh oh, readers... first mention of Ofsted!

My answer would be, no, you can't trust an Ofsted report because they are inconsistent as hell and, quite often, dependent on which inspectors are present and what bloody mood they are in.

During a weekend away with my wife to York, we were sitting in a café, having a coffee, when a couple next to us were talking about which school they wanted to send their child to. I'm a nosy bugger and as I was eavesdropping, they started discussing the school in question's Ofsted report. My wife gave me the death stare as if to say, 'Don't you dare!', but I couldn't help myself and had to interrupt them and explain how unreliable Ofsted reports can be.

My advice to parents like that would be to visit the school, speak to other like-minded parents (not the fusspots we will discuss later) and get a judgement from those who have been working with the school for more than two days if you can. You won't get a feel for a school based upon a few sheets of paper with one-word gradings at the end.

With the current framework from Ofsted, there is a big focus on interviewing children about their learning, and this contributes massively to the outcome of an inspection. Ask any parent or teacher and they will tell you that to base a judgement on what a child says is ludicrous. We know these children, and they are the most unreliable sources of information on the planet.

Easy, big fella! Save your ranting for the chapter near the end about modern education. You can grind your axe about the Big O later on. Although if Ofsted were to speak to some of the crazy crew that I get to work with, I'm not sure I'd still have a job.

Now, I love working with children. We like to refer to them as the most hilarious unintentional comedians in the world, which is great as long as your livelihood isn't on the line based on what they say. One story shared with us featured a child who mistook an Ofsted inspector with a bright suit, funky glasses and a terrible tan for... David Dickinson.

Oh no, what a Bobby Dazzler!

I mean, we've all got hilarious stories of the little misconceptions or misunderstandings children have throughout this book, but for the new readers, here is a little taster of things to come:

Teachers will experience such masterful insights from their younglings such as, 'Miss, did you know I was born on my birthday?'

That's a fairly jolly little comment to giggle at, but they aren't all as polite as that.

A Reception child was tapping a teacher's arm for about 30 seconds, and after finally turning around she was greeted with '... too late, I just pissed myself!'

I mean, how are you supposed to keep a straight face after that?

Year 4 were asked to name something that hibernates, and a child raised his hand to say, 'Michael Bublé!'

A Year 1 child learning about Remembrance Day was asked what a soldier is and he pointed out that you dip them into your eggs.

A pupil with a rash was asked one afternoon if he'd had chickenpox. Thinking the teacher was talking about his lunch he replied, '... no, fish fingers!'

With regular responses like these, teachers and school staff will wonder if the children are actual comedy geniuses.

Teacher: What are we working on in maths?
Child: Squared paper!?

Teacher: What is half of twenty?
Child: Twe?

Teacher: Yesterday was Tuesday so today is...?
Child: Threesday!?

An innocent pupil proudly told her teacher that the Bible is made up of two testicles. The old testicle and the new testicle.

Sticking with the Bible, one five-year-old thought the first two people in the Creation story were... 'Alan and Steve!'

It isn't just primary children with hilarious misconceptions; one Year 9 thought pioneering scientist Marie Curie was the person that sang 'All I Want for Christmas Is You'.

And finally, something that Adam would've potentially done as a child. A teacher asked the class if they knew what 'ordering numbers' meant, to which one lad piped up thinking they were ringing up to get a Chinese takeaway!

What's 25 + 79? Chicken chow mein and egg-fried rice!

Regular readers will be pleased to hear that, much like the previous books, we'll still be sharing plenty of funny classroom capers, talking about the modern school system and looking with rose-tinted spectacles at our own childhood school days.

Here's a shocking fact that someone brought to my attention... In *Back to the Future*, Marty McFly travels back in time 30 years to the 1950s, so if we were to travel back 30 years from now, Oasis and Blur would be starting their rivalry, WWE was still WWF (not the animal charity), and the Backstreet Boys were still, well, BOYS! Man, I feel old. But modern parents have no intention of feeling old and we're not ready to be considered the fuddy-duddies we thought our parents were, back in the day. Modern teaching and modern parenting have plenty in common – from the very good to the very bad, plus everything in between. More on this later.

In this book we're going to take you on a journey from harvest festivals in the autumn term, all the way through to sports day in the final summer term, exploring the trials, tribulations and tomfoolery that we all encounter along the way.

So, whether you are a parent, an educator, or someone that just likes silly stories about going to school, there'll be plenty in here for you to enjoy.

And a quick reminder (or a Who's Who for the uninitiated): if you see this font, you are witnessing the masterful musings of Adam (The Other Mr P).

Doubt it! If you see anything written in this font (and yes, it will also be significantly more coherent), then it is Lee **(Mr P)** speaking.

Enjoy!

Is there a worse feeling as a child (or a teacher, for that matter) than spotting the 'Back to School' promotions in the aisles at a supermarket IN JULY?!!

Obviously, there are worse feelings, but this is a gut punch that you can never be ready for. What kind of sick human being decided to pop Back-to-School stationery in a prominent position at the front of the store? Probably someone with kids they are already fed up with, I reckon. Seriously, it might only be the second week of the summer holidays, and mums and dads are sick to the back teeth of their little darlings spilling drinks, leaving crumbs on the sofa and getting Lego stuck up their noses. The general consensus about having kids is surely that it's so much easier to only have the little blighters for a few hours before and after school, before they (hopefully) go to bed and you can get your house up straight before the carnage starts again in eight hours' time. Sending them back to school in early September is a joyous event for many parents, and celebrating the moment with a G and T is borderline mandatory!

Not all parents will be feeling quite so chipper, because for many, it's a time of great anxiousness as their children find their feet with a new teacher. If a child had Miss Honey last year and now has Miss Trunchbull, it's a huge change for them and not uncommon for there to be tears on the way to school (from big people and the smaller ones). Similar anxieties exist for teachers and school staff. If you're a teacher and you were teaching a very competent Year 5 class that regularly aced times tables and spelling tests in July, only to move to a Year 1 class where little Ryan puts his own faecal matter in the glue sticks, then you're bound to get a little overwhelmed at the start of term. Equally, if staffing requirements dictate, you could have a Year 2 teacher moving up the other corridor and taking on a Year 6 class that includes 75 per cent of the little munchkins that they thought they had trained how to behave four years ago, only to be shocked at how some of them have not only regressed, but they are also 5 foot 8 and puberty is on the horizon! I guess it all depends on whether the headteacher likes that member of staff or not. 😬

But going back to school is something that children (and teachers) must do every year until they are of school-leaver age, or, in the case of those doing the educating... retirement.

To the parents reading this, ask yourself this question: how organised are you at this time? I'm giving people a binary choice with this one. If you have school-aged children, you can be one of two different types of people. The options are pretty much polar opposites, but you must choose one of the following. So, dear readers, which one are you?

A) Absolutely organised, with machine-level efficiency. The super-organised one who purchases everything they'll need for the following school year, WAAAYYY before the late August/September rush.

B) Like me.

If you are option A, I congratulate you, but I will go on record to say, I don't like you, because you're making the rest of us look bad. From my perspective, there is nothing like heading out on the hunt for all the things your child needs just a matter of days before the school year starts, which includes:

- Stationery (as in notebooks, pencils, erasers, sharpeners, pens and rulers)
- Backpack
- Lunch box
- Water bottle
- Uniform (more on that shortly)
- PE pumps
- Outdoor PE trainers
- Art supplies (such as crayons, coloured pencils, markers, sketchbooks and paintbrushes)

The last pieces of equipment on this list aren't *required*, but if you're in the supermarket with your child dragging along behind you, you can bet they fancy grabbing plenty of those items, too – just for fun.

There will, of course, be parents who are in denial about the rapidly approaching start of term. These are the sort that don't care, because they've still got two weeks in the Costa del Sol to enjoy before the start of September, and they are not ready yet to look at a maths set (with a protractor that'll hardly ever be used) and scented highlighters as part of a 2-for-1 deal. As far as they are concerned, they can all B.O.G.O.F.! (See what I did there?)

B.O.G.O.F.?

Buy One Get One Free. And while I'm on that subject, letting me near 2-for-1 deals is dangerous and probably why they don't offer them at my local KFC. I'd be permanently at the Colonel's mercy.

I doubt many families would entertain the idea of spending money in August on boneless bargain buckets, as they know it's going to cost them an arm and a leg...

A wing and a thigh?

Stop drooling over the keyboard again, Adam!

It'll cost an arm and a leg to get their kids kitted out for September, and this means the unenviable task of not only going shopping for new uniform/school shoes/PE kit, but the realisation that it's going to require one of the family to sell some vital organs on the black market in order to pay for it. As for the cost of school-branded sweatshirts... yikes!

Even worse is the fact that the children (especially our friend from the last book, the Muck Magnet) will potentially ruin their brand-new jumper with a mystery substance before the first week is over.

Don't get me started on the child that starts week one of the autumn term with three brand-new sweatshirts and by the end of that week has lost all of them. They will also come home, inexplicably, with someone else's. This will result in one of the parents posting on the class Facebook group, asking if anyone's child has accidentally taken little Rupert's jumper home instead of theirs.

Rupert? What school have you been teaching at to meet a 'Rupert'? Is there also a Cuthbert? A Tarquin?

Alright, bad example. Let's go with Alfie instead. The point is, once the children go back to school, you know there's a decent chance they won't be returning with all the uniform you sent them in with – at least, not theirs...

School shoes are another headache. You could not pay me enough money to work in a Clarks shoe shop in the final two weeks of August; it's absolute bedlam.

I can speak from experience on this, as I did in fact work in a Clarks shoe shop in my first ever job. Being the eldest, as soon as I finished my last GCSE exam my dad forced me to get a job, or I would otherwise be cut off. Adam, on the other hand, finally managed to get a job when he was 28 – only kidding, 18 – and that was after I had begged my manager at Next (where I was working at the time) to let him work a temporary position over Christmas.

When I got my job at Clarks, all was well for the first couple of weeks until I got trained on measuring machines for children. Little did I know that the next month would be absolute chaos working the back-to-school season. I can concur it was bedlam. I still have sleepless nights about that month of August 2001.

Many parents will ask themselves, why the hell did my child decide to grow their feet an extra few centimetres in the space of four weeks? How inconsiderate of them! And you know full well that they want the light-up shoes, but you also know that as soon as the first rainfall of September hits, they'll be covered in so much mud that it'd be impossible to see the lights anyway.

Shoes with gimmicks aren't anything new, though. During the mid- to late 1980s you could get glow-in-the-dark shoes for the lads, and for the young ladies there were shoes with magic keys in the soles. There was nothing stopping the boys having the keys and the girls having shoes with neon stitching, but very few that I know of tended to stray from the gender-specific footwear of the time.

Something 90s kids will remember is that certain brands were an absolute MUST for starting secondary school. Dragging your parents around looking for Dr. Martens that just about fitted the school's footwear requirements could lead to a few arguments. Then once the child had gone through that phase, there was suddenly the demand to upgrade to a pair of Kickers, which looked very cool but were impossible to play football in because they were pretty much moccasins! Try curling a free kick into the top corner with those on! Lionel Messi probably could, I guess, but I am not sure Jake in Year 8 could manage it.

Once your child is all kitted out for the new school year and you have had to cancel the aforementioned trip to the Costa del Sol to bloody pay for everything, it's time to discover the holiday homework you had never heard anything about until a day before they go back. Again, what kind of monster sets this stuff? It usually reads something like this:

'We hope you have a wonderful six weeks off school, and in that time we'd like you to complete a diary/create a sculpture/collect seashells for a collage/paint a masterpiece/write a poem/provide evidence that you've read 25 books/create an eco-brick, etc., in order to start our project next term.'

And you know you're going to learn about this when there's zero time to actually do any of these activities to a standard that looks passable. The child will get worked up because they don't want to upset their new teacher, and you're getting stressed out because Millie and Poppy's parents have already posted their child's creations on Facebook for you to be envious of. In fact, that's where you learned about the homework in the first place, because your child decided to turn the letter that came home at the end of term into a paper aeroplane or a fortune teller.

Will the new teacher take any notice of their new children's efforts? Probably not, but they were told to set that summer homework challenge to tick a parental engagement box just in case the Ofsted crew pop in for a little visit early on in the first term.

Another key issue for school staff at this time of year that will impact parents is any last-minute changes. Parents will think they've got everything in order and the children have adequate uniform (labelled), PE kit (labelled) and lunchbox/ water bottle (labelled, but probably going to wear off by October). Don't be lulled into a false sense of security, because after the school has its first INSET day(s) of the year, a guest speaker may have introduced a new initiative and the staff have agreed (or more likely the headteacher has decreed) that...

... every third Wednesday, the children will have to dress up as a historical figure, or bring waterproofs for the mud kitchen, or be given 50p as there's a cake sale to raise money for the Year 6 trip to the Isle of Wight. And no sooner have the PE days been announced, there are outside visitors from the local rugby club that are offering each class about 15 minutes' worth of coaching, but only for three weeks before the communal swimming pool arrives, and also the school

need volunteers to walk to another school for a drama performance about internet safety...

And... breathe!

Alright, that's an exaggeration, and the learning opportunities the children may experience will usually be fantastic, but if you've just about managed to get your sh*t together and then you're bombarded with 400 SchoolPing or Seesaw messages, I think it's perfectly acceptable to go a little bit crazy.

The start of term is hard for everyone, and some schools will run a 'Meet the Teacher' session in the first week, where they invite in parents and set out expectations for homework and behaviour, then put trips and events on parents' radars so that they know what may be coming up. It's polite and appreciated to give parents fair warning about these things so that they can budget for them, and also look at any potential clashes in the family calendar.

These meetings are usually quite a positive affair, but it also allows parents to decide whether they think their child's teacher is a b*tch or a d*ickhead; sizing them up to see if they are going to take good care of their little cherub or whether they will be on the receiving end of a sh*ttergram within the first week because they didn't know on what days spellings were.

Sadly, the parents that probably could do with the information on display during the Meet the Teacher sessions will almost always not be present, and there's zero chance they will be downloading the PowerPoint slides or PDF featuring all the details that have been shared. People have busy lives, but you know that some parents either forget these things, can't be arsed or they already dislike the teacher. This is because that teacher wouldn't let an older sibling be Mary in the school nativity five years before, and these people still hold grudges! Their little darling being relegated to Shepherd No. 5 was clearly a slap in the face for that parent.

I mentioned INSET days (In Service Training days) briefly earlier, but there is one thing that's absolutely guaranteed on the first day back after the summer break: one parent will completely misread the final newsletter of the school year and they will turn up on the premises with their children dressed in full school uniform looking very confused as to why nobody will take them in.

For teachers (as with ice-breakers on many corporate training days), the worst type of INSET days are the ones that start with something along the lines of:

'Just for fun, I thought it would be nice to go around the room and for each of us to say a bit about ourselves...'

You thought? Think again; it is neither fun nor nice! Whatever is said during that conversation can be used against you in a Secret Santa. Like dogs? You're getting a calendar with dogs on. Say you enjoy walking, perhaps you'll be gifted a snazzy snood to keep you warm. Like baking? You're getting a cookbook from the random basket of discounted books that sits in the staffroom that are surplus to the warehouse's requirements. Probably the same baking book you received when it came out 12 months ago.

If you fancy mixing things up in a situation like that, for a laugh, just say you like paddleboarding, philately or lion taming.

Phil Attley? Was he in the year above me?

Philately! Collecting and studying postage stamps, you fool.

If the new colleagues find it hilarious that you chose a fake hobby, you'll probably be mates for life; if they take it seriously, you can have a giggle if they buy you a book on stamp-collecting. Whatever you choose, it may lighten up the morning, plus it's health and safety next and you know you only just passed the online training with 79 per cent last time, so the school business manager is definitely going to be keeping an eye on you.

Now, most INSET days are in fact really useful. I've experienced plenty as a teacher, but some that particularly stand out are Alan Peat's training, John Murray's and, more recently, Andrew Moffat with his No Outsiders curriculum. I'd also like to think I've led plenty of useful and inspiring INSET days for schools myself. I know some parents struggle to understand why teachers have INSET training days, but they really are important for topics like safeguarding and are far from an extra day off for teachers.

The reason for having INSET days is so staff can receive valuable and up-to-date professional development training to make sure the quality of teaching in the school is the best it can possibly be. There is little to no time to even go to the toilet most days during the term, so having time to think, develop and implement new initiatives is almost impossible in the day-to-day.

Whenever we have asked teachers to share their stories about their worst INSET days, two themes usually emerge: well-being and anything related to Ofsted. Both of these themes will be explored elsewhere in this book, but here are some of our favourite submissions under the category of pointless INSET days:

'Being asked to come in on your non-working day to watch a video training session all about staff mental well-being and work/life balance. Ironic, much?'

'The ones where they make you think you're writing policies or deciding on a new way of doing something... then two hours later they whip out the solution "*Blue Peter*-style"... here's what we thought – boom! – waste of two hours!'

'So many team-building exercises... using dried spaghetti and marshmallows to build a bridge, newspaper to build a structure that could take weights, and newspaper to make an igloo that we could climb inside. All I wanted to do was get into my classroom and sort out my cupboards!'

'A mindfulness INSET... I remember we had to pretend we were different animals and roam about the hall. Then we had to roll a ball to each other and concentrate on it!'

'Council-led ladder training... to be told two weeks later that we weren't allowed to use the ladders.'

'Being told to wear your best underwear to work to make you feel better.'

'All teachers had to go round every classroom and name three things that weren't good. You then had to read your list out loud in front of everyone.'

'We had to spend time practising singing a song and then performing it through Google Meets to another school for an entire day.'

'Making wedding-table decorations for one of the teachers, for a wedding I wasn't invited to!'

'Skipping. For a whole day. 🤷🏽‍♀️'

The new term will bring new staff and I'd just like to end this chapter with two examples of school staff making interesting impressions on their new colleagues.

One teaching assistant moved counties, and as she was new to the area, she started doing some agency work at a local school. After a year in her school, she was asked to apply for a permanent role. While a temporary member of staff, the TA would park around the back of the school, but after what she thought was a reasonably successful interview the previous day, she spotted a space in the main car park next to a brand spanking new BMW. Excited at the prospect of landing her permanent role, she thought she would chance it. The day before, the TA was mentally rehearsing her answers to potential interview questions and thinking about her strengths. One strength that would not appear on her CV, however, was her ability to reverse park. Surely there was enough space to get into that spot...? Erm... turns out there wasn't and the gold/orange paint from her car was now very visibly down the side of the headteacher's (sparkling new and fresh from the showroom) BMW.

The TA entered the school, fearing she had blown her chance, and knocked on the door of the headteacher (who was expecting her) to confess her parking misdemeanour. The head greeted the TA with a big smile and a big CONGRATULATIONS as she welcomed her to the team. The TA was obviously delighted, but she quickly made her confession, in case the head wanted to retract the offer. Fortunately, the headteacher was absolutely lovely about it and they managed to get the damage repaired with minimal fuss. She definitely never parked out the front again, though!

On our podcast we've run a feature called 'diabolical leader of the week', which aims to shame some of the terrible headteachers and deputies that continue to pollute our schools with their cluelessness and downright nastiness towards staff. Not all school senior leaders are like that, and if you work in a school, hopefully you've got good ones.

Now, there's potentially making a bad start (like the previous story) and there's *actually* making a bad start. One story I was told by a friend of mine involved a TA starting at her school. The TA had literally never worked in education before, and on her first day, after a reasonably successful morning supporting the children, she made her way to the staffroom at lunchtime. As her first day was a special occasion, she'd brought herself a little treat.

Chocolate? Nope.

A Subway sandwich? Incorrect.

A doughnut? As if.

No, the TA reached into her bag and pulled out an Aldi own-brand can of cider, cracked it open and started necking it. After lifting their jaws from the ground, a few members of staff alerted the senior leadership team (SLT), who then removed the new TA from the premises. But rather than being apologetic, the lady complained, 'This is my own time, surely I can do what I want?!'

Just wow!

As with many school-related things, the songs you sing at certain times of the year in assembly often have a lot to do with the era in which you went to school, or (as we often say) may 'depend on your vintage'.

Christmas, Easter, end of the year – there will always be a few staples that most people recognise. There are thousands of potential Christmas songs (obviously), a couple of regular Easter ones ('We Have a King Who Rides on a Donkey'/'Spring Chicken') and so many leavers' assemblies have the tradition of singing 'One More Step Along the Road I Go'.

During the autumn term, it's time for the famous harvest assembly, or as many schools like to call it, 'harvest festival'. This is the assembly where the RE and Music coordinators in the school have about three weeks to put on an epic show so the local vicar can pop in and talk to the children about what it means to be thankful. He or she will also bless a bunch of tins of kidney beans, an out-of-date tin of fruit cocktail and a partially opened packet of pasta. OK, maybe that's a little facetious, but harvest festival will happen in so many schools throughout the British Isles, and usually part-way through the first half of the first term. It's important for children to remember that it's called 'harvest festival', because apparently one lad rocked up to school carrying a turnip, bragging that he'd definitely win! Turns out he was a little confused and thought it the 'hardest vegetable' competition. This is something Adam would've done, I reckon. I'd have loved to have seen the playground chat; instead of arguing about whose dad could win in a fight, I could just imagine hearing, '... no chance, mate, my cauliflower could have your parsnip, easy!'

Going back to the songs we sing, they have become arguably more cheerful as the years have progressed. Readers of a certain age will automatically think of the serious, plodding melody of 'We Plough the Fields and Scatter' as their staple harvest song. Think of Mrs Biddle plonking away on the school piano. Think about old Mr Hawkes booming out the first line to set the standard so that the cheeky little turds on the back-row benches upped their game and joined in with the rest of the school. God help anyone that didn't meet his level of participation as he peered over his bifocals with a steely gaze. Harvest festival was less about being thankful with that song and more about joining in appropriately so that the teacher (who was potentially born in the 1800s when the song started to become famous) wouldn't keep you in at break time and make you sing it again... solo!

If you managed to survive those days, you may recall your go-to harvest song being 'Autumn Days'. Written sometime in the 60s or 70s, many children will think incredibly fondly of this wonderful tune! Definitely more upbeat than 'We Plough the Fields', and far more relatable for the 80s and 90s kids and beyond – especially the part where you're allowed to yell a little bit on the line '... a win for my home team!'

The song 'Autumn Days' is full of metaphors and could easily be dissected as part of a Year 6 SPAG (Spelling, Punctuation and Grammar) lesson and, yes, I'm aware that some schools no longer call it that. Did we really know what 'whipped-up spray that is rainbow-scattered' meant at the time? Nope! But among all the interesting ways of describing the feeling of an autumn day (not sure why I'm smelling bacon as I tie my shoelaces), it's a really chirpy song that you can't help but tap your feet to before belting out the chorus of 'So I mustn't forgeeeeeeeet...' The best part of this song's legacy is that it's still an absolute favourite in so many primary schools, so if parents are invited to the assembly, they quite often join in for a bit of nostalgia.

Up next, and if you haven't sung or heard this bad boy before, did you even go to a school in the UK? Seriously, it's easier to not hear Wham's 'Last Christmas' on the radio from late November onwards than have missed this song. I am, of course, talking about the mighty...

'Cauliflower Fluffy!'

That's right, the harvest festival banger that kids who grew up in the 80s onwards can remember, including the lyrics, faster than the birth dates of their own children. You may have even seen a guy on TikTok (@JamesBPartridge) who plays school hymns as part of his stage show, and yes, 'Cauliflower Fluffy' is a crowd favourite.

Everyone knows that 'the apples are ripe', everyone knows that 'the plums are red' (even if not all plums are actually red, especially in the Eric Carle book *The Very Hungry Caterpillar,* where they are blatantly dark purple). Most importantly, the 'broad beans are sleeping in their blankety bed', which for the life of me I still don't understand, as I thought they grew hanging from the stalks of the plant above the Earth's surface. However interesting the lyrics are, it's a cracking little song that the KS1 children love. Will it inspire them to eat more fruit and veg as a result? No idea, but it's a song that you know an overworked Reception teacher will have had drummed into their skull as they model the actions to their new class in preparation for their first school performance.

I had a group outside doing a SPAG intervention in the morning and suddenly we could hear the rest of the class start singing harvest songs inside. One of the boys in my group got excited at this, and shared that the song was his favourite and he listens to it all the time at home in his bedroom. He said he asks his Alexa to play it and he twerks to it in his room – the song is 'Cauliflower Fluffy'. 😂 I then let the group go inside so the lad could enjoy the song, as I couldn't continue with the intervention after that. 😂

The higher up the school you go, the less enthusiasm there seems to be for singing this beauty. By Year 5, you can see the disdain on a few kids' faces as they give a half-arsed rendition of 'Cauliflower Fluffy'. They'd prefer a remix with a rap halfway through, but sadly that isn't an option so they must stick with the OG version. Don't worry, there's always the 'Harvest Samba'. No... really!

Regardless of what you sang at your harvest festival, the main message of this primary school mainstay is about being grateful for the things we have and thinking of others. It is a really decent message that should be taken seriously. Sadly, something that has become way more prevalent in recent years is the presence of volunteers from the local food bank.

While I've made light of the quality of the tins donated before – as being out-of-date stuff from the back of the cupboard brought in at the last minute because a parent missed the letter/electronic school reminder about it being harvest festival on Thursday – the sad reality is that the need for food donations in recent years appears to be greater and greater as families struggle to make ends meet. We don't mean fictional families on the TV, but actual children in the school. It's an absolute crime that food banks need to exist in this country, but sadly they do. It's heartbreaking but amazing to see how seriously the children take bringing in food donations, especially when they realise they might be going to help some of their classmates – even if indirectly. It is a sad state of affairs that at the start of my teaching career we spent years doing fundraising days for those less fortunate in other countries – I remember one particular year raising money to help build a school in a remote part of Uganda – but now, thanks to chronic underfunding and the cost-of-living crisis, most school fundraising days are held to support children in our own school, in our own local area.

Another thing that has become more popular over the years in harvest assemblies is the discussion about where food comes from. What does free-range mean? What is organic? Why is it important to think about buying Fairtrade products? As teachers, we're trying to train up some conscientious consumers, and that's pretty fantastic in itself.

Any local vicar or faith leader is very welcome to pop in and bless this lovely little tradition as our young people learn about why they should be grateful for what they have and why they should look out for those that don't have enough. This education around where our food comes from is also important so that you don't end up in a situation where a local minister is talking to KS1 in assembly, and when he asks them where pasta comes from, one little girl puts up her hand and says, 'TESCO!'

That's just one example of where an assembly turns to laughter, but don't worry, there are plenty more. We're going to end this chapter with a few stories submitted by some podcast listeners.

With every type of assembly there are always a couple of hilarious tales.

'One thing I will say is that it tends to be the smallest of the celebrations, so if your child doesn't get the biggest part, don't worry. Also, don't write a letter of complaint to a teacher; there are 30 children in the class at least, so everyone needs a go. One time a teacher received a two-page ranty letter because his kid couldn't remember if he was a carrot or a pea in the harvest festival. 😂'

'My husband was leading harvest assembly and I was sitting with my Year 3/4 class at the front. He boldly led the prayer... "Dear God, we thank you for our craps..." (It was, of course, supposed to be "crops".) I thought I was going to stop breathing! One of my class knowingly grinned on our way back to class. "Mrs F, I know why you're laughing..." It was a perfect moment.'

'Every year at harvest festival we take the school to the local church. Several years ago we had a rather unpleasant vicar. As the children were bringing their tins and packets of food up to the altar, he rudely ordered myself and a teacher to help receive the offerings and place them behind the rail. As the gifts piled up I bent forwards to take a tin of beans from a small child just as the vicar walked behind me to find space for the jar of jam he was holding. As I leaned forwards my bottom stuck out and knocked the vicar, who, caught off balance, fell backwards and disappeared under the altar table so that only his feet were showing. My teacher friend and I were in stitches and couldn't sing the next hymn for laughing. He moved to another parish eventually and we now have a really lovely vicar. 😁'

'I am from Newcastle (this is relevant for the story – trust me!). When I was an NQT, my school was in a small rural village about an hour and a half away from where I was living, so I didn't know the area at all. One time, after a horrible day, my boyfriend surprised me and picked me up to go out for food. We went to a local Wetherspoons near the school and were sitting at a table by the bar. I saw a man looking over at us. He came over to the table and said he was a parent of a child in another class and welcomed me to the school, so I said a quick hello and went back to my food. A few days later there was a whole-school harvest assembly. We had the children settled and parents came into the hall. The parent I had seen in 'Spoons made a beeline for me. He was holding a newspaper cutting and shouted across to me (so staff, kids and parents could hear), "I hope this isn't about you and your boyfriend, mind – we know what you Geordies get up to after a few drinks!"

'He then showed me the local newspaper cut-out about three people who had been banned from the local Wetherspoons for having a threesome in the toilets. One very awkward harvest assembly and a chat to assure my headteacher that she hasn't hired a Geordie, nymphomaniac, thrill-seeker NQT – it was thankfully all laughed off.'

'I was leading harvest assembly with a lot of parents watching. My heel got caught in the back of my dress as I stood up, which made me face plant into the Reception class, throwing the contents of a class harvest box at them as I did so! There was no way to style that one out. Knees were in agony, children in shock, dress ripped, and as I tried not to cry, I heard one parent say, "Well, she's been asking for that wearing those shoes!"'

‘Not from harvest time, but still on the theme of fruit and veg, one teacher working in a Church of England school used to have regular special assemblies and services in the local Church of St Edmund the Martyr. On St Edmund’s Day the vicar was talking to the children about the saint and asked what the word “martyr” means. One of the Reception boys put up his hand to answer (and it was pretty damn obvious he didn’t have a clue). The vicar selected him and he called out, “You put it in sandwiches with cheese!”’

Bless that kid. I mean, with that rationale, you could also enjoy a BLT (Bacon, Lettuce and To-MARTYR) for your lunch.

‘During a church harvest service, all children were asked to hold a letter to spell out “harvest water”. All went well during rehearsals, children stood in the correct place, read their words clearly, etc., but unfortunately when we were in the church, the child holding the “T” of harvest stood too closely to the children holding the “W”, “A” and “T” of the word “water”. A very flustered deputy headteacher was embarrassed to see the word “TWAT” spelled out to the congregation!!’

What were your autumn days like? Did you plough the fields and scatter? Were your cauliflowers fluffy? All we know is that harvest festival (hardest vegetable?) is a school event that seems to have survived the test of time and evolved into a showcase where we think about others before ourselves. Long may it continue.

By the time harvest festival has been and gone, you should have a full set of children in school throughout all the years, including all of the EYFS (Early Years Foundation Stage) classes. And, flipping heck, school staff don't half notice the difference in the playground when all of the Reception children are out.

This next chapter is dedicated to the funniest humans in the school, the children in our EYFS classes.

Once they've gone from doing half-day stints to going full time, those little mites are usually shattered each day and therefore wake up grumpy the following day. There'll always be a number of children that get to the end of their first full week in Reception and decide that school isn't for them, and they'd rather stay home with their little brother and watch *Peppa Pig* because they are already fed up with following rules and numberwork. Negotiating with these children is incredibly difficult, especially when you must tell them that after the week they've had, they have still got roughly another 180 actual school days before they finish Foundation Stage, then another six years of primary school, followed by five years of secondary school up to GCSEs and two more if they stay on to do A-levels or the equivalent after that. It's probably not the best time for that discussion while they are sitting on the sofa with a strawberry Calippo watching *Paw Patrol*. The child is thinking to themselves, 'Sod this for a game of soldiers.' Rubble on the Double and Chase on the Case don't have to learn phonics and put an apron on to use the sand tray.' By the time you think you can reason with them, they've fallen asleep onto their chicken dippers and potato waffles.

To help prevent this, most Reception staff will do a home visit during the last week of August or first couple of weeks in September and meet the students in their natural habitat (home). They pop along to introduce themselves to the student and also inform parents as to how best to get their child to school. As a teacher, these home visits can be eye-opening, as you can imagine. Fortunately, I have never had the pleasure of doing one of them, but I have revelled in the stories of others. So here are some of my favourites:

'I arrived for a home visit for a new Reception child. The mum had forgotten I was coming and was sunbathing topless in the garden...'

'I had to do a home visit and the mother was on a mattress on the living-room floor having electrolysis on her moustache throughout our meeting!'

'A lot of years ago, aged 21, I did a home visit. The mum opened the door in a see-through negligee with everything just there, for all to see. I politely asked her to get dressed while I spoke to her child.'

'Going on a home visit to be faced with a naked dad who was asking a genuine question as to what teabagging was in the staffroom.'

What? There's so much to unpick with this one! I wouldn't know where to start.

'While on a home visit, I had to speak to a mum while her partner was naked on the sofa opposite!'

'I was doing a home visit for a child starting our nursery. The dad was really lovely but got slightly overexcited when telling me about his daughter's talents. One thing he said was, "She can do a proper forward roll," and he kept trying to get her to show me. When she was too embarrassed he thought he'd model an example. Being over 6 foot and doing this across a sitting-room floor, the chap executed a fairly decent one but his finish left a lot to be desired as he landed on top of my feet.'

'On a home visit a dad answered the door with a tattoo gun in his hand, as he was tattooing himself. He offered me and my colleague one. We declined. Imagine!'

'Years ago, during a home visit, the little boy asked if we would like to see his room. On going upstairs he pointed to his parents' room and said, "Would you like to see mummy's special box? It's got things in it that do funny buzzy things but I don't know why she needs those toys. She's too old for toys!" We declined but were shown a box of vibrators anyway. 😆'

I don't even care if that one is true or not, what a little legend!

'So, on a home visit for new Reception children one mum invited us in and showed us through to the lounge. I sat on the sofa and I could hear a cat meowing. I asked if they had a cat and where was it – then she looked at me and said you are sitting on it. That poor cat! I am a large lady, and he did look a little squashed. I was so apologetic. Mum reminded me of that visit for many years to come.'

'I've been on a home visit for nursery and the mum was panting through her labour... Awkward!'

'While on a home visit to a soon-to-be Reception child, the parent popped out to make tea. I couldn't remember or find a note of Dad's first name so I asked the child, "What does your mum call your dad, what's his name?" The reply will stay with me forever, as the child said "Dickhead" just as the parent walked back in the room!'

'I had to do home visits before the child came into the nursery. It was to get to know the child, give the parents information and answer any questions they had about their child starting school. While I was there chatting to the parents the dad suddenly got up, walked in front of me, turned on his Xbox and started playing a game. I was trying so hard not to laugh while the mum tore a strip off him.'

'On a home visit prior to the Reception children starting school one year, I was sitting on the sofa chatting with the mum and child when the child started pulling at the mum's jersey dress. The mum was very calm and just kept removing the child's arm from her dress – she didn't really seem too bothered. I was worried that any minute the child was going to reveal the mum's bra, so I averted my eyes down just in case, to avoid embarrassment, however, this was the exact moment that the child then pulled UP the mum's dress and revealed, much to my surprise, that the mum, who was sitting legs akimbo, was also in fact fully commando and I was staring right at the wrong area!!! My TA and I were scarred for life!'

'I'm so ashamed to share this story but I think you'd like it... I'll take you back to my NQT year. I was eager and excited to be in Foundation and spent my first week on the busy home visits. I had my TA with me and was very aware as a new teacher that I needed to make a good impression. The day was going well, the children were lovely and I was able to answer all the parents' questions as we went from door to door. I had one visit left for the day. I knocked on the door as normal and was greeted by a friendly mum. I walked inside and suddenly the house looked oddly familiar. I shook it off and carried on with the visit. As we proceeded into the front room, I started to recognise more of my surroundings. I looked at the mum again. I definitely didn't know her from anywhere, so how did I know this house? Suddenly the front door opens and Dad walks in. To my horror, I instantly recognised his face... he was the douche bag that I'd met in a club a few months ago! I froze, not knowing what to do (they don't teach you how to handle these situations on your teacher training). I forced a smile as Dad went on to greet me as if nothing had ever happened. I tried to speed through the visit and get out of there as quickly as I possibly could. To this day I don't know if the dad actually remembered what happened, we've never spoken about it, but he came to EVERY parents' evening!'

That last one was awkward as hell, but we hope you have enjoyed these.

Starting Reception is a massive step up for the little ones, and the children that are going to be hard work for the rest of the school year (and possibly eternity) are easy to spot. I have only ever worked in EYFS sporadically, but I can easily say those are the teachers I respect the most, hands down, which is weird because they seem to be the ones who get looked down on the most. They do an incredible job at such an important foundational stage of development, especially since the government made that so much harder after scrapping all the Sure Start centres. In a recent article from the BBC News website, they reported that children from low-income families who grew up near a Sure Start centre performed up to three grades better at GCSE than their peers further away (according to the Institute for Fiscal Studies [IFS]). Why they thought getting rid of them was a good idea, I'll never understand. These teachers are exposed to some of the most disgusting things that these revolting creatures – sorry, children – do, and have to sit through staff meetings where 99 per cent of the stuff discussed has sweet FA to do with them.

EYFS staff have the most amount of respect from me because I don't know how they do it. The only way I can describe what being an EYFS teacher is like is going on a night out with all of your mates when every single one of them is leathered and you're the stone-cold-sober designated driver. To walk into an EYFS classroom is like walking into a packed Yates's or Wetherspoons on a Saturday night. The similarities between a 3- or 4-year-old and a drunk person is ridiculous. The levels of self-confidence are similarly unrivalled; when you try to tell them no, they just dismiss it, ignore you or just blatantly do it anyway. They are both unsteady on their feet, too; you will always see an EYFS child bump into stuff like they've had that extra shot, or falling over and either laughing like they're in a *Jackass* sketch or crying like they've just had their heart broken. I swear one of my EYFS staff said the other day, she turned to see a child standing on a chair with his pants round his ankles weeing into the sand tray while his friend was tickling his bum with a feather duster, which reminded me of rugby initiation night at uni! Have you ever done snack time with EYFS kids? Walk into the kebab shop at half two in the morning and watch a drunk person demolish a mixed kebab with sauce all over their face, debris covering their jumper, and that's snack time with nursery. They love going to the toilet together in groups as well. And have you ever been in an EYFS toilet? It's like a miniature version of club toilets; the floor is soaked, seats are broken – the only thing an EYFS toilet doesn't have is a gentleman at the sink with every aftershave, some lollipops and mints.

Another bizarre comparison could be the EYFS nativity play at Christmas; surely it is the 5-year-old equivalent of a stag or hen do. Think about it – everyone is got up in fancy-dress costume, stumbling about where they're trying to tell you something but forgetting, on their way to 'Seshlehem', trying to get in places but being turned away, and then a camel pees on the floor while a shepherd throws up.

There is one thing I think needs to happen on a night out that you'll see in every EYFS classroom, though. Imagine at the end of the night, the DJ is like, this is the last song now, but just before you go, we're going to have story time. They then proceed to read a picture book to the crowd. This always works with EYFS kids; you pick those kids up and they are chilled. Imagine that on a night out. Imagine how much the crime rate would drop – there'd be no fights, instead it would be: 'Leave it, Dave. Remember that guy might know the Gruffalo, you don't want to risk it, mate.' 'Yeah, you're right, let's get a taxi.'

Now for some stories about the brilliantly bonkers children that we come across in and around the school in those early years, starting with one KS2 teaching assistant who was on playground duty and was trying to get the new Reception children to line up while she waited to pass them on to their teacher – just to help out a little, as she knew her EYFS colleague would already be very busy mopping up

strange substances and checking if the children had put paint in her handbag. The TA was praising the children for making good choices and saying well done to any of the siblings of children in her class that were being good role models. You know, words like: 'Oh wow, James's brother is lining up beautifully and Samantha's sister is standing straight like a soldier!' One child will be obviously goosing around with his mate, and without knowing their name the staff member can't point them out and help them to line up.

'Young man, you seem to be being very silly, we're not at nursery now. What's your name?' The child did not respond and just carried on having the time of his life. Wanting to set the standard without being too strict, she asked his friend what he was called. 'Oh, that's Wedgie!' Wedgie? Who on earth names a child after the act of pulling underpants up from behind a person? The teaching assistant was puzzled as hell, so when the class teacher arrived, she asked her colleague if his name really was 'Wedgie'. It turns out that his name was 'Reggie' and the lad who spoke to her had some issues pronouncing his Rs. This staff member would never laugh at a child with a speech impediment, but on this occasion it was pretty funny. It was almost ironic that she thought a child was actually called 'Wedgie', too, as he was often walking around as if he had 70 per cent of his underpants up his bum. According to the support staff in the class, he definitely didn't wipe particularly well after using the toilet either.

At a completely different school, there was another example (sort of) of mistaken identity when lining up, which involved a child called Peter – a nice kid who is about 18 now but did tend to say things that weren't strictly true in his younger years. On this occasion, young Peter was one of the children making good choices and another teacher wanted to praise him for being a good chap. He was asked his name so they could report his positive behaviour to the TA collecting his class from the playground, and for some reason he told her his name was 'Tyrone'.

'Well, Miss Johnson, young Tyrone here has been very good at lining up today and I thought I should let you know!'

'Tyrone?'

'Yes, young Tyrone at the front of the line. Look how straight he's standing.'

Looking confused, the TA spoke to 'Tyrone'.

'Peter, why on earth have you said your name is Tyrone?'

'I just like the name Tyrone,' he replied.

Both grown-ups started to roll their eyes and giggle. It turns out young Peter's parents really like *Corrie*!

This chapter has focused predominantly on EYFS children so far, but children higher up the school are generally pretty hilarious, so here are a few more stories we think you'll enjoy, featuring other members of the school community.

One Year 1 child standing on the top of a climbing frame was reported to the teacher by some Year 5 children for swearing. Intrigued as to which swear words the little guy knew, she went towards the play area. Apparently, the little boy was singing about being the 'King of the Castle' and she remembered the rhyme well. She thought to herself that 'rascal' was hardly crossing the line as far as bad language was concerned. Approaching the little boy, she asked politely what he was doing. The Year 1 child declared, with one hand on his hip:

'I'm the King of the Castle...'
(then pointing at the teacher)
'... you're a dirty ARSEH*LE!'

Perhaps those Year 5 children were spot on about the swearing after all! A brilliant one came from a Year 3 child on a school stroll down to the local Sainsbury's. They were off for a session learning how to make bread in the bakery, and as they approached the site, there was a large truck from the company 'Bob Gay Plant Hire'. The car park was being resurfaced and the truck clearly had a large quantity of the materials required to do this on board. The problem came when only a section of the truck was visible, and the 'Bob' part was not on display.

One child at the front noticed and whispers were going down the line of children to look at the side of the vehicle that clearly read 'GAY PLANT HIRE'. Wondering why the children were giggling, the teacher stopped the line and enquired about what was up.

This is where little Sam stepped in and asked the teacher:

'Miss... why on earth would you hire a gay plant?'

Confused, and about to call out what she thought was homophobia, the teacher looked around and saw the truck. Immediately, she did a double-take. She turned around to see the whole class, including the TA and parent volunteers, laughing their arses off at what little Sam had just blurted out. Obviously, she started chuckling herself, pulled a funny face and proceeded to count the number of children. At least she knew where she could hire gay plants from now!

A little boy from a rural school, with some very traditional parents, had instructed their child (who had genuinely immaculate manners) to make sure that he made friends by introducing himself. He would come to school in a dark green waxed jacket that wouldn't look out of place at the shooting range, and in colder months he would even wear a tweed flat cap. In the 80s he would have been described as being dressed like a 'Hooray Henry', and ironically his name was Henry. His grandmother had told him to say hello by saying 'How do you do? I'm Henry.' It was a very sweet and pleasant gesture with which to endear him to his peers and the adults looking after him. Poor Henry took these instructions a little too seriously and forgot what his grandma had told him he was supposed to say. Rather than the suggested greeting he was given by his gran, young Henry walked around the school for the first few weeks (including when it became slightly chilly, and he was sporting his flat cap) spouting:

'How do you do, do you?'
'How do you do, do you?'

Lifting his cap just slightly above his head as he passed a new person:

'How do you do, do you?'

Word started getting round the pupils that there was small child who was hilariously greeting everyone in school by saying:

'How do you do, do you?'

Rather than take the p*ss, the Year 6 crew thought he was incredibly cute and would seek Henry out so they could look after him at break times. There's a scene in *The Simpsons* where Bart is famous for being the 'I didn't do it!' boy and his classmates are gathered around him begging him to say the line. It started to get to the point where Henry had achieved a similar status.

Word got back to the teachers that the 'How do you do, do you?' child was the source of great (but well-meaning) amusement, and while they were impressed that Henry was loving the attention, they also thought it would be nice if he could build relationships with children his own age. Henry's teacher brought it to the attention of his mum, who was initially mortified that her son was a playground sensation, but then she saw the funny side and suggested that he dropped his grandmother's greeting from his repertoire and just said hello to people.

By the time he was in Year 3 and his younger sister had started Reception, Henry talked very much like every other child, but enough time had passed that he could laugh at his former status as the 'How do you do, do you?' child. He'd even ironically greet the teachers he liked with the saying and they'd both lift their imaginary caps to do so. School kids can be amazing sometimes!

A few weeks into starting school, a new Reception child was having a lovely day with his pals until he felt his tummy rumble.

The two Reception classes at his school shared an outdoor area and this was the first day that Tyler had gone outside to explore the dedicated space. There was a sandpit, a mud kitchen and an awesome creation made of recycled pipes and plastic containers, where if you added water at the top it would cascade down and flow into the different parts of the course until it reached a grow bag full of tomato plants at the bottom. It was a beautiful idea and an ingenious way of watering the plants.

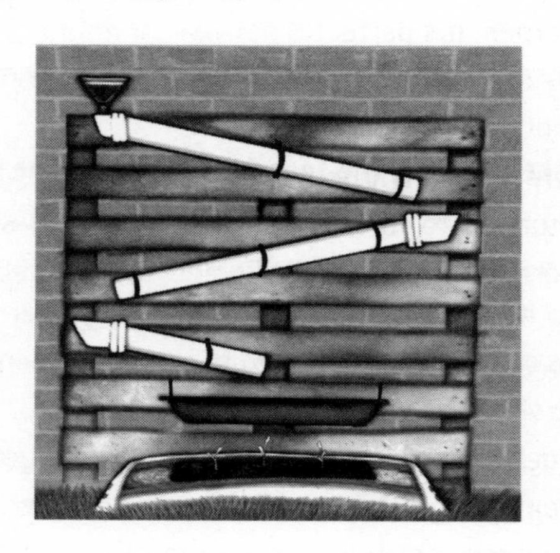

For such wonderful outdoor play activities, it was essential that the children wore the communal waterproofs to ensure they didn't cover their school uniform in mud, water and sand. As well as communal waterproofs, there were communal wellies that any child could put on. Lots of Foundation Stage classes will have areas like this because of the opportunities that outdoor play and exploration give the children.

Back to Tyler, who was sensibly decked out in his all-in-one waterproofs and wellies, which were a little tight but at least they'd keep his socks dry. As this was in Yorkshire, young Tyler looked 'reet grand' in his outdoor kit. He had a wonderful time in the sand, with the mud, and the tomatoes were grateful for a drink as the weather was still fairly warm. Being out for the first time, Tyler didn't quite have his bearings and wasn't sure how to get back to his own classroom. In his Yorkshire drawl, Tyler was walking round saying 'Where's t'teacher?' Tyler was in a fix as his tummy was rumbling and he'd eaten an entire box of strawberries for his breakfast. He needed the loo.

He didn't spot that the supervising staff member was helping a child near the sandpit, and he wandered round, holding his belly. Muttering to himself, Tyler was striding around saying: 'tollit wit'perper, tollit wit'perper'. It's perfectly normal for young EYFS kids to be having a lovely conversation with themselves while having a play, but Tyler was not quite as jolly.

'Tollit wit'perper, tollit wit'perper!'

Tyler was starting to fart as he walked, and he was becoming increasingly worried that he was not going to reach the bathroom in time.

'Where's t'teacher? Need tollit wit'perper,' he continued to grumble, while getting redder in the face. His friend spotted Tyler was in some discomfort and alerted the teacher near the sandpit that Tyler looked upset.

'What's wrong, Tyler?' she asked.

'Need tollit wit'perper!'

She asked him to repeat what he was saying because this teacher was new, and from Kent, and she didn't recognise what he was saying in his broad Yorkshire accent.

'TOLLIT WIT'PERPER!' he exclaimed, but it was too late for her to translate it to meaning 'I need the toilet with paper,' which is an old-school phrase, possibly learned from his grandfather, that means he needed a POO! It was definitely too late to learn what that phrase meant. I'm reliably informed that this can be known as a 'Scarborough warning' among some from the Yorkshire area, which means 'with very short notice/warning or none at all'. Fairly apt in this situation.

By the time his teacher had worked out what the issue was, poor Tyler (fuelled by the entire punnet of strawberries) had managed to fill his britches with a volcano of unpleasantness. Not only had he filled his pants and shorts, it had spilled further into the bottom of his waterproofs where, ironically, it was being kept in by the slightly too-small wellies. It looked like he was wearing sh*t-filled bell-bottoms from the 70s. If you're a TA and were tasked with helping clean up poor Tyler, you'd best be getting a huge bunch of flowers and a gift card for Hotel Chocolat!

If you are reading this and you work in a school, you'll now be very aware of what 'toilet with paper' means. This is clearly a warning to any newly qualified teacher or early career teacher (ECT), as they are known nowadays, that they need to make sure they learn the regional variations for 'I need a poo' to avoid such situations. They don't teach you that on the B.Ed. or PGCE courses!

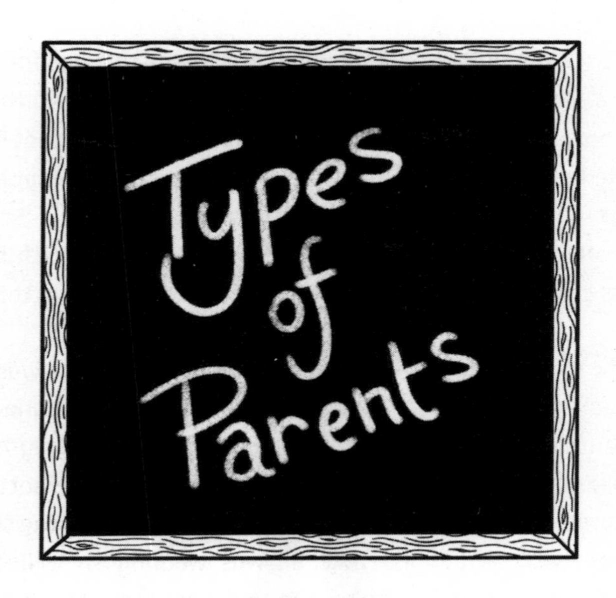

Once the year is starting to normalise and all the parents that decided to take their children's first days of school off work – as it's such a special time – have returned to the office, you are left with the pick-up/drop-off crew of parents and carers.

Some of them may work full time with hours that allow childcare commitments, and some may work from home (which is far more common post-pandemic). Some of the parents may be on a career break after having their children, and some may not work at all. Depending on the size of the school and where it is situated, you may have a very diverse group of parents.

PTA Mum

Three letters: PTA – The Parent–Teacher Association (PSA for some schools) should do exactly what it says on the tin, as it's an association between the teachers (or school staff) and the parents. When it works, it REALLY works; when it doesn't, it's more of an us versus them, where very little money is raised and the children don't benefit from a potential alliance that could make a big difference.

Think I'm being cynical? Sadly, there are some schools where the PTA is non-existent due to poor relations with parents, or because the parents are limited in how much they can give/help, or because of stinking attitudes from school staff. Well, we're not here to dwell on the bad stuff, we're all about celebrating some of the most fantastic members of the school community, and the person we're celebrating here is the PTA superstar.

Whatever role someone has in the PTA, everyone's help is welcome. Try to think of them as like the residents of Hundred Acre

Wood. You'll get some characters with some strong thoughts on how they should go about things, like Rabbit, and a few Owl-type characters, who have sensible and cost-effective ideas. There may also be some folk with good hearts who like sweet things, like Pooh (so they bring plenty of biscuits to the meetings). And yes, you'll get a few Negative Nellies like Eeyore and slightly timid folk like Piglet, and you'll undoubtedly have a few Tiggers with bat-sh*t bonkers ideas too (we do appreciate the enthusiasm, though).

The PTA superstar is almost certainly the Christopher Robin of the crew, who is the glue that holds everything together. They manage to enthuse the doubters, empower the worriers and filter out the ridiculousness of some of the brain-fart suggestions. Hopefully you know a PTA superstar at your local school, and if you do, you're very lucky. This lady doesn't even need to be the chairperson, she'll have just as much impact if she's only a helper, because there's no ego and she'll muck in with everything. She's at her best when she's in the vice-chair role, as she can help run the show but doesn't need to be the big cheese or take all the plaudits.

She's already done a stint as treasurer and secretary, and as good as she is at counting the money and taking the notes, it's nice to share out the jobs to the Piglets and the Rabbits. Probably best not to entrust those roles to Tigger or Pooh, though. We know how that might end...

These PTA superstars will plan out the PTA calendar on a very colour-coordinated Excel spreadsheet, which will be shared at the first meeting of the school year. During that meeting, they'll hope to obtain a few new additions to the PTA crew, especially among the new intake of Reception parents. It's essential that they are tempted into the fold early so that they can tap up their mates. The plan for the year will contain:

8 × cake sales
7 × tuck shops

6 × non-uniform days
5 × school discos
4 × ice-lolly Fridays
3 × sponsored bounces
2 × film nights
And a partridge in a pear treeee!

Don't forget Santa's Grotto, the panto, Easter egg hunt, treasure hunt, quiz night, race night, ladies' night and silver Smarties. Silver Smarties? Yep, silver Smarties. It's where you buy the whole school a tube of Smarties and they need to earn silver coins (20-pence coins, hopefully) to fill the Smartie tube, then bring it back into school. Easy money! As long as you keep reminding the classes to bring in their money and reward the year group that brings in the most returned tubes with a prize.

I say easy money, but this is one of the occasions where you DON'T want to be the nominated treasurer, unless you just so happen to have access to one of those counting machines. Despite asking for 20ps, you'll get whatever change they can find down the back of their sofa. It must be quite an old sofa, because who uses cash nowadays anyway? If parents don't regularly have cash and the office asks them to pay for all their trips and school lunches using a parent-pay app, how are the PTA supposed to fundraise? You can't buy new iPads using a few coppers, a Polo mint and a button.

Don't worry, the PTA superstar understands the modern world, so she's convinced the committee to invest in a couple of wireless card machines. It potentially puts more pressure on your families, though, as now they can no longer skip Ice-lolly Friday because they've got no change, as the card machines make it easier for people to pay by card or phone. Damn you, PTA!

The PTA superstar has got lots of fantastic qualities, but her most useful trait is her networking abilities. She's a PR queen and has contacts everywhere. One huge moneymaker for the school fête is the raffle. This isn't just any old raffle like the ones at a quiz night, where the first ticket out gets first choice of the prize table. You know the ones – if there are 30 items to choose from, the first ten tickets drawn get a decent selection of the wine and beer that's been donated (although a lot of the beers will probably only have a shelf life left of about two weeks, so read the bottles carefully). There's also the chocolate that's been donated, but if you're attending a quiz in June and the tub of Celebrations still has a Christmas design on it, someone definitely found it at the back of a cupboard. Clearly, they panicked when they remembered at the last minute that they had agreed to bring a prize for the event. As the draw goes on, the quiz night participants will come to the front and select from the remaining prizes, which are diminishing in quality with every ticket drawn. One bloke will 'hilariously' select the nail varnish set for his partner, and then your ticket is drawn when there are only five prizes left to choose from.

You're left with:

- Poundland pedicure set
- DVD of *Chicken Run* (which you won't be selecting as you no longer have a DVD player)
- Some bath salts
- *Shoot* annual from 2018

and finally...

- *Mrs Brown's Boys* bar of soap and flannel set (damaged packaging)

Trust me, if I'm the final ticket drawn and there's only that bloody *Mrs Brown's Boys* gift set, my ticket is going straight in the bin and they can draw again so someone else can have it! I don't care how many shandies I've had, I wouldn't wipe my arse with it (even though that's probably one of the primary functions of that prize).

Anyway, the raffle I'm really talking about is the big one at the fête. In the prizes donated, you'll still have the booze, the sweeties and the bath salts (re-donated after the quiz night – they'll probably end up on the tombola). But in addition to these, there'll be some impressive prizes thanks to the PTA superstar and her networking skills.

She'll tap up local businesses, so don't be surprised to see a voucher for a meal at the local carvery, Indian restaurant or tea rooms. She's a member of the gym, so they'll happily give her a month's free access as a prize, even though everyone already gets a month free when they are new. There will be free taster sessions as well from all the different people that have come to the fête to do a demonstration. I'm not sure Bobby's nan will use her voucher for a free tae kwon do session, but don't rule anything out!

It's not just vouchers. Down to the PTA superstar's amazing prize-hunting skills she'll manage to wangle (that's right, wangle) signed football shirts/footballs, tickets to the theatre/cinema, a day at the races, cocktail making, a SodaStream, a bike and a top-of-the-range shower. Prizes like these make the raffle worth entering. The more people that buy tickets, the more money they make, therefore the better the chances that the school can afford a new cricket kit, more library books and a classroom that actually has glue sticks!

She's a whiz at making posters and her marketing materials are top-notch. PTA superstar loves new ideas and will spend plenty of hours scrolling Pinterest at night, looking for inspiration about how they can raise money in the most creative ways. Lying in bed, she'll poke her husband in the back to show him some super-snazzy wristbands she can get to sell at the summer disco. Her husband is sick of her sh*t, truth be told. But because he loves her, he'll nod, give a thumbs up and roll over to get five more minutes' kip before she discovers another brilliant idea that he couldn't care less about. To counter her late-night enthusiasm, he'll break wind loudly and turn over again, giggling to himself. He'll get a back-of-the-head punch, but it'll be worth it. The short-term pain will at least mean he doesn't have to approve all the other crap she discovers on the PTA ideas Facebook groups. He's usually quite supportive, but not after 11 o'clock on a Sunday night when it's his turn to do the school run in the morning.

Deep down, hubby knows he's lucky to have her, and the school PTA are incredibly lucky she's on the team. I said earlier that she's a Christopher Robin figure, but she often displays the qualities of the rest of the characters from A.A. Milne's classic books. Sometimes she's wise like Owl and pedantic (for the right reasons) like Rabbit, while she's also got Pooh's heart and Tigger's energy, but, make no mistake, if she doesn't have her coffee in the morning she'll be a right mardy-arse like Eeyore.

Daddy Big-B**locks

There are some parents you meet and you'll wonder quite why they decided to procreate. Seriously, some mums and dads should be given some sort of test or at least be interviewed about their suitability to bring other versions of themselves into this world.

I'm not talking about a parent with a few annoying habits or tendencies to cause a little bother, I'm talking about the self-righteous arses who are so convinced their own opinions are correct that if they saw their reflections in a mirror they'd probably argue with it! Not only are these types of parents obnoxious, they are also bloody loud.

Think of the *Looney Tunes* character Foghorn Leghorn (the giant rooster starting his sentence in a Southern states' drawl with his catchphrase 'Ah say, ah say, boy...'). The giant rooster says absolutely nothing of substance every time he opens his enormous beak, but it's very loud and it draws attention. Same goes for Mr B-B.

He's the gobby knobhead at parents' evening who busts out the old clichés about bringing back corporal punishment and getting the cane at school. He boasts about how it didn't do him any harm, even though he was born in 1988, a full year or so after it was banned in state schools.

He's the sort of oaf who belittles his child in front of staff and other parents, and mocks the fact that they can't read particularly well. It's almost as if he's given up on his child already. Sadly, every school will have multiple Mr (and Mrs) B-Bs and they are often the ones that make huge complaints over minor issues but take no notice of things that significantly affect their child's learning. Mr B-B will have plenty of excuses like, 'Yeah, I was crap at times tables as well!' when his child's difficulties in maths are brought to his attention.

He himself may have had a particularly difficult upbringing, but it's hard to feel sympathy and unpick his personal issues when you're overwhelmed by his brash and obnoxious demeanour.

Does he watch GBeebies (GBNews)? Probably!

Does he share dodgy Facebook posts? Frequently.

Does he weirdly see haunted Victorian pencil (as he's sometimes described online) Jacob Rees-Mogg as a man of the people? Weirdly, yes!

OK. That's a fairly unkind generalisation, but you know the type of parent I'm describing. The 'I say what I like, and I like what I bloody well say' approach to life means he definitely gets noticed but it's never for the right reasons. Daddy Big-B**locks seems to have quite strong opinions, even when he hasn't even thought through what he's about to say. Much like Homer Simpson, his modus operandi is:

'Better say something or they'll think you're stupid.'

Trust me, Daddy Big-B**locks will ALWAYS be saying something. In fact, here's a bingo card of clichés that may come out of his cake hole.

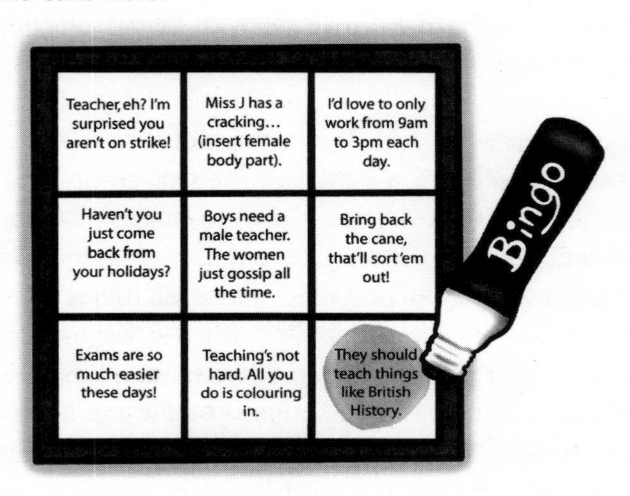

Honestly, I've genuinely heard most of these from typical Daddy B-Bs. The one in the middle is pretty offensive to my female colleagues, but also completely untrue. The awfully outdated tropes of gender stereotypes, I have heard them all. The number of parents who have commented about needing me to be their child's teacher because I am a man, like I can do anything better as a teacher because I am male, is ridiculous. 'Well, you know all women do is sit around and gossip!' Erm, I hate to tell you, the worst person for gossiping in my school is... ME! I'm terrible. I live for the gossip.

Back to Daddy B-B, the bottom-right square is one of those lazy comments made without realising it's complete rubbish. We DO teach British History in schools, and perhaps if Daddy B-B took an interest in his child's homework rather than blanket statements and falsehoods, he might have a clue. It's not uncommon for these berks to recite whatever they are told by the *Daily Fail* and dodgy Facebook pages with too many British flags (despite not really caring about the British Values that are taught in citizenship lessons).

Perhaps Daddy B-B could do with Twinkl worksheets to help him know that these lessons cover:

- democracy
- the rule of law
- individual liberty
- mutual respect
- tolerance of those of different faiths and beliefs.

This is the sort of guy that would be fuming if he heard that his child's school was using Hindu–Arabic numerals in their maths lessons, despite the fact that it's the exact same number system that has been used in daily life since the twelfth century.

The parenting blogger known as Man Behaving Dadly posted a picture of a slip he created, pretending it was from his child's school, gaining permission for the children to be taught Arabic numerals – you know, 0, 1, 2, 3, 4, 5, 6, 7, 8, 9. It was, of course, satire, but the number of reposts it received from angry right-wing folk, disgusted that children in British schools were learning foreign numbers, was worrying. They literally had no idea where our number system came from because apparently history started in 1945.

Actually, Daddy B-Bs probably doesn't know the significance of that year, and the only Churchill he knows is the dog that sells insurance!

Not all Daddy B-Bs are bigots and chauvinists, but plenty will be. The sorts of fools that tweeted during the Women's World Cup about staying in the kitchen. Paddy Power did a great advert mocking the ridiculousness of such attitudes, although I'm not entirely sure Daddy B-B would understand the satire. In fact, I don't think he knows what satire means.

Daddy B-B will have something in abundance, and that's courage of conviction. If he thinks he's right, he'll convince himself so and won't budge from that position, even if presented with, you know... facts! He'll have strong opinions on most things and will make it known that if you don't think the same way as him, then he needs to say it louder. There'll be strong opinions on the curriculum (with zero research into what is actually being taught), strong opinions on discipline and very strong opinions on why HIS son should be captaining the school football team. He is the type of parent who coaches his son's football team. He'll get his FA Level 1 coaching badge and automatically assume that he's José Mourinho; 'special one', my arse! I can't tell you the number of issues I've had in the 16+ years of coaching school football teams from dads like him. While many are supportive and wonderful (just like our pitch-side legends), there are the occasional ones who believe that their Saturday morning coaching experience makes them far greater experts than me (despite my lifelong involvement in the sport, my coaching qualifications, and my collection of trophies and accolades).

There was one memorable incident when, after I had selected the school team, a dad insisted on a meeting with the headteacher, who, without my knowledge, agreed to it. During the encounter, the dad slid a piece of paper across the table to my headteacher, revealing a list of names and saying, 'There's your team.' My headteacher promptly returned the paper and sternly stated, 'Don't ever waste my time like this again.' Funnily enough, that very year, the team I selected reached the national finals and came incredibly close to victory, losing only by a golden goal in the semi-finals.

But whether he's thinking he's a footballing tactical genius, spouting tripe about kids these days being too soft or generally causing verbal noise pollution, do approach Daddy B-B with care – if at all. The thing is, this kind of chap is not just ill-informed, he's deliberately ignorant. While teachers preach the importance of listening to both sides of a story to make sure you have a decent perspective, it's almost dangerous to listen to the bullsh*t that comes out of Daddy B-B's gob. Sadly, there's no antidote to this creature, so the best thing to do is to not engage with his provocative nonsense, otherwise you may plummet down to his level.

Once you meet Daddy B-B, you'll appreciate why his son or daughter may be the way they are. As mentioned before, Daddy B-B may be a product of his own environment. Like

Darth Vader, he could be full of good deep down underneath, but it's REALLY hard to stomach him when he talks (LOUDLY) so much sh*te!

Grandfolk

Let's hear it for the grannies, the nannas, the grandads, the grampies and millions of other variations that sound weird to everyone else but to your family make perfect sense, such as:

Bampy
Pops
Mamaw
Ohpah
Nain/Taid (popular in some parts of Wales)
Moma
Pumpa (I bet he knows the 'pull my finger' joke)

Special mention to the grandparent who has been deemed such a whinge bag that they are affectionately known as 'Grumps'. To have that as your grandparent name and to embrace it should be applauded for services to being a deliberately miserable old sod! 😂

In this day and age, with childcare costs going through the roof, where would we be without grandparents?

Not all families live close enough to help out, but for some families grandparents are a lifeline that enables the parents to work enough hours to feed and clothe their children. For those parents who do have this luxury, it's invaluable to have these silver-haired superstars around to help pick up and drop off (some do both) their grandchildren.

Gone are the days of a typical family with 2.4 children where father goes out to work while mother stays at home and takes care of the house and children. Thank goodness we no longer live in the 1950s, because as great as all the traditional family values may seem to some, it doesn't wash in twenty-first-century Britain... and neither should it! Modern times call for modern grandparents, and we've long said goodbye to a time when Nana or Pops told stories of the Blitz and rationing. You'll still hear 'back in my day', but the current crop of sexagenarians and septuagenarians are younger than The Beatles (well, two of them) and were lucky enough to experience Queen, ABBA and AC/DC in their prime.

Grandparents these days seem far more active and still have their own teeth. They volunteer at food banks, run charity shops and even take part in some amateur dramatics in primary schools. Your local school may not experience this, but around the country there are plenty of pensioners that visit schools and tell stories in assembly while acting out parts of the Bible. Granted, the word 'acting' is doing a lot of heavy lifting and they should not be expecting Oscar nominations in the post, but it's lovely that they are dedicating themselves to making such a positive contribution to society. These are the lovely grandparents we're talking about, not the pink-faced horrible ones that pop up on *Question Time* and try their utmost to give the elderly in this country a bad name.

What is age anyway? One male teacher informed us that while there were plenty of yummy mummies at pick-up, there were also increasing numbers of what he would class as GILFs. Yes, you read that correctly, he has replaced M for mum/mom in MILF with a G for granny. That dirty dawg is sweet on the over-50s!

You're only as old as you feel, and there's a way to check. The test is where you may fall over in public, and the reaction decides if you're old or not. As per usual this wisdom came from the front of a birthday card, but apparently if you fall over and people laugh you're still young. If people go 'ooooh' and run over to check on you, I'm sorry, but you're officially OLD! Another way of checking if people deem you to be a senior citizen is if you go to the checkouts at either Aldi or Lidl, you'll be able to find out (potentially the hard way). If the cashier slows down enough for you to pop your purchases in your bag, they believe you are officially ancient. If the person on the till scans your items at 100mph, you are deemed still young enough to receive the bombardment of cornflakes, yoghurts and frozen pizzas being pinged at you faster than a speeding bullet. I just hope you still have the reflexes.

One person who definitely doesn't let advancing years get in the way is our beloved Nana Maureen. She spent her eightieth birthday dancing with an Elvis impersonator.

Here's a story about a grandad getting into some bother. At one school, there was a 'no guns' policy, which meant that children were discouraged from acting out games with guns or even making them using Lego or Unifix cubes. The danger of gun violence in the UK is no laughing matter, so it is understandable that schools in certain areas may have such a policy.

So this was a policy in place at the school in our story, but despite this, one child, called Gavin, was really upset with the ruling. For some reason, he wouldn't go to school unless he could bring his toy gun with him. To avoid a daily meltdown, the mum had to make the compromise that 'Gav the Gun' could have it with him on the way to school, but he must hand it over when they reached the little bridge before the entrance. Surprisingly, this worked fine for many weeks and there were no tantrums when the boy had to give back the toy weapon.

One day, though, it did not go quite as smoothly, as the child had been driven to school by his grandfather. Rather than taking the gun from the boy, the toy firearm was left on the front seat of grandad's car, in full view of the rest of the parents at drop-off.

While little Gavin was being dropped off, one of the mums spotted the gun and called the police. The local police station was only two minutes up the road and they swiftly surrounded poor grandad's car, with the old chap crapping his pants because the feds were worried he'd bust a cap on someone's ass!

David Walliams can keep his Gangsta Granny, we've got 'Gav the Gun's Gangsta Grandpop' with a plastic Glock 17 on his front seat!

With more and more families relying on grandparents for childcare, quite often these legends get to know the school staff better than the parents do. One grandad, whose grasp of polite language was somewhat lacking at times, used to do the pick-ups for his daughter's children, where he would often forget himself and blurt out a few things he often regretted. If his grandson hadn't had a decent day and his behaviour necessitated a chat from his teacher, as he approached them he'd grumble, "... not another b*llocking Georgie-Boy, yer mum told yer not to be a dickhead this morning." Coupled with 'rats' cocks' every time he dropped something or hurt a body part, this grandad was apparently comedy gold. The teacher had to report that the child had used the less-polite version of 'rodent appendages' a few times in school, and when the grandad realised that he himself was the bad influence, he apologised to the teacher and said, 'It could've been worse, his gran usually says "SH*TBAGS".' For the rest of that family's time at the school the grandparents were affectionately known as 'Grandad Rat-Cock and Granny Sh*tbag'.

Not all grandparents will have such colourful nicknames and certainly not such an interesting vocabulary. When a visiting grandparent from another country with minimal English picks up their grandchild, the interactions at the end of a school day can be interesting. This is especially humorous when reporting that little Anya's wellies went missing after forest school. This will require lots of eye contact, repetition and dodgy acting, only to be greeted with nods and smiles from the grandparent who is making out that they have processed the news about her missing footwear. Don't worry, the child will immediately translate the information, rendering the conversation between the adults completely pointless.

The one thing that I find hilarious is observing the transition from being a parent to a grandparent and the change in the person graduating to the position. Plenty of mums and dads would consistently dish out roastings to their kids for untidy rooms, incomplete homework activities and failure to pronounce the 'T' in certain words.

Oooh, Mum used to hate that! Apparently, it's Manchester 'U-ni-**ted**'
(rather than 'yer-nigh-ed').

Then the parents that give you so much grief for minor indiscretions suddenly turn into the most fun humans on the planet. Here's a picture of our dad (Big Mike) and our mum, dressed as Minnie and Mickey, announcing that we're all off to Disneyland as a family one Christmas.

Where the hell were these two jokers when I was growing up?

Anyway, if you know some awesome grandparents and you are lucky enough to see them frequently (or as much as you can tolerate in some cases), then obviously, that's a positive thing. If you are a grandparent reading this book, we thank you for your service (and please can we go to Disneyland again?).

The Keyboard Warrior

Are you a keyboard warrior? Can you think of anyone who is? This is one of those people who do their damage online; they frequent the school Facebook pages, say controversial things on the parental WhatsApp groups and are equally active with their nonsense on the hilariously bad community noticeboards.

The three words that send shivers down the spine of any teacher in this rich digital world we live in has to be 'Parents' WhatsApp Group!' As an avid *Star Wars* fan, it was only recently that I discovered that Obi Wan's infamous line, 'You will never find a more wretched hive of scum and villainy,' was actually about parents' WhatsApp groups. Of course, I jest, and for the most part they are useful and helpful, but when the keyboard warriors infiltrate, it can soon turn toxic.

For any parent reading this who is yet to be added to the class WhatsApp group, please let this section be a cautionary tale so that you aren't radicalised, because it can happen to the best of us. It nearly happened to me, and I'm a bloody teacher! My kids didn't go to my school; sometimes it's better what you don't know, if you get what I mean. I don't know if I could sit there and take criticism about my children from someone when you know what they get up to at the weekend.

Anyway, I'm in this WhatsApp group, playing the role of the lurker, just observing, finding my feet. It starts innocently enough; there's that parent who is unable to read the bleeding email/text/Seesaw post/tweet asking things that are clearly stated. There's a busy parent who needs to get a job, you know – they're organising play dates, PTA stuff, the lot. Then it begins. One parent starts querying things, you have no idea what's happened but you're seeing certain things – the odd comment from the parent questioning and being negative towards the school. You give them the benefit of the doubt – why would this parent speak like this unless there is an actual issue? Your only reference point is your own child's judgement of the other parent's child, and at the age of six, you know your kid is a dodgy enough judge of character at the best of times. Then this one parent recruits a couple of other parents and it starts snowballing, and before you know it you want the school closed down. You finally speak up and write something, but only in the side group about the main group – a couple of trusted parents are in that one, so you ask them. And believe me, if you're in a parents' WhatsApp group but not part of the side group, that side group has your face as the group photo and you're the reason they've got that group.

Here is my advice, because I learned the hard way and it was only when I'd almost forgotten the fact that I am indeed a teacher and was ready to go full gung-ho protest against the school when Facebook suggested that I befriend the initiator parent who started everything, and once I had a look at this parent's profile immediate regret sank in. You only have to look at the profile picture; there she is with the kid, but we can't really tell as the profile picture is layered full of Facebook profile frames. There are at least 50 of these frames on the one profile picture. You can just make out some poppies for the Lest We Forget frame, which is laid over with a Pride flag, with a Ukraine flag to show their stance on Putin, followed by 'I've got my vaccine,' 'Stay at home, save lives,' which has now been cancelled by 'My body, my choice'.

These humans are not quite troll-level because they aren't really targeting individuals with an intent to bully or harm them, they are just virtual busybodies who should wind their necks in.

Such folks clearly think their opinion matters and, in their defence, they can sometimes be on the right side of the argument. For example, people whose dogs crap outside the school gates do deserve a calling-out. If a dog owner misses a tiny drop or nugget that popped out of their pooch's poo place, then I'm sure they just missed it; however, if there's a pile that looks like it was produced by a lion, then I'm all for the owners being named and shamed.

This is one occasion where a keyboard warrior may be a force for good, but that doesn't give them free licence to be a knobhead permanently. If they are on a parents' WhatsApp group, you can bet they will be incredibly contrary over minor issues. If the parents have collectively agreed to club together to buy the teacher a gift card and some flowers as an end of year present, the keyboard warrior will object and suggest there should be a poll to see what they do with the money they all chipped in.

If the majority of parents want to organise a get-together outside of school and have found a date that suits 95 per cent of the group, the keyboard warrior will make clear that their dog has a dentist appointment, so they need to change the date to one that suits them. They'll often start messages with, 'I thought we agreed that...' and 'Sorry to be THAT person...', knowing full well they are going to be THAT person and they aren't sorry at all. They'll take screenshots of previous conversations to prove their points. If someone forgets to do something they'll point out that the forgetful person not only read the text but they gave it a thumbs-up emoji, so they shouldn't deny knowing about it. It clearly takes a lot of effort to be that pedantic, but from the keyboard warrior's point of view it is time well spent to prove how right they are.

If they themselves are proved to be wrong, they will double down and spin the situation so that it's someone else's error. Fortunately, the rest of the WhatsApp group aren't too bothered about the trivial stuff, so they generally leave the argument there, which unfortunately gives the keyboard warrior a sense that they have won. The perfect antidote to this smugness is to have an equally pedantic person in the group with whom they will trade text-message barbs. If this happens, just snooze the conversation and ask your mate who is also on the group to let you know if anything hilarious is said between them.

WhatsApp isn't everyone's favourite way of communicating, and some parents don't particularly want their personal phone number to be available to every parent in the year group just because they produced humans within the same 12-month period. Don't get me wrong, groups like that can be very useful, especially if you've got some eagle-eyed superstars that remember everything on the school calendar and spot if there's a change in date for when the children are doing swimming or a class assembly. We definitely need folks like that in the school community.

Some schools have year-group Facebook pages. Usually titled 'Y4 parents 2023–24', or if the school has cool class names based on birds it'll be 'Wrens and Finches parents'. Whatever the name of the group, you can guarantee that the keyboard warrior is on there and probably stirring up sh*t.

These sorts of Facebook groups can sometimes be monitored by a member of staff to make sure the parents aren't slagging off the teachers too much. While some teachers are a complete pain in the arse and parents are entitled to their opinions, on those sorts of groups the teacher in question gets no right of reply, so perhaps it's good to have someone connected to the school on there. There's nothing stopping parents from starting their own rebel page called 'We Hate Miss Palmer', but the sort of people who would do that are usually d*ckheads that need to look in the mirror anyway. There's a serious element to some of this, though, and way too many teachers are bullied out of their schools by particularly nasty parents. This chapter is more about making light of parental quirks rather than a big exploration of what's wrong with social media and education, so I'll not go into any more on that point.

The class Facebook groups can be incredibly useful for parents panicking at night because their child said they needed to bring in something for the following day. You can guarantee that some parents, despite being signed up to the chosen communications app, will miss everything. Like, I'm not even joking – everything.

The sorts of things you'd find on there include:

Has anyone got Mrs Goodwin's email address?

Yes, you do. It was in the comments below your last post when you asked exactly the same question. In fact, you could look in your sent emails and it would be there.

When's Children in Need day?

This is a national event that simple googling would answer.

Is it swimming today?

A perfectly normal and useful question but the children have swimming every Thursday so I'm not sure why they'd change to a Tuesday just for one week?

I'm being slightly harsh here – there are far more stupid things on parent Facebook groups than these examples – and most people will just give the answer and laugh about how it's always the same parent that never has a clue what is going on. The keyboard warrior, however, will not only reply to the post with potentially some sarcasm, but might also correct their spelling and grammar (yet wonder why they are never invited for a drink with the other parents). Grammar and spelling are incredibly important, of course, but shaming folks on an online parents' group isn't always the best idea, especially if the parents reaching out for help have difficulties and insecurities themselves. If you're having an argument on Twitter/X, though, go for it (especially idiots that troll others).

Keyboard warriors take all forms and, obviously, this type of human is not just limited to parents' WhatsApp groups. Outsiders will still kick off about school-related things. One dweeb moved to an area directly behind a school and complained – get this – about the noise! Despite having no children at the school, he'd regularly complain on the school's Facebook page that music should not be played during school hours when he was trying to work, and after school when he was trying to relax. For three years he'd complain; every sports day, every school fête day, every... well... Thursday! Staff members would have a sweepstake in five-minute intervals as to when he'd pop on the school Facebook page for a whinge.

'OK, who had between 10:20 and 10:25? Grumpy B*llocks is moaning again!'

Sharon in the office was delighted to win a tenner that day! It was only an outdoor Christingle service because Covid restrictions were still in place. I mean, you can hardly sing 'O Come All Ye Faithful' via Zoom. How dare they?!

Another place where the keyboard warrior chooses to stick their nose in is in the community Facebook pages. It's mostly full of adverts for fêtes, knit and natter sessions, baby groups and quiz nights. Like the parent groups, they can be really useful – but they can also be ridiculously entertaining. So entertaining, in fact, that you may even question if some of the commenters on the page are actually professional comedians trying out new material. Will the keyboard warrior be in the mix on these sites? Damn right!

If you've never been on these sites purely for entertainment value, you're missing out. It's a sea of self-righteous twerps that fall out over anything from fireworks to wheelie bins. The big question is, are you the person that says the stupid stuff or are you the person that grabs a bucket of popcorn just to read someone kicking off about the teenagers that broke the swing in the local park?

Some of the groups are tame, but some in a neighbouring area can be far more spicy. Your mate Jacqui (who is just as evil as you are) may even join one of those groups purely to laugh at the comments, take screenshots of the insanity and send them to you. That's a good friend right there!

Here are a few posts you may find on such sites featuring our keyboard warriors (names and exact wording obviously changed to protect identities), and yes, some of the comments are brutal:

Post: Is there a Stephen Smith of 103 Jersey Road on here? Your parcel was delivered to me by accident.
Comment: Yes, he lives at 103 Jersey Road. Knock on his door and ask for Stephen Smith.

Post: To the teenagers that kicked over my son's snowman… I'll call the police next time.

Post: Any recommendations for a decent local butcher? Thanks
Comment: @jamesbutcher and @sallybutcher are local.
Comment: Ffs!

Post: To the person that pooed in our child's pumpkin last night, we have CCTV footage.

Post: After all the positive comments I received during my clarinet recital after we 'clapped for carers' last week, shall I do it again this Thursday?
Comment: God, NO!
Comment: I'll pay you not to!
Comment: Any ideas where I can get cheap earplugs?

Staying with this topic, here's a story we must share that was featured on the podcast. It seems like an age ago that we were clapping for carers each Thursday night at 8pm during the pandemic. Remember that? The NHS staff could've done with PPE and safer working conditions rather than just applause, but clap we did. It was funny that the street all congregated each week and then you'd catch the eye of your neighbour across the road and nod towards number 18, who didn't join in.

Our podcast listener's auntie was an absolute stickler for the whole community joining in, and one evening she went to her door with pots and pans ready to show her appreciation for our brave keyworkers. Auntie opened her door and was flabbergasted that no one on her road had bothered to join her in showing respect and appreciation for NHS workers. Disgusting behaviour! Fuming at her neighbours, she took her frustration out on social media. Channelling her inner keyboard warrior, she typed the most epic rant to post on the local Facebook group, slagging off her neighbours for showing utter contempt for those key worker heroes. Within seconds of tapping the post button, a comment appeared simply saying, 'It's Tuesday, clap for carers is Thursday.'

I'd have loved to have seen Ring doorbell footage of her clapping and banging pans on a random Tuesday; it would have been a sight and a half.

The moral of the story here is whatever your keyboard warrior says in a public forum can easily backfire, or even better, be countered by someone as bad or worse than them. Some are objectively funny, and some can be cruel, but it's amazing that whatever they will say from behind a keyboard may not be how they would talk in person. Some people feel power, some feel anger and some just get a kick from being an arse. The final part of our keyboard warrior's plethora of flaws is that they don't half post some b*llocks on their own social media platforms. Don't be surprised to see:

'I just deleted a whole load of Facebook friends that were clogging up my timeline. If you can read this, you survived the cull and you're one of the lucky ones.'

'I've just been on a litter pick with my children, and we collected three large bin bags full of rubbish.'

'Be kind.' (When you know full well that they are not.)

And some of them with no sense of irony still post...

'Live, laugh, love.'

The most unforgivable of all, however, is:

'New series of *Mrs Brown's Boys* starts tonight! Lolz'

Alright, the last one is a personal peeve of mine, but you get the picture.

We're all secretly keyboard warriors, I guess, but the ones at your local primary school can be particularly annoying, especially when they seem to be on such a mission to make others dislike them so much.

Active Mum

Active mum will be sporting activewear permanently, even on non-gym days. Even if it's just coffee with her girlfriends after school drop-off. It may be force of habit or it may just be that she is so committed to her persona as the school's parent fitness queen. Active mum is usually very focused and will potentially have a very 'active' presence on LinkedIn. She'll be posting all the time about 'goals' and 'the journey'. Some mums will be in awe of her, some mums will hate her, but all mums know that they couldn't beat her in an arm wrestle; she's got bigger muscles than half the dads on the school run. Being an active mum can be a lifestyle choice, but beware, other active mums may hang out in groups. I don't know what collective noun you would use for a group of active mums? A Lycra? Because goodness me, don't they love their Lycra?

Active mums in a group may have weekly or daily routines with regards to their exercise regimes:

- Monday: cycling
- Tuesday: jogging
- Wednesday: spin class
- Thursday: hill walking
- Friday: swimming

Plus, exercise with the family at the weekend. If you are an active mum or an aspiring active mum, I must warn you to approach these groups with great care. Not because of the potential dangers of socialising with such strong-willed women, but more along the lines that once you're in the active clique... YOU CANNOT LEAVE!

One poor mum got caught up in it and now goes walking every Thursday and bloody HATES it! She quite likes a stroll in the morning with the dog and will happily meet at a local beauty spot to get some steps in, but the commitment to the group is something she can't get out of. The problem is, despite being 28, she doesn't want to not be part of the cool group. Think *Mean Girls* but with less pink on a Wednesday (mostly because it's on Thursdays). The dress code is more about Lycra, big sunglasses and Skechers. If you miss a week of going on a mini hike up the hill, then you'll often miss the coffee and b*tching session afterwards. As we all know, if you're not part of the session, they'll be b*tching about *you*. In the words of the band Bowling for Soup... 'high school never ends!'

There's a great video (which you can probably find on YouTube) by an Australian sketch comedy group called Skit Box, where loads of mums are gathered doing various activities while wearing their activewear even if activewear is not even slightly required – like for grocery shopping, waiting for a bus, and buying more activewear while wearing... activewear. It's really funny and if you see lots of mums (and dads – the ones that should have to obtain a licence for putting their knobbly knees and hairy legs on display in public) wearing activewear on the school run, you can start chanting 'activewear' at them to amuse yourself. Active mum, however, will definitely be using her chosen attire at some point during the day, and if she's too sweaty from the first activity, not a problem – she has the same outfit, but in blue!

Active mum will walk to school with their child on their scooter, then on the way home she'll feel confident enough in her own skin to ride that scooter home. It's great cardio if you switch which leg you use! Active mum has no concept of weather. She adapts to her surroundings but will exercise in sun, rain, snow and even extreme winds. As long as she gets in her steps and feels like she's had a decent workout, the weather is of no consequence.

She may double up as a personal trainer, and she has some fantastic local clients that love her, but she's also potentially a qualified sports massage therapist, so if you overdo it she'll be able to sort your back out and revitalise your dodgy hamstrings. To have such drive and mojo to maintain a high level of fitness is admirable, but don't expect the rest of the parents to be able to keep up with her. With great perseverance comes great competitiveness, and she's constantly competing with herself to reach a new personal best. As soon as another active mum appears on the scene, you can bet she'll be sizing her up for when June/July comes, and sports day is on the horizon. They will start training in January in preparation, and don't be surprised if they attend the school fête purely to check out the condition of the running track on the field. She needs to know how hard the ground is and whether to wear her spikes or not. This isn't about showing her daughter that she's a great role model for having a growth mindset, this is about smoking Shaniqua's mum on sports day as she's the only one that came close to beating her last year... the b*tch!

Active mum will also still play competitive sports such as hockey, rounders or netball, so when the school are looking for parent volunteers to help with clubs, she's there in an instant because she wants the children to share the amazing opportunities for being active. Her positivity, focus and energy can be annoying, but you have to respect her tenacity and dedication to maintaining her body, mind and spirit. That said, I bet she's never munched an entire packet of Oreos on a Friday night because the kids are doing her head in!

The Juggler

Bloody hell, being a parent is tough sometimes and even the best of us struggle to keep the plates permanently spinning. There are some folks that are fairly straightforward and have no additional dramas. Wake up, feed child, drop them off, go to work, pick up child, feed child, put them to bed – REPEAT. They'll probably listen to their child read, pay the dinner money and help with homework. It's a pretty simple existence. Know anyone like that? Nope, neither do I! And if there are parents on the school run who look like that's what they do each day, don't be fooled. They are as stressed as everyone else, they just hide it well.

The most honest representation of most parents is the juggler, or JAM (Just About Managing). The juggler will have anywhere between two and five children of various ages.

There used to be these reality series about families in America with multiple children. Shows such as *Jon & Kate Plus 8*, *OctoMom* and *18 Kids and Counting*. They were pretty big during the 2000s reality TV boom, although if you google for yourself and see how these families were affected by being surrounded by cameras 24/7, and how the actions and relationships of some family members weren't entirely positive, you may be shocked (or unsurprised).

I had my 15 minutes of fame with my triplets on the local BBC News over a decade ago and that was more than enough exposure with the three of them, thanks.

Are you a juggler? Do you have more than just spinning plates to get on with? Does it sometimes feel like you're riding a unicycle while playing 'God Save the King' on a kazoo and balancing a vase on your head? Alright, that's extreme, but there's so much going on for many parents that managing to stay on top of any of it is quite a brain ache.

Many modern parents have multiple roles at home and at work. The years of having 2.4 children, one car and a parent that stays at home are long gone. Despite all of the depictions in Hollywood films about how perfect life in the 1950s was, they are forgetting the paranoia about nuclear war, the misogyny and the casual racism – but as long as you have a white picket fence and a Cadillac, you're all swell and peachy.

There's earned respect for a juggler or a JAM parent, mostly because they genuinely love their kids, their house isn't Instagram-perfect and every meal isn't organic. They care about the environment and are very careful in sorting their recycling each fortnight, but they don't preach to others who fail to wash out their Marmite pots.

Their cooking is perfectly adequate and most nights the family do eat chicken dippers, potato waffles and beans – or some other beige variation – but there's always plenty of fruit in the house, as evidenced by the children's bowel movements and ability to break wind. Any child invited for tea won't care that they aren't having lobster thermidor; bring on those Aldi pizzas (not forgetting that garlic bread you can still taste a week later). They'll also get a chance to play Dad's retro Super Nintendo that he got for Christmas in 2018 and still uses regularly now.

You see plenty of dreadful adverts with adults pretending to play video games with their children and grandchildren, they're laughing hysterically like Peppa Pig's family when Grandad gets something wrong by pressing the buttons. Those type of adverts are cheesy as hell and very annoying, because while it's great to play *Mario Kart* as a family, there's no collective laughing at doddery old grandpop, it's sh*thousery of the highest order and probably tears. If someone hits me with a red shell right before I'm about to cross the finish line, they'd best watch their back! The juggler will join in with such activities and the children will be so impressed with how she manages to give them a run for their money on *Mario Kart*, as she's been practising since 1992. The children, however, refuse to play her on *Street-fighter II* as Chun Li because she is UNBEATABLE and her trash-talking is UNBEARABLE!

While we're on gaming trash-talk, there's a video by Irish TikTok star @mammybanter where she highlights the absolute b**locks spouted by young gamers these days. It's bad enough that a nine-year-old refers to their mum as 'brah' but what in the blue hell is a 'Sigma-Skibidi-Toilet-Rizla'? Yes, I'm paraphrasing, but there'll be plenty of parents reading this that recognise the verbiage yet are as clueless as I am about what they bloody mean. And it's not just heard while online gaming. I can assure you that the children continue this waffle in the playground too.

As well as having multiple children, the juggler may have multiple jobs. Some jugglers even work in the schools at the breakfast club, as a TA, as a lunchtime supervisor and at the after-school club. She cleans people's homes at the weekend and is often called up to pull pints in the local pub when they have staff off either on holiday or through sickness. Her brother has an ice cream van and will often be at events as well. Her Mr Whippy skills are quite impressive, and she knows how to create every sundae on the board in under a minute.

Everyone tries to juggle, although some parents are more successful than others. In a perfect example of trying to keep all the plates spinning and failing miserably, one parent was on autopilot and clearly on another planet as well. She drove to her child's nursery, and just as she pulled in and got out of the car, she realised there'd been a big mistake. No little tiddler in the back of the car. He had been dropped off that morning at her mum's house!

The mum felt compelled to ring the nursery manager to explain why she had pulled up in the car, then she had a cry and drove off again. What made it worse was that on the same day, she arrived to pick the child up and had already rung the doorbell before realising that the child was, once again, at her mother's house.

It was awkward as hell explaining her mistake to the staff, who clearly thought she had lost her marbles.

Another wonderful example of trying to juggle life and failing involved one podcast listener forgetting something important. We're all in a rush sometimes, and just remembering your keys, wallet and phone in the morning can be seen as a win. One morning, this listener was getting ready to take a train. She had a decent routine most of the time, but mistakes happen. When brushing her teeth, she managed to drop some toothpaste on her skirt. We've all done something similar, but sadly the skirt was dark and the splat was very visible. She took off her skirt, gave it a good scrub and popped it onto the radiator while she packed her bag and lunch. It would be a quick turnaround, but the good news is, the lady managed to get out of the door on time and get to the railway station with minutes to spare. Good work!

One would almost forgive this teacher for a little bit of self-congratulation, but unfortunately for her there was one major issue on the horizon that she was yet to discover. Two trains later and strolling towards her final destination, the wind was starting to pick up and her legs were feeling the breeze. She reached down to make sure her skirt was in the correct place but there was one glaring issue... NO SKIRT! The flipping thing was still nice and toastie on her radiator at home, and she had been flashing her tights and knickers to the general public for the best part of half an hour.

A great start to the day!

At the end of the day all parents are jugglers, and just-about-managing is a common trait. If it means she can help her family to the best of her ability, then she's worthy of much praise.

Business Mum

Yep, that's right, business mum is a mum who works... in business.

She loves her kids, absolutely adores them, and she works bloody hard to ensure she gives them nice things and wonderful experiences. Look on her Facebook page and you'll be loving her holiday pictures with her crazy kids and idiot husband. I say 'idiot husband', because he's more interested in ruining the family photos with silly or grumpy faces. Why can't he just smile properly?

Business mum is incredibly good at her job and can make very bold and serious decisions about very bold and serious things. Don't be mistaken, she's not a Corporate Caroline – you know, one of those incredibly driven women who are probably equally good at their job but you're not sure why they bothered to have kids in the first place because they hardly talk to them or care what they are doing at school. Business mum lives for her children, even if she doesn't fully understand every aspect of what goes down at school.

There are some parenting aspects she's got nailed; she always pays for school trips straight away, the nasal flu vaccination form is completed immediately, and she won't be ordering school photos at the last minute. The school office is very grateful for her timeliness, and they'd be happy for as many people as possible to be as efficient as her.

She'll also have her parents' evening slots booked before she's even consulted her husband (and, sorry, teachers, it'll probably be the penultimate one of the evening).

Her level of financial and business knowledge is an asset to the PTA. Affectionately known as the 'ball-breaker', it's no wonder she's nominated as treasurer every year. She's the perfect ying to the overly excitable chairperson's yang and will need to see a SWOT Analysis (Strengths, Weaknesses, Opportunities and Threats) of running a fundraising event.

She wants to know what the financial benefit of 'Wacky-Hair Day' will be when the families spend more money on coloured hairspray, bright pink extensions and jazzy headband accessories, yet only charge 50p for the privilege. She also wants to know why they are buying burgers for the school fête from Waitrose rather than at the wholesalers, where they already have an account.

Her work pattern is usually very intense, and she may be away quite often, but she always tries to get involved. While helping out at one Halloween disco she ended up sitting at a colouring-in table chatting to the other business mums, and when it came time to run the tuck shop, the business mums gathered and worked together as a retailing machine, calculating the change before the Year 3 child had pulled her 50p out of her LOL Surprise wallet.

One thing that is potentially a common theme with parents that are high-flying business folk is that they can be their children's best friends, but weirdly their worst enemies as well. This juxtaposition can be explained by the theory of 'The Middle'. The Middle, or lack thereof, is where a business parent (or any parent for that matter) is on a scale.

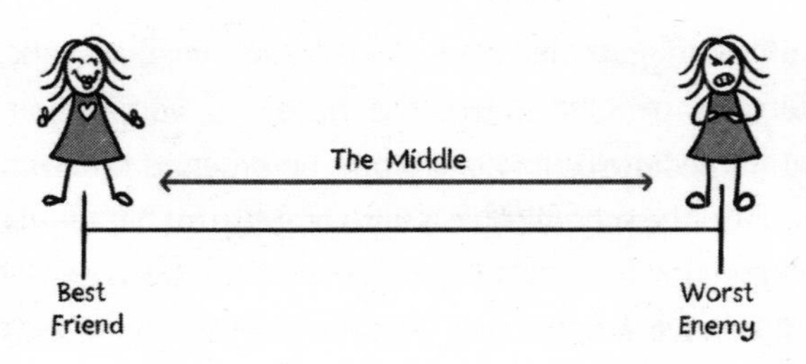

As you can see, there is one end on the left where parents are the children's best friend. They book the best holidays, they take the children on days out to lovely places and they are single-handedly keeping the ice cream van that visits their road in profit! If there's a teachers' strike day and the children need to stay home, boring dad may make the children fill out a worksheet, practise their spellings and play a few maths games, followed by a quick spot of exercise in the afternoon and then some reading to keep the children on track. However, if the children are off with business mum, you can bet they'll be getting breakfast delivered by Greggs, a trip to the cinema and possibly a Maccy D's for lunch! Her cynical husband will humorously accuse her of buying her children's affections with fun and fast food, but she will respond by blowing a raspberry and sticking two fingers up at him when the children aren't looking. Also, she's a nightmare with bedtimes. If the children aren't being dropped off by her in the morning and Dad is out playing football or at the pub, you can guarantee that bedtime has gone out the window. If she's not on duty to get them to school the following morning, she'll happily spend a good hour and a half buggering about showing TikTok videos and training Pokémon. This is why business mum is often the favourite parent.

At the other end of the scale, though, is the worst enemy part. Because she is so focused while in the business world, she may struggle to communicate in the most appropriate manner over the little things. If she walks into a bedroom after a very annoying Zoom call with bad clients or team members not pulling their weight, she may start pointing out the breakfast bowl still half full of Coco Pops, the un-emptied bin and the towel from this morning's shower still on the floor.

In summary, the business mum is the most fun, but she also gives the biggest b*llockings! On the scale, she has no middle, no median, no halfway point; she's either the greatest human alive according to her children or the biggest grumblebum/tyrant (depending on how messy the room is). Business mum does have an off switch, she just needs to exchange it for one of those circular ones used for dimming lights.

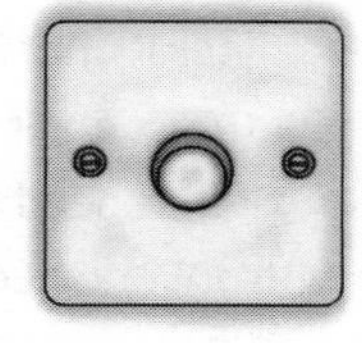

Pitch-side Legend

Some mums and dads will support the school in many ways, and whether they are on the PTA, regularly volunteering or even part of the school's governing body, it makes a huge difference to the life of the school. Budgets are tight, so decent parent volunteers during school hours are invaluable to help listen to readers or support groups in lessons.

Not all parents can contribute in this way, but plenty have skills to share. The pitch-side legend is so-named because of the contribution he makes to the enjoyment of children's sport at the school. First and foremost, he and his wife have very kindly produced three children and they are reasonably spaced out across the year groups, so a school that is lucky enough to have a character like him should get at least a decade of his support. All of his children enjoy sporting activities and he's very happy to contribute.

His actual name is perfectly normal, like a Mr Dobson, Mr Ryder or Mr Jones, but the children will affectionally know him by his nickname, something like 'Dobbo' or 'Tug'. That's how he was known in the fire service and on the rugby field, so that name has stuck. He's already got a DBS from coaching his children's sports team, so gaining one to help out at the school was easily obtained.

This guy will be pitch-side for all the sporting events he's needed at. Very vocal, yes, but never disrespectful to the officials. Back in his day you still called the referee 'Sir', if you knew what was good for you. He had a decent footballing career as well, so when the teacher is having to referee a home football match, the pitch-side legend will help run the substitutes or even run the line. No job is too small for him and he's genuinely happy when the children are enjoying their sport. You wouldn't be able to tell this, however, as he's a right grumpy bugger and incredibly sarcastic. Once you peel back the layers you realise he's one of the best dudes you'll ever meet, but he'll never let on that he's actually quite a sweetheart.

Guys like him are VERY helpful, as there are few teachers in modern primary schools that have enough time to commit to running a sports team or club, let alone multiple ones. One guy that qualified in 2007 as an NQT/ECT took over as the school's PE co-ordinator and at the same time ran all their predecessor's clubs. His week went as follows:

- Monday – Boys' football
- Tuesday – Netball
- Wednesday – Staff meeting (a couple of pitch-side legends did rugby that night)
- Thursday – Girls' football
- Friday – Key Stage 1 Skills Club

There's plenty in this book that we exaggerate and embellish for comic effect, but this anecdote is factually correct: he really did have to do all those clubs. I was the same in my first few years of teaching. There's no way I should've been expected to do that number of sports clubs, but there was an incentive, namely opportunities and competitions that were funded and run thanks to all the investment into the 2012 Olympics and through things like the School Sports Partnership. I'll say more about this later in the book, but I definitely remember a time when sport was held in much higher esteem as an educational priority.

Pitch-side legends aren't all big, burly, former rugby players, though. If you're a parent and your children play a sport like rugby, football or hockey at the weekend, you'll understand that it's great fun when the sun is out but less fun when it's December, cold and p*ssing it down. Some parents bring the brollies, some sort the kit, some do the coaching and the ones that do the refereeing get huge kudos in my book. If the parent is a coach, it's quite a big responsibility, so they need the support of the parents from the sidelines. Our pitch-side legend will do anything to help out: with coaching, lifts, to step in as ref – and he's a qualified first aider. He gets a lot of respect for that too.

As a quick aside, I spend a lot of time on the sidelines and I support my children with their team sports. I've done this as a teacher and I obviously do it for my own kids. You would think I would get some respect too... nope! I went with my two lads on a mini tour that ventured to Wales. If you've been around rugby at all you'll know that there's a lot of banter. You play hard on the pitch and enjoy the camaraderie off it. At school-age level, obviously there's none of the famous drinking games and stealing golf buggies (that I'm aware of), but there are plenty of tour traditions and shenanigans as part of the evening's entertainment. One night on this particular tour, I ended up with both my lads wielding custard pies that were apparently destined for my mush. If it was anyone else's kid it would only be one pie, but because I have two boys, I was going to be punished twice.

You'd think as their father they would respect me enough to place the edible missiles in my moneymaker gently. Did they do that? Did they b**locks! Both little gits smashed me so hard in the face with the custard pies that I thought they'd broken my nose. I suppose I deserved it for making them reluctantly appear in some of my social media videos. We'll call it a draw for now.

Back to our pitch-side legend. One I can think of is a former rugby lock/2nd row and a centre-half; he's an imposing figure so I'm not sure my kids would dare pie him. He helps to run the after-school tag-rugby club. Everybody is welcome as long as they've got a good attitude and will give it a go. He starts with a game of 'British bulldog', wearing the tag belts he managed to blag from the local rugby club. He's very well known in the local rugby community and has contacts everywhere. He's kitted out the whole school with balls (he knows a bloke who runs rugby tours and they donate plenty of items they no longer need), he's got sponsors for the PTA-purchased rugby kits. He even has a contact at the closest Premiership rugby team, who'll send players to visit, present awards and run curriculum sessions. The greatest acquisition he made was having a tackle bag and pads donated, as they are the absolute highlight at the end of his club, where the children get to smash him as hard as they can (he only pretends to move for the little ones, then they get to wipe out the tackle bag). An absolute Bobby-dazzler of a parent and the school will be absolutely gutted when his youngest child leaves. That said, there's every chance he'll keep volunteering, because he really is a legend.

The Fusspot

All parents have the capacity to be fussy, and a lot of the time they have every right to be concerned or to want to make sure that their child's experience is as positive as it can be at school.

Some parents have a very laissez-faire approach, where they are inclined to leave things to take their own course without interfering. It doesn't mean they don't care about their child, in fact it's the opposite; they want them to have fun without too many boundaries, but if they step over certain lines, then they get what they deserve. Those sorts of parents will never quibble if their child has to stay in at break time for doing something wrong. Do the crime, serve the time, is their attitude.

Not the fusspot... The fusspot will not only ask how their child's day was, she'll also take notes as evidence. If her little prince or princess reports another child's behaviour to her, you know she'll be down in an instant to report that child. This parent will request that their child is moved in the classroom on a near-weekly basis as the other children stop her little cherub from learning. To be fair, some of the children she takes issue with can be annoying or bothersome, but her child has managed to systematically fall out with around 75 per cent of the class, which begs the question, is it her child that is the problem?

Ask the teacher... yes, it bloody is!

Ask the fusspot... no, it's everyone else.

She'll constantly request meetings with the teacher to discuss her child's progress, but she's never interested in how he's doing academically, she just wants to slag off the other kids, especially the children whose parents she doesn't like. She may have good reason to take issue with certain children and/or their parents, but because she's well known for causing problems, people don't take her quite as seriously.

Many times over she has applied to be a parent governor, but she can seldom find someone to nominate her, and if she gets on the ballot, she's overwhelmingly defeated, much to the relief of the staff and the headteacher.

Parents should be praised for taking such an interest in their children, and there are lots of children from a school perspective that could really do with greater engagement from their guardians and caregivers, but there is an unspoken line between being interested and being annoying.

If there's a school open morning, where parents are invited to come and see their children in action, the fusspot will definitely be in attendance. Teachers will start the activity for the whole class and their visitors, and if fusspot hasn't appeared, the staff with be quietly celebrating inside. Don't worry, though, she'll appear just before they kick off the sentence-writing task and make loads of noise as she enters. Fusspot won't even sit near their own child, but they will audibly talk during the instructions, much to the teacher's annoyance.

If you've ever been to one of these open mornings, the teachers will prepare an activity for their children to excel at that the parents may struggle with. Just so the parents can be impressed that their children understand modal-verbs and commutative laws.

Fusspot is never impressed. They just flick through the children's school books and point out missed full stops and capital letters. Make comments like, 'What has happened to your handwriting this year?' loudly enough for the other parents to hear. The fusspot is also unsurprisingly pedantic and will point out that 'practice' is spelt with a 'c', despite the fact that it's the verb form that requires an 's'. Funnily enough, she doesn't appreciate being corrected by the little boy sitting next to her. That kid's definitely going to be swimming in house points once the parents are gone.

The fusspot will always be on the lookout to correct any communications that they receive, but even the fusspot might find this error to be funny. Actually, she probably won't, but I'm going to share it anyway. We get stories all the time on the podcast about schools trying to do the right thing with their communications and translating for the parents with English as a second language. In one bizarre example where the translation app should not have been trusted, a school sent home a message about sickness procedures to a Romanian parent that read:

'If your child is stupid, please do not send them to school for 48 hours.'

If that was the case at our school, Adam would have missed a lot of time in class!

One thing fusspot would've spotted straight away was a mistake in a school newsletter. One faux pas that an eagle-eyed parent spotted was when the teacher writing the newsletter used an emoji to accentuate some exciting news but didn't spot that the smiling face was actually smoking a joint.

Talk about having 'HIGH expectations' for the kids!

While we're on the topic of correspondence going home that the fusspot would be ALL over, one school had to send a letter to parents to apologise for something displayed on an interactive whiteboard during a class music lesson.

Teachers have to be careful because whatever is on their laptop screen will be displayed for the whole class to see. This is why many teachers freeze their whiteboards when using their computers for sensitive information (emails, data) that they don't want their class to look at. I bet this teacher wishes she'd frozen her screen or turned off on this occasion, as you are about to find out...

During the music lesson, the class were singing about a grandfather clock and it became apparent that the children had no idea what that was. A child asked if they could google it, and due to an unfortunate typo the search engine results were not quite as expected. 'Grandfather clock' was missing an 'L' and incredibly, the school's internet filter had not detected the image of an old man's penis, which was in full view of the entire class of children!

Can you imagine the fusspot's response to that? Yikes!

Fusspots come in all shapes and sizes, and can be found all across the country.

One fusspot from north of the border made it known she was not happy with her child's P7 (Scottish Year 6) teacher after their leavers' assembly.

A quick bit of context here. Year 6/P7 staff will do their utmost to ensure a smooth transition to secondary school and make a huge deal of the little legends on their way out of the door during their final days of primary school. Since teachers really started embracing technology in the last 20 or so years, there is usually a PowerPoint to music or mini highlight video created for the children to look back on during their leavers' assembly and remember their primary years fondly. One quite sweet activity is to make a video of the children 'then and now'. Parents will submit photos of their child when they are tiny so the teacher can create a cool little video that shows how much they have grown physically and as people.

There will always be a few families that leave it until the last minute to provide photos, ALWAYS! One parent did just that and their child's photos missed final edit. It happens, but what the teacher doesn't expect are emails from irate parents containing lines like:

'You have spoiled their last day of school.'

'You have ruined this milestone.'

'Thank you for being the worst teacher they have ever had.'

Where fusspot's disagreeability stems from is anyone's guess. Perhaps she was picked on at school, perhaps she was overly corrected by teachers and parents as a child. There's every possibility that it is a combination of both and more. Deep down, you know she probably dislikes herself a little, so on the VERY rare occasions that she lets her hair down, it would be great to see her smile and enjoy herself. So a plea from teachers to parents: if you ever see a known fusspot frequent a public house and you're in there, please buy them a beverage or two and help them to have fun. To paraphrase Austin Powers (badly): 'It would be a shame for that bug up her arse to die!'

Bed-hair Magee

We've all seen these parents on the school run, and we can all think of one or more people that would fit this description. This is purely a jolly look at those parents that don't have their sh*t together – almost the complete opposite of the business mum.

Nobody is even doubting that Bed-hair Magee loves her children. In fact, she probably spends more time with her children than business mum, who may be constantly travelling as part of her work, but Bed-hair Magee definitely isn't as organised. I'm talking about the mum that rocks up to school late, parks on top of the sign of the little child on the tarmac that says 'Please don't park here' and runs in with her children four minutes after the bell has gone, hoping that the gate is still open.

Bed-hair Magee is aptly named due to her hair looking like she has just jumped out of bed. Chances are, she hasn't at all, she's just been too busy trying to get everything else ready in the morning because 'prepping the night before' is not a concept she is familiar with.

Yes, she will come to school wearing her pyjamas, a pair of Ugg boots, a huge puffer jacket and big sunglasses, and, yes, she may still be smelling of fags/vapes and a bit of Malibu a couple of times a month, but her children are actually quite nice little scallywags and their homework is always done. Done in spite of their mum's help or not is another question, but to their credit, they are pretty unfazed by their mum's inconsistencies, and if anything they are being taught the valuable lesson of being organised enough so they don't look like her in the future.

One HUGE thing to point out about how unfair this judgement is on Bed-hair Magee is that the same standards of presentation are not expected of the male equivalent: Scruff-bag Magoo. If Scruff-bag is having a bad hair day, he just shoves on a baseball cap and wears shorts and flip-flops. Nobody is judging his make-up or lack thereof.

Bed-hair Magee will not always look like this, though. Some days of the week she is immaculately dressed (usually when she's dating again) and scrubs up incredibly well – you might not even recognise her initially. It's the same person there, it's just that her alarm clock was working that day or she hadn't partaken in a few Proseccos the previous evening. It's REALLY funny to see the parent besties that were heavily involved in 2-for-1 cocktail Tuesday at their favourite bar and how they are all sporting bed hair, big sunglasses and minimal make-up the following morning. They had a great night but you can bet they've all got banging head-aches and no amount of coffee or a fry-up is going to bring them back to life for the rest of the day. So rather than judging their life choices, you just smile and utter, 'Good night, last night?' as you know full well it was as they posted it all on Facebook until about 3am.

There are some variations on Bed-hair Magee that are less savoury, and lazy words like 'chav' are often thrown at them. Don't get me wrong, some deserve the reputations they get, whereas others are just working with the cards they've been dealt. They don't need people looking down on them, and that's not what we've been trying to do here.

Yes, there are plenty of parents that do drop their kids off late, wear pyjamas and swear audibly outside the school with a dog that will take a massive dump that won't be cleaned up. You've seen them and you know who they are in your local area, but we're not here to make light of that sort of person or suggest they should be allowed to produce other humans. We're celebrating the majesty of the bed-hair crew and how they manage to function perfectly well sometimes but have no shame the morning after a sesh with their girlies. Whoop whoop!

So there we go, plenty of characters that you may have the pleasure of encountering on the school run, at parents' evening and (if you can't avoid it) the supermarket. These are just archetypes of some of the humans that teachers interact with over the school year and quite often bring great entertainment when we do. Did you manage to recognise yourself or someone you know?

These characters aren't specific to any particular gender, though. Maybe you're an active dad or even a Brenda Big-Bollocks. Fusspots are equally likely to be men and mums are definitely pitch-side legends too. Now you've read this chapter, you can go on the school run and start noticing some of the crazy characters we've been talking about and giggle to yourself. Don't giggle too loudly, mind, otherwise it may scare the children and the other parents. Perhaps just treat yourself to a little chuckle.

Back to the school year, and now we're into October. What the hell happened to the summer? You might be asking yourself this when it hits 7:36 on a weeknight and it's almost dark. Don't worry, you'll be in for a bigger shock in a week's time when it's getting dark at 7:27. I say 'shock' – we all know the evenings get darker earlier each autumn, but if we try to suspend our disbelief just a tiny bit we still think we can prolong summer by about five minutes at least (science teachers reading this, we are aware that this is total b**locks, but please bear with us as we come to terms with the changing seasons).

In Britain over the last 15 or so years, it's not been uncommon for there to be a decent spell of warm, sunny weather into September and, if you're lucky and you like that sort of thing, even into the start of October. This is commonly referred to as an 'Indian summer', but any aspect of summer is welcome to stick around for a tiny bit longer. I've known PE lessons go on outside up to October half term some years, where you can still be in shorts and T-shirt on the field teaching some football or tag-rugby skills. It's not guaranteed, but any opportunity to pretend it's not winter yet is always worth taking advantage of. To test this theory, by all means have a little jog around on some grass, and if you trip trying to avoid a twig or a fox turd and you land and it's soft, you know it's gradually turning autumnal. Try that in July and you may end up with a bruised gluteus maximus!

Children will often switch from shorts to trousers as it starts to get colder – it depends if the school has to choose between heating the school or employing some more support staff. Both are incredibly important and valuable, but worryingly, there are schools that have literally had to make that choice.

As the shorts are switched to trousers, there's a considerable possibility that the mood will start to become a little testy. Some children, teachers and parents feel that shift in early September, and while it may not be as severe as the January Blues, there are many that find this period hard to deal with. The children that are not happy with the drop in temperature and the reduced daylight hours are those that love to play outside. It's a tight window between September and mid-October where summertime becomes more and more distant. Lots of 'This time two weeks ago, we were still in Majorca' talk will soon be replaced with 'Why can't I go out on my bike for another hour?' Once the initial shock of embracing autumnal conditions is out of the way, families can plan a few more trips to the cinema/bowling alley rather than the beach and the local outdoor pool.

This is the perfect time for school coaches, PE leaders and parents to try to fit in their fixtures before the conditions are too bad (dark/muddy). Depending on the size of the school, the person in charge of their inter-school sports fixtures (football, netball, hockey and tag rugby are common at primary level) will be frantically trying to pencil in matches between themselves and other schools.

But as term progresses, the behaviours we are all used to will start to need tweaking. Is it acceptable to have a school-night barbecue where the kids can splash around in the paddling pool? Well, nobody's stopping you, but it's not particularly advisable. Certainly not when it hits NOVEMBER!

This is the time of year when children are disgusted that they are not only back in the process of reading regularly to their parents again, but they also have to provide evidence in a little yellow book. The comments at the start of the year tend to look a bit like this:

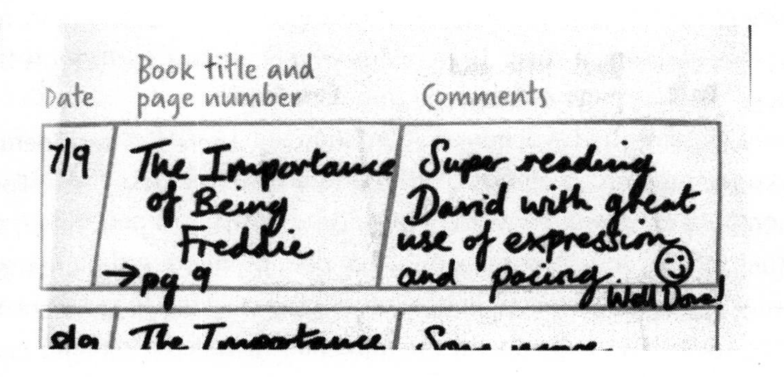

Date	Book title and page number	Comments
7/9	The Importance of Being Freddie →pg 9	Super reading David with great use of expression and pacing. ☺ Well Done!

Yet we know that by June, they look like this:

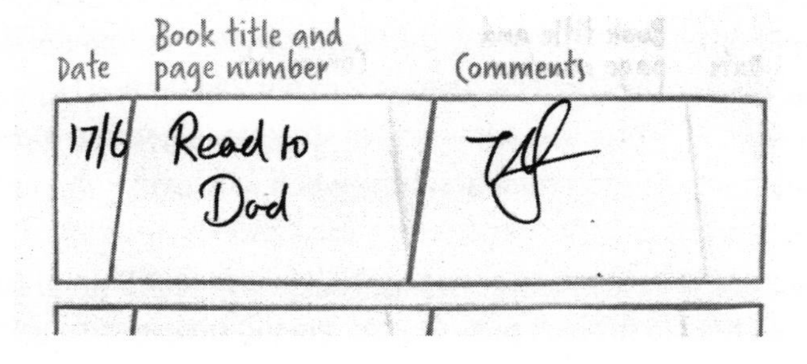

Date	Book title and page number	Comments
17/6	Read to Dad	[signature]

The children will start learning spellings again and there will always be moaning about the lack of consistency in the spelling words. Why has little Hannah gone from learning the word 'onomatopoeia' in her

Year 3 spellings but her first set of words in Year 4 contain 'ghost' and 'ghoul'? There's probably a good educational reason for it, but from a teacher's point of view, they just need to learn them as best they can. As the children go up the year groups, there's a potentially greater expectation on home learning, especially if the school had crap maths results. You can bet there'll be extra times tables practice if that's the case.

Everyone has a morning routine (well, unless you work nights, in which case you're either asleep or just finishing work). What's your morning routine like?

Are you one of these keen beans who is up at 5:30am for a run/dog walk/gym visit before a fabulous homemade breakfast of granola, smashed avocado on sourdough toast with freshly squeezed orange juice and a hint of chilli? If you are, fair play to you, but the majority of us will be just about getting our sh*t together and our fuel for the morning may be a handful of Frosties that the kids couldn't be bothered to finish before they decided that they can't find their shoes and now their reading book is covered in milk.

Mornings are HARD WORK with little ones. Teenagers aren't much fun either, but at least you don't usually have to physically dress them before kicking them out of the door so they don't miss their bus. Primary-aged children are the biggest bunch of dossers. There, I said it. Tyson Fury would be calling them out, big time.

It's hard in September when you're starting to get into a routine, but at least it's potentially sunny when you wake up and the temperature is a little fresh rather than bloody freezing. Getting into a routine in September has its own issues, but trying to wake up when it's pitch-black outside and leaving your warm bed to go and make sandwiches that'll probably end up in the bin isn't too appealing.

Even if you don't have children and you're a teacher, your morning routine could be equally grim. Some teaching staff will be up at the sparrow's fart and into school (depending on their commute), printing off Twinkl worksheets at 6am because the Year 6 crew were bashing out 62 practice SATs tests the night before.

Whatever your routine, it's a huge task to take children from a state of sleep to being ready to start their day and manage to get yourself ready in the process. Your own personal waking-up and getting-ready process may be vastly different, but how many individual things from this routine can you relate to?

5:30 Alarm goes off (ignored)
5:45 2nd alarm goes off (also ignored)
6:00 Zzzzzzzzzz 😴
6:07 Sh*t! I best bloody get up then.
6:09 Cat is chewing on your toe because it needs feeding while you're trying to make breakfast.
6:15 Wake up secondary school-aged child and pop on a classic episode of *The Simpsons*. Bring in their breakfast, including a chewy vitamin for them to consume.
6:17 Watch *The Simpsons* with child while scrolling through and deleting all the emails you received overnight from companies whose Wi-Fi you used once while on holiday and you've forgotten how to pop them in the spam folder since the last iOS update came through.
6:19 Stop watching *The Simpsons* as you can hear your cat making that gagging sound before vomiting up his Felix: As Good As It Looks tasty shreds on the kitchen floor.
6:20 Slip in cat vomit and swear as quietly as you can so as not to wake up the entire house.
6:21 Wipe up the cat spew, then swear that the cats eat better than you do in your house. Start wishing you had a dog because they'd happily clean up their own vomit.
6:24 Wash your hands thoroughly.

6:25 Empty the dishwasher from the night before because you need the Tupperware pots to put the children's sandwiches in. You'd usually just give them a quick wipe but when you opened the lunchbox yesterday after school, it was caked in banana peel and yoghurt.

6:33 Put the kettle on.

6:34 Treat yourself and go for a wee!

6:36 Make yourself (and partner, if you have one) a cup of tea.

6:39 Sit down to see the end credits of *The Simpsons* rolling. Your teenager will roll their eyes and tell you you've missed a good episode. Teenager goes upstairs to have a shower and watch their phone.

6:40 Start making packed lunches and checking the children's timetables to see if they have Forest School, PE or swimming that day and they've forgotten to tell you.

6:41 Retrieve wet swimming stuff from last week's bag. More swearing.

6:45 Quickly cobble together another set of swimming kit as a replacement.

6:55 Discover that the older child needs a replacement shirt as they have just remembered that a pen leaked in their pocket yesterday. Grab another shirt from the back of the wardrobe that still smells nice because of the wild orchid fabric softener used on it last week. Get out the ironing board and iron out the creases.

7:00 Wake up primary-aged children.

7:02 Burn yourself on the iron that you forgot to unplug. Even more swearing.

7:05 Plonk younger child in front of TV and ask them why they don't want to eat the cereal you've bought them today as they ate it perfectly fine yesterday and you've only just opened a new family-sized box.

7:10 Give the older child a reminder to get their arse moving as they should be dressed by now.

7:15 Reset the Wi-Fi as the younger child is part-way through an episode of *Bluey* that you are streaming through your phone.
7:20 Finish making packed lunches just as the younger child remembers that it's roast dinner day at school. Very quiet swearing under breath.
7:25 Drive oldest child to the bus stop.
7:26 Turn back as child has forgotten their swimming kit AND bus pass.
7:29 Drop child at bus stop, seconds before the bus arrives.
7:35 Return home and pop in the shower.
7:40 Dry yourself off and take a breath but don't get too comfortable as there's a shout from downstairs that there's been a spillage.
7:50 Clear up spillage and lay out the younger child's clothes. Make sure both shoes are present.
8:00 Finish getting yourself ready, brush your teeth, then remind your youngest to do theirs.
8:05 Remind your youngest to get dressed.
8:10 Remind your youngest child to get dressed AGAIN.
8:15 Point out that your youngest child's toothbrush is still dry and to get off their iPad and get dressed.
8:20 Child dressed, one shoe missing.
8:25 Still searching for shoe.
8:30 SHOE FOUND.
8:35 Walk to school.
8:36 Run back to house to get reading book that was left out of bag.
8:37 Start walking again.
8:40 Phone call from older child as the shorts packed for swimming are actually his brother's.
8:45 Youngest child in school!
8:55 Discover previous cup of tea... NOW COLD!

This is an example for a family or person that doesn't have to be in work for 9am themselves. For people who do, perhaps wake up 30 minutes earlier, and add a lot more shouting and spilling things. Don't even get me started on dustbin day!

OK, here's a huge decision at this time of year... when do you put the heating on?

From *The Simpsons* to *Family Guy*, to hundreds of TikTok comedians, there's the joke that a big row usually ensues when the house thermostat is touched by anyone other than Dad. Almost as if there's a sixth sense about when someone is adjusting it.

The reason for this is because it costs money to heat our homes (obviously) and lots of folks don't want to pop on any form of heating until the seasonal climate makes it entirely necessary. The issue with putting the heating on is because the weather in the UK can't make up its mind at the best of times.

A quick but important aside, because it's a touchy subject and something I don't want to make light of, is that there are families in our school communities who are actually having to choose whether to be warm or fed. It's very wrong in the developed world that this is even an issue. So, the decision to pop the heating on is huge for them.

Back to the silly stuff, popping the heating on for most families is an admission that it's wintertime, and while the orange, yellow and brown leaves on the ground act as a warning, it's a big decision to admit that it's cold enough to have your radiators on again.

By the way, don't trust those leaves. They are not evil, but as beautiful as they are, they are not for playing in, as the movies, cartoons and comics may suggest. You never know what's lurking in there and you don't want to find out the hard way. Yes, there may be a few conkers among them, and yes, when I see a horse chestnut seed I feel like I'm eight years old and ready to battle the world, but lurking inside the leaves there may be something else.

One teacher recalled a time when they were on a Forest School session and the children were playing in the leaves while trying to identify which tree they had come from. In one group, the children spotted a small pile of leaves and decided to make it into a bigger pile by kicking more and more on top. It was close to a little mound of earth-covered grass and a child reckoned (when his teacher's back was turned) he could do a front flip into it. The move is what wrestling fans would call a 'Swanton Bomb'. The child's calculations about whether he'd reach the pile of leaves were decent. With enough push off the mound, he was able to hit the leaves back first. Well done him. What he didn't anticipate was the surprisingly large hedgehog trying to sleep at the bottom of the leaves. Let's just say that Mrs Tiggywinkle had a rather rude awakening and the flying wrestler wannabe was in quite a bit of pain. Ouchy!

To be honest, every family has had a go at kicking some leaves on the way to or back from school at some point in the autumn. It is quite fun, but it's not funny when you slide your foot through a massive pile of dog sh*t. Obviously it's hilarious if it happens to someone else (especially if they are wearing pristine white Reebok Classics), but it does bring me back to my point about why you shouldn't trust leaves!

Anyway, from untrustworthy leaves back to turning on the heating (seamless link...). With falling leaves, dropping temperatures and darker mornings, it presents such a nightmare decision for some because of how difficult it is to wake up in the morning anyway! If you pop your heating on (even on a timer) and it kicks in about an hour before you've got to get up, then you stand a much bigger chance of sleeping through your alarm. While it's hilarious to watch the family rushing around when they sleep in during *Home Alone*, it's not so funny when it's your family and you don't live in a massive house in suburban Chicago. (There have been some theories online about exactly what job the dad did to be able to afford a house that big for his huge family. Not to mention how much it cost to take his ungrateful brother and his equally huge family to Paris for Christmas. Let's just assume he's the head of a drug cartel and then it all makes sense. I bet they didn't care what level their thermostat was on!)

Sometimes known as your 'pit', trying to get out of bed on a cold day is soul-destroying. You may be one of the people that have an alarm set in five-minute intervals from about 6am onwards, but you know full well that you'll be snoozing through every bloody one before you finally manage to raise your carcass from said pit.

If you have tiny children, you'll be awake at 4am anyway because those selfish little creatures can't take care of themselves yet. How dare a one-year-old still require feeding and changing so early in the morning? As for entertaining them... CBeebies doesn't start until 6am so you're stuck with Baby TV or something similar while you're still half asleep and using your foot to simulate a rocking movement in their bouncy chair. Top parenting!

Then you need to try waking up the bigger children... For those of school-age, some little ones may have internal alarm clocks that spring to life at 5:30 every morning. I'm not talking about those little cherubs, though. Plenty of children will almost require a spatula to remove them from their bed to stand any chance of making it to school on time. Parents will think back to the previous evening, when the child deliberately forgot to brush their teeth, asked for multiple drinks and started a conversation about the meaning of life, the universe and everything at 9:03. Nice try, little Hannah. Get to sleep or you'll be a nightmare in the morning!

Alright, it's a first-world problem, and once you get into the swing of things it's fine, but the initial few weeks of balancing the paranoia of not waking up on time and going for a wee when the house is freezing cold is nobody's idea of fun.

This time of year is far from all doom and gloom, though; there are plenty of folks that love the crisp autumn mornings, crunchy leaves underfoot and rosy cheeks. As soon as there's the possibility of a pumpkin spice latte, folks will be digging out their Halloween jumpers before you can say 'spooky scary skeletons'. They love it. Don't be surprised to see an autumnal wreath on their front door either. And pumpkins on their doorstep on the first day of October. And you can bet they are planning a trip to B&M or Home Bargains to grab bat-, cat- and witch-shaped items a full month before they'll use them. Plus a spooky-themed fleece blanket for the front room. If it's you I'm talking about then you are a very strange human, but given how early the Halloween items end up in shops (yes, August) and the fact that they don't have a lot of it left in November, this may increasingly be seen as normal behaviour. Perhaps it's me that's just a whinge bag.

Halloween at school is interesting. Depending on when your local school's half term is will dictate how 'Halloweeny' it all gets. This event has become a staple of British culture for a week or so at the end of every October and, as annoying as it is to see Halloween-themed cakes and sweets on the supermarket shelves in the first week of September, the kids mostly love it – and so do the big kids. Do you enjoy Halloween? Do you have any traditions? What are your go-to Halloween movies that you watch with your family? If *The Exorcist* is on your watchlist then I'm slightly concerned about you.

As for school activities, there's usually a spooky maths starter or some creative writing based on a ghost story, which builds the excitement a little. There may be a child or two that doesn't fancy colouring in a pumpkin because they have particular types of religious beliefs that prevent them from celebrating Halloween. That is perfectly understandable and must be respected, but most of the children will usually be buzzing about the festivities. None of the children have any idea about the origins or relevance of Halloween and, to be fair, neither do most of the adults, but as long as they get to see their mates, eat enough spider-shaped Haribo and neck about ten Fruit Shoots, then it's happy days.

Speaking of Haribo (and as we know, kids and grown-ups love it so), they are one of many brands that definitely jump on the Halloween bandwagon. In fact, it's arguably their most lucrative time of the year. It's fairly easy to see that Halloween is on the horizon by looking down the supermarket aisles in their seasonal section. You'll be greeted by a sea of spooky-themed items in a combination of purple, orange and bright green – the official colours of Halloween. Jaffa Cakes are suddenly flavoured with 'green slime' and 'blood orange'. Cake bars that look like Frankenstein's monster, gingerbread skulls, pumpkin-shaped crisps and yoghurts that look like Dracula.

Another thing that has increased in popularity in the last 30-plus years is pumpkin carving. Families will dedicate entire days out to visiting a local farm shop to select the pumpkins they want to attack with a blunt knife ready for trick or treating. These farms aren't as common if you live in central London, but lots of places now offer pumpkin trails, ghost hunts and haunted activities to entertain the children during half term. These events happen at places that offer pick your own strawberries in the summertime. Any excuse to get families in and sell them hot chocolate and overpriced crisps. This is a nice opportunity for families to meet their pals and justify their purchase of £75 Hunter wellies as they find out that some of the ground is firmer than other parts. Learning the hard way that a grassy patch is actually a mud bath is a lot funnier when you're not the person going arse over tit wearing a posh new outdoor coat and a knitted jumper with a ghost on. Alternatively, you could just grab a pumpkin off the shelf at the local supermarket – just make sure you don't leave it to the last minute or the good ones will be gone, and you'll be forced to carve a butternut squash with some very p*ssed-off children.

Pumpkin carving can be great fun and, depending on your artistic abilities with a knife, you can make the designs as complicated or as simple as you like. Schools may run a pumpkin-carving competition for the children. As for the quality of the entries, it's pretty bloody obvious when the parents have done all the work. I mean, little Amy is currently in Reception class but she has still managed to enter a carefully sculpted head motif of the Demogorgon from *Stranger Things*. Quite an achievement considering she's not started split digraphs in her phonics yet!

Alright, these competitions are just a bit of fun and they do encourage families to engage in a nice activity together. It's all pretty harmless stuff unless it goes to a public vote on the school Facebook page where the 'best' pumpkin isn't necessarily the winner. It's usually the kid with the parent that messages all their mates and family members and begs them for votes because 'there's no way Jenny Bloody Smith's winning the competition again!'

Remember, remember the fifth of November...
Gunpowder, treason and ... what the what now?

British festivals are all over the shop. Yes, Christmas is a religious festival and Halloween comes from the Celtic traditions of Samhain, which symbolises crossing the boundaries of the world of the living and the dead (and yes, I had to google it). Easter is obviously a religious festival as that has been hijacked by a rabbit and chocolate makers (more on that later), but Guy Fawkes Night is just ridiculous.

Americans have Thanksgiving and Mexicans have Día de los Muertos (Day of the Dead), which is like Halloween with lots more skulls. There's a story behind every tradition and there'll be plenty more strange celebrations around the world that we'll happily laugh at, but how on earth did Bonfire Night become a thing?

I won't do a history lesson, as the story is too complicated, but can you imagine explaining to someone who has never heard of Guy Fawkes why we effectively commemorate a treasonous plot to blow up the Houses of Parliament? You'd think people would want to forget that it happened, but as Brits we just go along with things because, well, tradition!

What do they do near you to mark the fifth of November? Do you have a local firework display? Do you grab whatever last-minute rockets and sparklers you can find from the special counter at ASDA and put on a display in your own garden? Obtaining them in the first place is near impossible, as the one person trained to safely sell them is usually on their break, off sick or hiding in the produce fridge with the broccoli.

Some schools will put on a display with a big bonfire made from donated pallets and scrap wood. These sorts of displays started popping up to discourage families from holding their own firework gatherings and burning down half the neighbourhood. Or there may be a massive firework display put on by the local council in the town or city where you live where there's a fun fair (and yes, it's ironically neither fun nor fair and it costs £3.50 a ride and a burger and chips are £11.75. That's before the extortionate entrance fee). Even if you've only got a small family, you're looking at a huge bill to watch some pretty explosions. These events do have some decent fireworks, though (no wonder the tickets were so bloody expensive), and it's properly marshalled and safety precautions are followed. So it's slightly safer than a firework display in Uncle Derek's garden where he nails a Catherine wheel to his fence and wonders why he has to creosote the thing the following January when he notices the damage. A teacher friend once got into a fair bit of trouble at family fireworks display when one of the 'fountains' blew over slightly and started spewing sparks in the direction of the spectators. Did he shepherd the family members to safety? There were no children present, but did he ensure that older family members were protected? The answer to both of these is a big NO! What he did do was panic and hide behind his MOTHER-IN-LAW. Safe to say he was in the sh*t for the rest of the evening. This does highlight how dangerous fireworks can be and potentially why public displays are perhaps the safer option.

If you are of a certain vintage (here we go again) you may remember those terrifying adverts from the 70s and 80s about firework safety – you know, kids blowing their faces off and scorching their hands on sparklers. I'd say look it up on YouTube, but it may scar you for life, just like most of the public safety films that were repeated for many years after they were first broadcast. John Carpenter and Wes Craven would have been proud of some of the horror depicted in those adverts.

If it's a school or community bonfire event, some places will have or used to have a 'guy competition'. Children and their parents will stuff old clothes with newspaper, put on a mask that was left over from Halloween and enter it into a competition. Whoever wins the competition will get a little prize, but their afternoon's work will ultimately get slung onto the fire. There's often one kid (or parent who is a terrible influence) who will pop a couple of aerosol cans inside and a few packets of those little bangers just to get the party started. Whatever the guy looks like, the fact that we create effigies of a historical terrorist and lob them onto a fire says a lot about how strange we are as a nation.

Years ago, they used to have children knocking on doors saying, 'Penny for the guy', and random strangers would give the children a few pence for their guy-making efforts. That was unless you came across one of those old chaps who thinks they are a right funny guts and will wind up the children. If guy-makers ever come to his door and say, 'Penny for the guy?', he'd say 'Nah, it's worth far more than that!' chuck them 10p, take the guy inside and close the door. That prank only really works if the person pulling it actually returns the guy to the children, otherwise it's technically theft. The sort of humorous old geezer who would pull that stunt would also be prepared on Halloween. When the children say 'Trick or Treat?' he'll respond by saying, 'Oh thanks, I'll have a treat, please!' then steal a child's bucket of sweets. Again, it can be hilarious, but it's important that they return the bucket of sweets, because if they don't, they may be getting dog sh*t smeared on their windows as a result. And rightly so!

Schools dip into the Guy Fawkes traditions as well. Depending on when 5 November falls each year, you may have a single day in class creating some lovely artwork or acrostic poems about what you can see, smell, taste, touch and hear. Be careful with the tasting and touching near mini-explosives, mind!

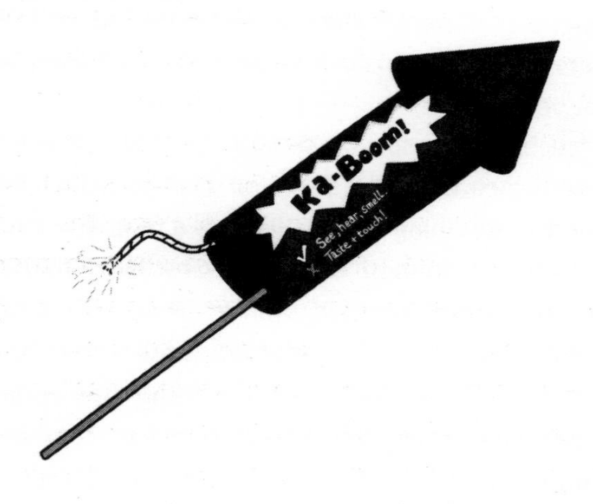

These activities can be really fun, and from a teaching perspective, it's always nice to try to get what we call 'cross-curricular links' in, where lessons are linked with other subjects. Describing interesting scenes or settings while creating artwork can give children context and inspire their word choices.

Anything to liven up the teaching of some aspects of English is probably appreciated by staff and, as a result, the children. So, to finish this chapter, and while we're on the topic of exploring the English language, either with our senses or our thesauruses, here are a few word-based classroom funnies.

One vocabulary lesson involved a teacher working with children to learn about idioms. A 'piece of cake' or 'a barrel of laughs' are commonly used, but not everyone recognises them as idioms. To help the children get to grips with these, one teacher asked the children to act out their idioms and whispered in the children's ears what they needed to perform. A fish out of water was a pretty good one, but one lad came up and was asked to act out 'hit the sack'. Rather than mimic sleeping, the child raised his arm and clenched his fist, then proceeded to punch himself IN THE NUTS! Doubled over in pain, after hitting himself harder than he had expected, he looked up at the teachers with near-tears in his eyes and said, 'Please don't make me do that one again!'

When teaching a lesson on similes, the children were asked to come up with their own that featured 'like' or 'as' while making a comparison to something else. 'As light as a feather' or 'running like the wind' will be common examples. One child said something 'shook like my mum's vibrator'. Ooh-er! That's embarrassing, but what made it even more cringey is that the dad worked at the school as the caretaker and the mum was a lunchtime supervisor! I bet they ended up with nicknames after that, with Dad as 'Buzz' and Mum as 'Miss Rabbit'!

There's one final story for this chapter where a teacher definitely regretted her choice of words, or at least the way they came out, while teaching a music lesson. During a session on using recorders, one teacher was teaching the notes and finger positions for 'London's Burning'. She went through each finger position for each note and loudly declared on the (fetch the) 'en-gines' part that the children should 'put your fingers on your A-holes'!

Thinking before speaking is a must in primary schools, because you never know quite what the children will hear. Fortunately, the children only followed the teacher's instructions when using the recorders this time!

So...

What kind of person are you when it comes to Christmas? You can decide for yourself where Ebenezer Scrooge, John McClane and Clark Griswold fit in on this scale but where would you be?

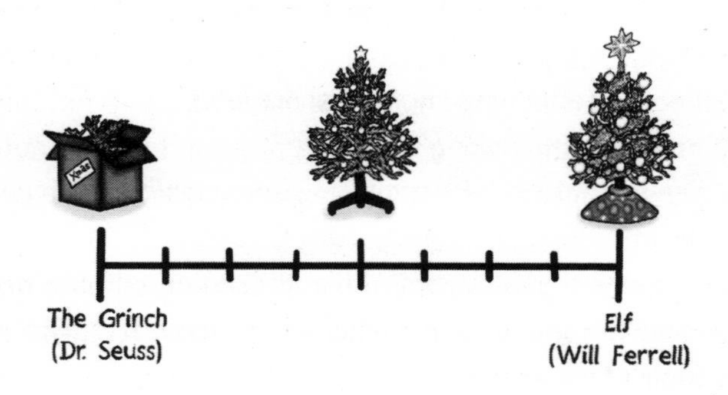

Me, I'm definitely Elf level. Some people adore Christmas, like I do, but there are some that really don't. Wherever you are on the scale of Christmasiness (yes, I know that's not a word), there's a school-wide understanding that as soon as you hit the first of December there are some things that are acceptable and some that need at least another week before you can give them the green light.

Some schools start practising for Christmas productions before November has ended. It's such a massive rush in December, and how much you have to cram in before the children break up depends on the day of the week on which Christmas Day falls. I think there are schools that broke up on 23 December last year, whereas other schools may be done by the 17th/18th, leaving a week or so of build-up at home. If term ends on 17 December, that leaves approximately 10 school days to fit everything in, so if parents are a little overwhelmed by the calendar of events over a short period, I promise it's even crazier in the classrooms.

If a school is expecting a visit from Ofsted, you can guarantee that the children will still be completing a full timetable of Maths and English up until the last possible date that the inspectors can make 'the call'. And yes, Ofsted *do* visit schools in the last week of term before Christmas. I think the lead inspector's name for such inspections must be Ebenezer, but I doubt they have been visited by three ghosts yet. Hopefully that's to come...

There's so much to fit in, and that includes:

- School performances (more on those later)
- Christmas card making
- Calendar making (with those tiny unreadable calendars at the bottom)
- Decorating the classroom with paper chains and lanterns
- Writing to Santa (with enough time to receive a reply)
- Google's Santa tracker
- Christmas Talent(?) Show
- Acrostic poems that make no sense but look quite sweet
- Class Christmas parties

Not every school has exactly the same Christmas routine, but most schools will have some form of class/year-group party. It's these 'parties' that promise so much yet deliver so little. I mean, they deliver plenty of leftover food, but that's about it. Unless the teacher or teachers are particularly enthusiastic, it involves children rocking up to school wearing their own clothes with multi-packs of crisps, biscuits, cakes and chocolate (plus some child potentially signs up to bring in cold pizza or samosas, which usually end up in the staffroom) and a few classic party games before watching a Christmas film. While watching a film that 75 per cent of the class have already seen, the teacher or TA will be cleaning up after the messy little buggers. It's a bit of fun, but here's a top tip: when booking the date, make sure there's enough time to work through the leftover food before the class breaks up.

Some smart schools will gift the leftover grub to either a food bank or some of the families in their community that may need it more. If not, it'll end up in the staffroom, and the last thing school staff need to see when they return from the Christmas break having started a diet or made a New Year's resolution to give up sugar, is leftover Quality Street, boxes of mince pies and multipacks of off-brand Pringles (Prongles?).

One other thing to note is that there's only so much energy available from the children and the school staff, so if the morning is full of party games, quizzes and craft, the afternoon will often be spent with the grown-ups filling bin bags while the children watch Christmas movies. Sadly, they must have a U certificate otherwise the teacher will need to send a slip home that requires a signature because the movie requires Parental Guidance (PG). Now, which are the best Christmas films in my humble opinion?

THE OTHER Mr P's TOP 10 CHRISTMAS MOVIES	
THE SANTA CLAUSE	This is Tim Allen at his finest (sorry, Buzz). The sequels aren't up to much but this first film is magic. If you have a child who is wavering in their belief in the big man (Santa, obviously), stick this movie on. It made me a believer again when I rewatched it at 16.
HOME ALONE	This is a stalwart of any Christmas moviethon. The traps that this young kid could make are mesmerising and probably required a degree in engineering. It gave me great inspiration for pranking my family members and may also explain why I'm the least-favourite child.
ELF	This movie has gone from strength to strength over the years. I remember seeing it when it first came out and I loved it. Despite being over 20 years old now, it seems as popular and incredibly quotable than ever. SANTA... I know him!
HOME ALONE 2	This movie made me fall in love with New York. In a similar way to *The Hangover 2*, it's pretty much the same movie as the first one, but it's such a festive feast and I love it regardless. Not even an appearance by Donald Trump can spoil it.
LOVE ACTUALLY	Love truly is all around; I love this movie. I'm not sure about Keira Knightley kissing her new husband's best mate, and I swear Mufasa dying in *The Lion King* has nothing on Emma Thompson opening that CD (expecting the necklace from her husband), but it's all I want for Christmas.
JINGLE ALL THE WAY	Any movie where Arnold Schwarzenegger screams, 'Put the cookie down!' has my vote every day of the week.
THE HOLIDAY	I'm a straight, married man, but Jude Law in this movie had me seriously questioning everything in my life. A great, festive romcom.
MIRACLE ON 34th STREET	My dad has watched this movie over 40 times and cries each and every time. It's an absolute classic and Richard Attenborough has got to be one of the GOAT (Greatest of All Time) Father Christmases.
DIE HARD	I don't care what Bruce Willis says, I had to put this film on this list as it **IS** a Christmas movie. Mind you, I could watch it all year round. Best action film going.
THE MUPPET CHRISTMAS CAROL	There have been so many adaptations of this classic Charles Dickens' tale, but for some reason, none hit home as much as Kermit and his crew. Add Michael Caine playing Scrooge and it is EPIC!

That's a bold move, Adam! *Muppet Christmas Carol* at 10? Some people will see that as sacrilege. Plus I'm doubtful that you'll get enough signatures for *Die Hard*. We don't want the Year 2 kids going home yelling 'Yippee-Ki-Yay, Motherf**cker'!

Another staple for so many schools is the ironically named TALENT SHOW. That's not to say the children don't have talents, it's just that some of the choices of talents to share are questionable. One stunning example of this involved a child (a keen swimmer) who decided to place herself, belly first, on a chair and perform a very well-demonstrated breaststroke. She was definitely talented but it was unclear to all the children and staff as to why she felt the need to perform the action for nearly three minutes. No music, just a kid swimming on a chair.

In the last ten years it's usually been called '(insert name of school)'s Got Talent'. In some schools there are usually no auditions as they feel it's not fair to deny the little ones a chance to take part, but some schools will insist upon it to make sure the acts are worth showcasing. One kid may stand up on stage and play the saxaboom like Jack Black, but a Year 1 might go up in front of the whole school and play a squeezebox for about 10 seconds with no discernible tune. It's the taking part that counts and it's the job of the MC for the day (usually the headteacher or member of staff that likes the sound of their own voice) to make sure these sections don't go on for too long, as the 'talent' has already been 'shown' and the school hall has pretty much seen all they need to of the performance.

Sometimes the teachers will get up and 'do a turn', as it's called at posh dinner parties, but not all staff are as keen, so they're the ones you will see slinking out of the hall and starting to double-back their boards for next term's display. I started creating videos for our school talent shows like my parody of *Frozen*'s 'Do You Want to Build a Snowman?' and my 'Whip/Nae Nae' routine, but with marking pens and highlighters. They seemed to go down really well and helped encourage me to make more videos to share on my social media.

The timings of the school talent show can vary. If you do auditions and only send through the best few acts from the year group, you can often get the event over in a couple of hours, but if you just let anyone sign up to empower the children and give them a shot, you can probably make the whole thing last until lunchtime. It's a complete waste of a day but the kids love it and look forward to it.

There are a few memes that come around every year on social media about the impending festive period. Ones about thawing out Michael Bublé in time for the start of December, any number of *Elf* (Will Ferrell) or Mariah Carey ones, plus a picture of a pair of feet with holes in their socks and some similarly overworn pants saying, 'Hang on in there, lads, it's almost Christmas.' Obviously, it's implying that the only time they get new socks and underpants is at Christmas. What makes it funny is that it's mostly true. Have you ever seen a man shop for underwear before? Unless he's sh*t himself while being out and about in town, chances are he'll be on the countdown for his wife, partner, mum or gran to restock his selection of socks and pants.

Speaking of memes and countdowns, another fun one we often see has words to the effect of:

'I don't care if I'm 28 with a mortgage, if my mum doesn't have a chocolate Advent calendar for me, I'm legally divorcing her!'

Advent calendars have changed over the years, from the beautifully crafted wooden delights of the 1850s to the snowy-scene pictures where you peel back the doors to reveal some sort of religious imagery. By the 1990s chocolate Advent calendars had become commonplace and were pretty much the norm for many children's childhoods. Another meme on this topic made me laugh the other year:

'According to my chocolate Advent calendar, there are only 2 days until Christmas. 🤷▒♂'

It's hard to know where lots of these memes come from, mostly because they have been stolen, copied and shared so many times over, but we're grateful for them so keep them coming!

Something I've noticed since my kids were born is the increasing numbers of Advent calendars with toys in: Lego, Playmobil, Barbie, Turtles – you name it. Huge Advent calendars where the children will get a mini figure to add to their collection or a piece of a sculpture or model that will have something new in it every day. By 24 December you may have even built Hogwarts or Optimus Prime! What a fantastic little thing to look forward to for children getting excited about Christmas. For the parents potentially buying them... how do they cost 35 f*cking quid?!? Don't raise my expectations of being seen as the best dad ever by bringing home something so cool for my children only to be smacked round the head with the price tag.

As we said at the start of this book, neither Mr P is an expert at parenting, so we're not dishing out a lot of advice on that front, but – top-tip alert! – if you want to get your child (or, let's be honest, yourself) one of these calendars, do it in January when there's loads of leftover stock in Smyths or The Entertainer. They'll be a fraction of the price, and you just need to hope that the kids still like *Paw Patrol* the following year or it'll be going on eBay!

Advent comes from the Christian tradition of preparing for the birth of Jesus, and the story has been told so many times that children probably know it better than their teachers. Some classes have Advent calendars where either a child whose name has been drawn randomly or whoever has behaved the best that day gets to open one of the doors. As I mentioned previously, if there are only about 2.5 weeks of term when the children are actually in school, the teacher will probably not get through the whole class. It sounds completely trivial, but to children of a certain age it is the ultimate privilege to be selected for the task.

If there's been a weekend and there are two unopened doors for Saturday and Sunday, teachers, don't you worry, little Toby will remind you at least five times on the Monday that this is the situation. Granted, Toby can't remember to put his reading book away or learn his spellings, but if there's chocolate involved, his teacher best be up to date! By the end of term, it's usually the children that have miraculously behaved the best for the last few weeks that get their names 'randomly' drawn to open the remaining doors. What are the chances?!?

Some schools go BIG (literally) with their Advent activities. I seem to remember a school where they had a huge Advent calendar in the infant hall. The older children had provided some Christmas pictures in November and the teachers had created a grid to hide them behind. Each day during December (yes, Toby, we know we missed the ninth and tenth at the weekend) the children will be selected to come and open the doors. As we know, it's a huge flex if you are the child selected to do that in front of the whole school.

I think these may be slightly less common, but not because the children don't want them anymore, more because they are a hell of a lot of work to create and they will be out of date by January. If a teacher wants to keep it low key but still thoughtful, there are always Advent candles. It's smart to entrust certain children with making sure it only melts the number of the days that have already passed. Some teachers quite like to do this during story time as it helps provide a mellow atmosphere for when they are about to read.

Everyone will have experienced Advent in some way or another, but only children and parents of a certain age will have had the pleasure of encountering...

... this little b*stard. The elf on the shelf!

It was so lovely when it first came to these shores a decade or so ago, and the original book and story are really sweet, but on behalf of every parent currently on their seventh year of doing it... DAMN YOU, ELF ON THE SHELF!

Most people know what the point is anyway, but families across the world will pretend that the magic elf is a representative of Santa, and he will keep an eye on the children of the house. The elf will report back to Santa each night before appearing somewhere else.

In theory, that's what happens. In theory, it sends an extra message to the children to make sure they are brushing their teeth, eating their vegetables, and saying 'Please' and 'Thank you'. For a few years, that's exactly what the elf did. He (or she) would pop up in some random places that would make the children chuckle.

'Look, Mummy, the elf is on the tree!'

'Dad, I think the elf has climbed up the curtains!'

'Oh no! The elf is sleeping in the cat's bed!'

Lovely innocent ideas and something brilliant for the children to look forward to. For years Santa's little representative was one of the highlights in the build-up to Christmas. If children were badly behaved, there may be a note from Santa telling them that he was disappointed with them, but they can still make his 'good list'. It's hard to tell children off for lying during this period, as technically the entire elf show is one big fat lie. If parents can keep telling themselves that it's all part of the magic of Christmas, then suddenly it's perfectly OK to bullsh*t children into behaving.

A few children went viral in recent years due to Christmas-related shenanigans:

- One child threatens to give Santa an uppercut if he's on the naughty list;
- One child calls the elf on the shelf a 'greedy bastard' for eating his sweets;

(And in the most Mancunian clip ever...)

- A girl has a pair of glasses drawn on her face as a prank by another elf and she's grumbling, 'Nah, nah, it's not funneh... I've got school!'

The elf on the shelf works pretty well for the 24 days up until Christmas, as long as whoever is in charge of moving it moves it! Have you ever had a late-night conversation like this?

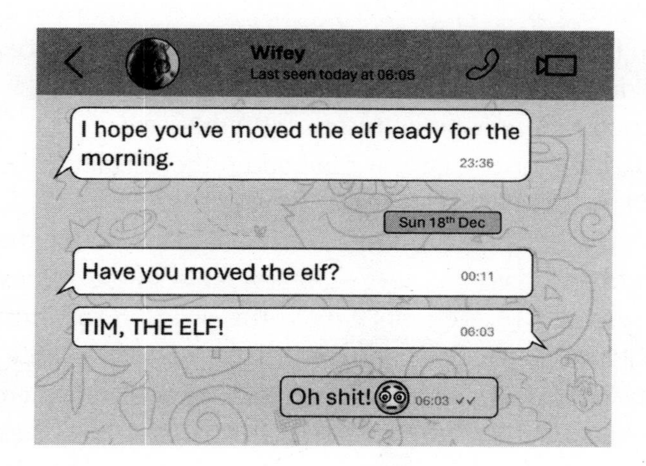

Schoolboy error! Surely everyone knows that you need to set an alarm on your phone to remind you every night. The worst words you can hear during this period are:

'Why hasn't the elf moved? Have I been naughty?'

If there's a dad in your household or you're the one responsible for moving it, you know you've f**ked up royally if you hear those words. It means you've got approximately 30 seconds to come up with a good excuse about the elf having Covid and taking a rest, or he'd done his hamstring and couldn't move. Funnily enough, the elf will definitely be remembered the following night, once the missus has forgiven you for almost ruining Christmas! Sound familiar?

Most of the first few years of elves on shelves were a bit like this, then it got competitive. The elf went from appearing in random places to being slightly cheeky and playing pranks.

'The elf has spilt some sugar.'

'The elf has taken the batteries out of the clock!'

'The elf has drawn a picture on my whiteboard I use to practise my spellings.'

Oh that cheeky little elf. What will he do next?

I'll tell you what he'll do next. I've run out of sensible ideas, so he's now going to be a little b*stard!

Toilet paper everywhere, snow angel in flour and leaving a few chocolate drops on the side to make it look like he's done a poo! The elf is getting naughtier and parents are starting to steal each other's ideas from Instagram and Facebook.

The worse-behaved the elf is, the bigger hypocrites the parents are for telling the children to make good choices. That all gets lost in the fun of it, but it doesn't just stay at home. The good news is that some teachers will use the elf for a couple of weeks' writing activities. The excitement from the children in Mrs McGregor's Year 3 class when they come home on 1 December and tell their parents that they have an elf in their class as well!

Result! Parents don't get to take the year off from doing the elf, but with an elf at home and at school, the children may reach maximum elf tolerance by mid-December, so the likelihood of them wanting him back has reduced significantly.

So, with only about 2–2.5 weeks of actual days in school during the month of December, there's a shedload to cram in. The Reception nativity performance, which is always good for a laugh, seems to take absolute priority over everything, and the question is, do you include it as part of a whole-school performance (much easier if you only have one class per year group) or do you do a separate Reception nativity and KS1 and KS2 performances? If it's the latter, planning for these needs to start around... August?!?

There are only so many Christmas ideas and it's really important that teachers negotiate who is doing what. Will it be a variation on *A Christmas Carol*? Will it be *La Befana/ Babushka* (the one with the old lady that helps people) or will it be the famous *Grumpy Shepherd* play? (If you've not seen *The Grumpy Shepherd*, it's usually a treat because the most eccentric child from the infant classes usually gives a barnstorming performance while the rest of his or her peers are barely audible with the rest of the dialogue.)

Some schools do a whole-school performance where each year group gets to represent a different time period to see Christmas through the ages. If you've got a particularly enthusiastic DT co-ordinator, they may even knock up a time machine with flashing lights and a clock that goes backwards on the front. Or just do a PowerPoint with timed sound effects.

This is a fabulous one, but teachers shouldn't be surprised when parents question the costume request letter, which reads:

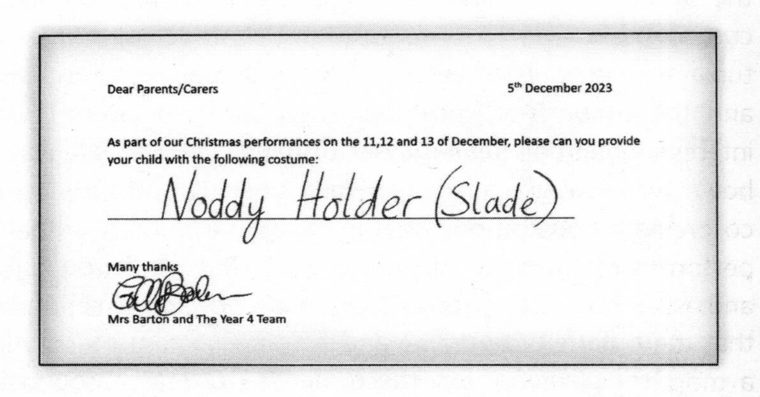

Dear Parents/Carers

5th December 2023

As part of our Christmas performances on the 11,12 and 13 of December, please can you provide your child with the following costume:

Noddy Holder (Slade)

Many thanks

Mrs Barton and The Year 4 Team

Something as epic at the time-travel performance can live in the memories of every child/parent/teacher for years, but do bear in mind that if the grumpy teacher that all the parents hate is in charge the following year because the enthusiastic music teacher retired in the summer, it may just be a carol concert with readings. Don't get me wrong, everyone loves a bit of 'Before the Christmas Daybreak…' by Christina Rossetti and some 'O Come All Ye Faithful', but after the *Bill & Ted*-style extravaganza the previous year, the parents are allowed to feel a little underwhelmed.

Another theme that could be good for a whole school is Christmas Around the World, where each class takes a country and shares its traditions for the festive period. You can have a lovely cultural exploration and compare and contrast the different traditions between France, Germany, Finland, Italy, etc… There's plenty of learning to be had during a performance like this.

One teacher was part of such a performance, and at the time his Australian section had gone down a treat. Comparisons were made between how Christmas is celebrated in the UK and in Australia, and how strange it is that a barbecue at the beach is more common Down Under than a turkey dinner round a table. The performance went so well, and the children and parents would still talk about how interesting and entertaining it was for years. One child, however, did not appreciate that legacy. The teacher who co-ordinated the Australian Christmas part of his school's performance bumped into some parents many years later and asked how their children were doing. The parents replied that the older sister was very happy and off to university in a month, but the younger brother was not overly pleased with the teacher....

Standing nearly 6 feet tall and looking grumpy, the now 16-year-old was pulling a face of scorn towards his former teacher. There was clearly a grudge, but what could it be?

'Remember our Christmas performance in 2008?' boomed the offended teenager. 'The one where you made me play ROLF HARRIS?!'

Oh dear! This teacher had forgotten that he'd cast the young lad as the wobble-board-wielding, cartoon-drawing, eccentric TV presenter and musician. Of course, 2008 was a long time ago, and many years before the Australian entertainer was arrested and convicted of being a 'wrong 'un'. How could he have known?!?

Turns out that the poor boy's nickname for quite a bit of his school career was 'Rolf' and there's no way he was ever going to forgive his former teacher. Awkward or what!

There's a beautiful story during a school nativity where Mary, clearly delighting in her role as the designated mother of the Messiah, was not appreciative of her Shepherd Number 3. When it was his turn to leave the stage to go back to class, he instead stayed on where he was playing with his baby lamb (which was actually a furry Build a Bear Pokémon called Wooloo – no, really). Five-year-old Mary offered her sheep-herding friend a little stage direction. She called his name while trying to maintain eye contact with her audience. Clearly the parents were starting to giggle as the boy stayed onstage in his own little world, holding up the rest of the class as they tried to leave. Mary went from sweet little starlet to crazed director and proceeded to yell:

'Oi, Leo... move it, yer d*ckhead!'

Parents were gobsmacked as little Mary gave her command with such gusto, but also the realisation that it probably wasn't the first time she'd called Leo a d*ckhead. Fortunately, the child moved and everyone got off the stage safely, but nobody could remember the nativity as they were still laughing at Mary cussing out Shepherd Number 3. The teacher who shared this story confirmed that Leo lived up to his moniker on a fairly frequent basis, and while Mary probably shouldn't have called him out publicly, it was definitely the highlight of the performance.

One school had a very interesting final day of term before Christmas. I say interesting because it wasn't even supposed to be the final day at school... Nope! This should've been the penultimate day and the festivities were in full swing. It had snowed a few days before, but the lovely little snowflakes had compacted into ice and it was still bloody freezing. Children watch films and see Christmas cards depicting a white Christmas (including the film... *White Christmas*) and as the majority reading this book will be UK residents, they will appreciate that it's not very often that it happens.

If you can cast your mind back to 2010, you'll remember that the snow was so heavy that it turned the British Isles white. Satellite pictures looked like someone had forgotten to colour it in!

With regards to this school, as parents popped in during the Sunday to turn the indoor PE shed into Santa's Grotto, they thought they would be simply having a wonderful Christmastime, because on the Thursday before school broke up they were holding their annual Christmas Fayre. It was an opportunity for the Year 6 children to run fun stalls for the little ones to buy things and play games, and for all classes to go and visit Santa. It's a fundraising activity that most schools do, but rather than only take the children whose folks had paid, some parents and grandparents had kindly donated a few quid to make sure every child in KS1 got to see jolly old St Nick and would get given a book and a little bag of sweets. The true spirit of Christmas.

It was a fantastic day and the children were so excited to meet Father Christmas, even though most of them had already met him at their parents' work party or the local garden centre. It didn't matter, this Santa was at THEIR school, so clearly he was the real one. With one of the teachers as the chief elf (because Santa was a random grandfather without an up-to-date DBS) and another parent dressed in a furry Rudolph costume, this was not just any Santa visit; a lot of love and thought had gone into the experience. Surely nothing could go wrong...

Oh yeah, the snow. It had been a few days since the initial snow had landed and on the day of the Christmas Fayre everything was still pretty frozen... including the water pipes. The morning had gone rather swimmingly (I might regret using that word) and from about 9.30am up until lunchtime, the National Elf Service/PTA managed to get through Nursery, two Reception classes, two Year 1 classes and sneaking in the Year 4, 5 and 6 children whose parents didn't want them to miss out on seeing Santa before they stop believing in the big guy (Santa, not God). Halfway through the Year 3 children there was a loud howling sound in the cupboard next to the school kitchen. It wasn't a sound that they had heard before, but everyone carried on regardless. Santa, Rudolph and the Elf Squad were pretty pleased at how they had managed to get through the children so efficiently, and at the same time give them a very positive and personal experience. The howling noise was back and this time even louder – so loud that the second Year 3 class thought the *Titanic* had arrived (it had been their topic last term). Santa managed to get through the rest of the Year 3s, but just as the elves were walking up to collect the Year 2s from their classroom, the howling was back. Rather than dying down, it became even louder and then – CRASH! The school shook as if it had been hit by an alien ship. A loud THUD and subsequent SPLASH from the cupboard by the kitchen as water started pouring under the door and into the school hall. 'OH SH*T!' was overheard from some of the staff present as they realised that the frozen water pipe had burst and water was gushing everywhere. A frantic headteacher informed the chief elf that he had 30 minutes to get through entirety of the Year 2 cohort because they were closing the school.

What could be done in the situation? The PTA couldn't realistically give refunds and the lovely little Year 2 kids had been patiently waiting all day to see the bearded wonder! They couldn't postpone until January, and how sad would it be to be the only year group to miss out on seeing Santa?!?

With the water still gushing and the headteacher still swearing, they managed to get all 61 Year 2 children into the PE shed/Grotto and out (having told him what they wanted for Christmas) in 23.5 minutes! Sadly, the representatives from the *Guinness World Records* (definitely not Norris McWhirter, as he popped his clogs in 2004) weren't present and if they were, they wouldn't have been overseeing a record-breaking attempt, they'd have been using buckets, mops and boxes upon boxes of paper towels to stop the tsunami getting as far as the carpets.

Funnily enough, the school wasn't open the next day. 😬

One last story before we break up for Christmas, which involves a present from a parent.

I've said this many times in my career but can I please state for the record that teachers do not expect presents at the end of term? If a parent thinks a member of staff has done a good job then we wouldn't say no to a bit of chocolate or a beer, but as parents ourselves, we know that life is expensive enough without having to buy teacher or TA gifts. Over the years, we've both had some amazing ones, but we cannot stress enough that they are far from expected by most teachers.

That said, if a parent really insists on purchasing something, mugs with lids are always very much appreciated. It's a cliché, but it's true; teachers don't half like a cup of tea. They love a brew. If you can't make a good cuppa, then perhaps working in education is not for you. For safety reasons, school staff have to use mugs with lids on if drinking a hot beverage outside of the staffroom. Every school staff member will have a favourite or preferred mug and certainly won't stick it with the communal ones in the staffroom.

One teacher was gifted the most fantastic stainless-steel mug (with a lid and handle) that she absolutely adored. It was very distinctive and the teacher was devastated when it went missing from her classroom among the Christmas chaos, having only managed to use it a few times before it disappeared from her sight. Initially, the teacher blamed a cleaner for nicking it and taking it to the dishwasher, but after a few weeks she decided to buy a replacement in exactly the same design. These super-modern safety mugs are so advanced that they keep liquids hot inside but the outside is cool enough that a child cannot be hurt if they accidentally touch it. Smart, safe and useful; they are a must in the modern classroom.

The teacher, while tidying up the classroom after school on evening, reached behind her flip chart to grab her mug full of piping hot tea and have a quick slurp. She took huge GULP of what turned out to be...

... four-month-old tea! 🤢

The teacher should've been delighted to discover the mug she thought she'd lost, but sadly her tastebuds were rather preoccupied with bacteria, sour milk and potentially some penicillin. Grim!

I'm not sure the elf on the shelf could be blamed for that one.

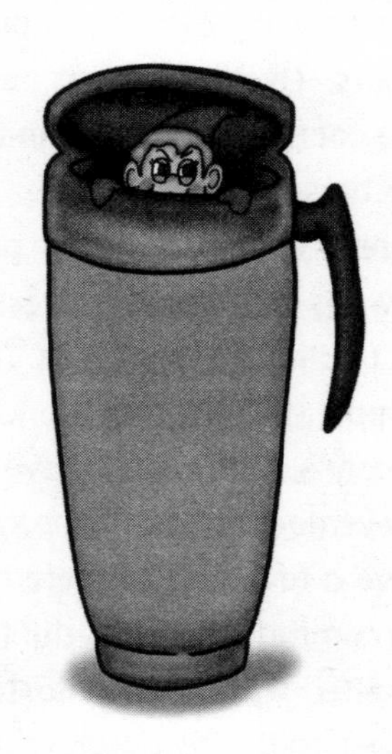

Bloody January! What a month!

If we could all hibernate for a month and wake up in February, that would be much better. Although we'd all probably start hating February instead.

In fact, January gets a bad rep. And that's because it comes directly after 'The Most Wonderful Time... OF THE YEEEAARRR', and if you love Christmas as much as many folks do, you are obviously going to be fed up, grumpy and downright depressed as you approach the return to school/work/life and you get used to no longer seeing flashing fairy lights, having a sumptuous breakfast of Quality Street and hearing Mariah Carey on repeat. To go from that to having to switch your body clock back on and recommence your routine can be demoralising. Children are equally grumpy when they realise that their days will be spent learning adverbs and angles rather than playing *Mario Kart* and eating Pringles. Damn you, January!

Joking aside, the return to routines in January can be really hard for some families. After over-indulging throughout Christmas, you must embrace the start of the new year. You can see it in the exchanges between parents and teachers. The parents (while semi-delighted to be passing their little darlings back to school staff) are as miserable as can be because only a week earlier they were wearing their *Home Alone* PJs watching Clark Griswold and his oversized tree. They know it's back to the daily grind and they can see the teacher feels exactly the same. 'Where did the last two weeks go?' is a fairly universal response from both parties as they meet at the school gate.

The small talk at the gate isn't entirely necessary, but it is fairly unavoidable. Parents can't just shout 'They're your problem now... ha ha!' and then leg it from the school premises. Actually, they can, but it all depends on whether there's a shared sense of humour. With some parents, if they were to say that you know they mean it!

Back to school is not great fun for the children a lot of the time, either, but they do get to see their mates after what feels like an eternity, and there are hi-fives, hugs and general merriment as children are reunited with their classroom chums. It feels like years since they were last in each other's company, yet they were on Roblox together about 12 hours ago so really they shouldn't be that ecstatic. But they are kids, so they can show their emotions if they want to.

What makes January so hard is its stark contrast to December, when everything is going on, as the month when literally nothing is happening. From a teaching perspective it's really hard to go from party hats and paper chains to parentheses and improper fractions, plus booster groups because there's no way little Ralph is going to get through the SPAG test in the summer.

Payday in January is usually the 158th day of the month (yes, I know that's not legit but that's what it feels like), but lots of people are already spent up before even halfway through the month because Christmas (as it does every year) maxed out their bank accounts. There's very little chance of booking in many social events in January as everyone is pretty much brassic. If you've had a particularly hectic festive period, you (and your liver) may be very grateful for the rest. On the other hand, it's hard to go cold turkey if you've got used to letting your hair down. (Speaking of cold turkey... it's January, check your fridge, as I'm not sure it'll still be safe to eat it now.)

There's also the despair of waking up in the morning with Friday feeling to realise that it's only flipping Tuesday! Tuesday can p*ss right off. Some people are so bored with the monotony of the week that they are calling Thursdays 'Friday Eve' and counting down the 'getty-ups' until the weekend. I think they secretly hate themselves when they say it, but they are holding on to quirky little stuff like that as they've got nowt else to chat about other than work and their kids (and how both are doing their heads in). I bet the people that invented those little names are probably behind (or at least spotted the terms on Twitter and started using them) calling the Queen's Platinum Jubilee 'Platty-Jubes' and Her Majesty's subsequent death then state funeral the 'Statey-Funes'. Perhaps they need to permanently sod off on 'hollibobs' because it's January and I'm not in the mood!

I mentioned that there's not much to chat about among colleagues, but do you know what's worse than not chatting to colleagues? That's right... chatting to colleagues! This is made even worse by nattering about New Year's resolutions, and in particular diets. January diets? They are tricky to start when your house is still full of Quality Street and Twiglets. We all need a fresh start, but if you've decided to switch from shop-bought sandwiches to rice cakes and oily fish that stinks up the staffroom, then you'd best open the window and clean up after yourself. I swear the fish brigade wouldn't dream of making their home microwaves smell like that, so why are they forcing their foul, fishy fragrance on my nostrils. Get in the bin!

By all means have New Year's resolutions, especially if it's going to help you to achieve more in life – a better diet, greater levels of fitness and losing old habits that are a hindrance to your existence. Go for it! Some class teachers will start afresh with their children in January and reflect upon what has been going well up until the end of the previous term. There may be some children that need to feed into their own behaviour pledges and agree what will work best going forward.

Reflection in the new year by the children is actually something to be encouraged, even if the same level of reflection from the grown-ups about new, faddy diets and fitness plans is less appreciated by the grown-ups you work with. A picture of something healthy or a gym selfie is perfectly fine on your social media because the people that want to see it will deliver all the likes and comments. The people that don't, however... they hid you from their timeline anyway years ago. In person, however, this is slightly more difficult. You can't tap on your colleague's forehead when they are preaching about calorie-deficits and cardio, then select 'Snooze Gemma for 30 days' like you would on

Facebook. You can try it, but you may end up in an HR meeting discussing the appropriateness of your actions. January does that to people.

There are the post-Christmas conversations as well, where you feel obliged to ask people how their festive break was, despite the fact that you either already know they went to New York and you're jealous because it was all over their social media, or the ones where you're just being polite but you don't actually care. There'll be staff you actively avoid because you don't want to hear about how marvellous their annual skiing trip was, and plenty of colleagues that want to tell you about their new pet. There's only so much of other people's lives that you can stomach.

'Hey Tom, do you want to see my new kitchen?!'

NOPE!

It's like show and tell for grown-ups, but unfortunately you can't hand the fellow staff member a sand timer and tell them they have a full minute before it's someone else's turn. I mean, you can, but there's an increased chance of said sand timer being launched at your head or possibly shoved up your ARSE (plus, you know how busy A&E is in January). To save your sanity, perhaps just nod and smile, because the necessity for that sort of chat will diminish the further you go into the month.

As there seem to be 95 days in January, it is definitely a month of the academic year where levels of teacher tiredness are at their highest. Now we feature this regularly on the podcast, because everyone gets tired, but the level of mental fatigue caused by teaching means that teacher tiredness is a whole new level. I think there is only one more level of tired above this, and that is teacher-on-a-residential tired. But we have often been in hysterics sharing stories of ridiculously random and hilarious things teachers do when they are so drained from teaching their brain struggles to function.

'I know I am tired as I've just said "good girl, have a house point", to the cat !!!🐈▦ 😂😜😂'

'Drove to school one day (don't normally do this as I live close enough to walk), then at the end of the day I walked home as normal and went into panic mode when I got home and saw my car wasn't there. It then dawned on me that I'd driven to school so had to do the walk of shame back to collect my car!!! 🤦♀'

'I sat down with a glass of wine, picked it up and blew it like it was a hot cup of tea 🤣🤣'

'Many moons ago I used to live around the corner from school, I nipped home at lunch to collect some resources, sat down on my sofa for 5 minutes and woke up an hour later to my (sixth form) students ringing me wondering what had happened to me!'

'I once got to school, opened the car door and reached over to get my work bag (containing all essentials such as laptop, keys, lunch, etc.) only to find I'd brought the hoover instead. 😂'

'I went to a member of the SLT to request some time for a funeral. I passed her my request form, which she opened and found a picture of a snowman drawn by one of my Reception children. Wrong pocket.'

'Asked a school nurse how to use an epipen for a student. She demonstrated with a dummy. I had go but I had, unknowingly, picked up the real one and jabbed myself in the hand with it. Ambulance called and I was wheeled away. 😂'

'PE teacher here. I work at a different primary school every day over the week, but I keep consistent over the term, so same school Monday, same school Tuesday, etc. One day during the last week of the school year, I needed to go and cover at a school I've never been to before, so I wanted to get there in plenty of time. I arrived there at 7:45, signed in, had a tour around and started getting the equipment together for my first lesson. At 8:50, the office manager came out and said, "Excuse me, but we aren't actually expecting a PE teacher in today, who are you?"

'Turns out I went to the wrong school, and I should have gone to the school a mile up the road.'

'I was telling my headteacher that I had worn my top inside out until someone noticed and told me at lunch time. She laughed and said, "Don't worry, last year someone came to school with odd shoes on." Then we realised that was also me. 😂😱'

'Marking a child's book with "Great so fart" instead of "Great so far". 😳'

'While marking after school, I realised I was dunking my biscuit (I needed the sugar!) into my paperclips pot which was next to my mug of tea! Then I tried to swipe my car door lock with my school entry pass to open it at the end of the day! 😂'

'I had a nap under my desk before a parents' evening. I awoke to find a number of people standing around me. Apparently the cleaner had found me and thought I was dead. They were discussing who was brave enough to poke me and see.'

'I went swimming after work and couldn't undo my padlock that I had attached to the locker. I tried all sorts of numbers to unlock it and failed. I asked at reception if someone could break the padlock off for me. I waited an age before a manager came with bolt croppers. We returned to the locker and were just about to remove the padlock when a lady came up and asked us why we were trying to break into her locker. Turns out she had the same padlock as me and I'd put my things in a different locker with my padlock that I was able to open with my code. 😳🙄'

'I put my marking and bags into the car and walked home! Then I wondered where my bag was and realised it was in the car park. I cried on the doorstep – the neighbour saw me and drove me to school to collect my keys and car. 🤦‍♀️'

Lots of things can make people rather testy at the start of the year, and from a teaching point of view, there's always the drama of PE in January. Many teachers will send the children's PE kit home at the end of term to make sure it is washed and brought back in at the start of the new term. A wise move, but there's always some child that never remembers to pick it up. At the end of term. You could ask a TA to duct-tape the bag to the child and it still won't make it home. I'm not advocating the use of duct tape on children, of course, but how on earth do they still lose their kit?

For the first week in January, roughly two-thirds of the children will have their PE kit. Teachers in the upper part of the school will lecture the older children about preparedness and how forgetting their kit could be a black mark by their name followed by a detention at secondary school. Half the time it's not even the children's fault, so it is wise to ping the parents several reminders, otherwise there'll be a group of only 19 children taking part while the other members of the class have to sit out and/or read/practise times tables. Of course, 19 is a great number for a PE lesson from a teacher's perspective, but from a learning viewpoint, that's too many missing.

Let's talk about PE slots in the winter months. If the school is large enough to have separate halls for KS1 and KS2, there's a good chance the school may be able to fit everyone in. Every class should have enough time to get their PE sessions in (especially when the weather is crap). If it's a two-form-entry school and there's only one hall, it's a nightmare, and mostly because the teachers schedule in gymnastics and dance during this time. There are never enough slots to cater for every class, so plenty of outdoor PE still takes place on the school playground, or, if the school is modern enough to have one, a rubber tarmac space – otherwise known as a Multi-Use Games Area (or MUGA). There was one parent that heard their child speak of the MUGA in school, but because of the child's pronunciation, they called it a 'mugger'. She did question what her child had told her when she came and spoke to the teacher, but the parent was relieved to hear it was a place to carry out sports rather than a dangerous criminal. Two very different things!

Now let's talk about something that is really criminal... having to do gymnastics in the hall AFTER lunchtime. The hall is gross! Despite the lunchtime supervisors' best efforts to clean before the afternoon's activities begin, there's always something they miss; a few peas, a grape, some yoghurt, half a bloody shepherd's pie!! What kind of human (child or not) wipes their dinner on the PE mats when nobody is looking?!?

This caused problems for one teacher modelling gymnastics once. She used the Year 5 sports leaders (Year 6 were in SATs mode and therefore too busy) to set up the hall, ready for a KS1 gymnastics session. Her sports leader helpers were some of the most trustworthy and helpful children. They made sure that the mats were carefully spaced apart, the sections of the box/vault were safely placed in position and the hooks of the benches were properly placed onto the rungs of the metal tables with the padded tops. There was no way she could've set that up so efficiently after roast dinner day in the hall without their help. She was too busy helping 29 Year 1 children to get changed and therefore very grateful.

With the apparatus set out perfectly, she led the children into the hall on tiptoes. Quietly, they made their way to the mats, trying their best to sit in a gymnastic seated position with their toes pointing towards the teacher. This teacher clearly knew her onions and how to get the best out of her class, despite the room still smelling like broccoli and flatulence. Perfectly modelling the balances she was looking for, our teacher gracefully tiptoed across the equipment and made her way onto the top of the table, ready to carefully walk down a bench before finishing with flourish. Stunning!

Her school still had the brown benches that had been in that hall since at least 1984, and over time their colour had faded to the point where they were the same beige colour as, I don't know... roast pork in gravy. Oh yes, one of the children had taken a lump of meat from their plate and plopped it in the middle of the bench. This was probably done so he or she could look like they had finished their dinner and so go out to play football before their mates. And however diligent the Year 5 helpers had been in the poorly lit school hall, they must've missed the meaty hazard on the benches they set up. I think we all know where this is going, don't we...?

Yep, the lady in this story, while making good eye contact with the children and modelling excellent form as she approached the bench, placed her toe, then the front of her foot, onto the gravy-soaked (now cold) slice of swine flesh. The texture felt hideous, and the gravy provided lubrication as she skidded then fell onto her ARSE! The children all gasped as their teacher went from graceful to painful in less than a second. Slapstick gymnastics of the highest calibre. As the Chuckle Brothers would say, 'Oh dear, oh dear oh dear oh dear!'

Many years ago (or at least pre-YouTube), if it was pelting it down outside, the children just had to either get wet or do something else. Now that teachers have access to the internet, they can still keep the children active with a bit of improvisation. Hockey lessons that are interrupted by the heavens opening and dousing a class of 30 children can be saved by relocating into the classroom, moving a few tables and popping on a JustDance video for the class to dry themselves off to. The headteacher may walk past the class and wonder why their head of English and Lower KS2 Phase Leader is channelling their inner Kevin Bacon while bopping away to Kenny Loggins's 'Footloose', but at least the class will be getting their exercise.

Another activity teachers may use is putting on a video of some children's yoga. If you've followed our podcast for a few years, you'll know that we're not a fan of yoga staff meetings. This is when an outside company will pop in and make the whole staff practise breathing exercises and downward dogs as part of a well-being push, when the teachers would much rather be getting their marking done so they don't have to take 60 geography and handwriting books home. Yoga staff meetings? Grrrrr!

Now I've got that off my chest (again), we can go back to the emergency yoga session brought on by the unexpected rain shower. Cosmic Kids Yoga can be quite popular, and there are some great stretches and poses that are perfect for the children. But teachers need to also be aware that doing yoga on the floor of the classroom may still have potential hazards. One teacher thought they had covered all the bases by moving enough of the tables to maximise floor space, but there's always a child or two that will hide under the tables despite the staff's insistence that they shouldn't. Even though it might be good for them to 'learn the hard way', there will still have to be a conversation as to why a child has a bump on their head that wouldn't look out of place in a scene with Itchy and Scratchy on *The Simpsons*.

The teacher in this story thought she'd taken all necessary precautions, but she missed the fact that her moveable flip chart only had three out of the four wheels present. Flip charts on rollers can be very useful in class as the teacher can move between small groups and model perhaps some maths calculations or sentence starters. Sadly, they always need all of their wheels and on this occasion a child secretly started moving towards his mate and sat on the bottom of the base. The flip chart toppled, sending magnets and whiteboard pens flying everywhere. It tipped and fell towards the class sink, which had pots of paint covered in cling film balanced on trays to be used again the following day. The corner of the flip chart smacked the trays of green paint and catapulted them all over the sink, the display board, the stack of children's reading records and... one child. SPLAT!

The bright-green paint on top of his white PE T-shirt made it look like he'd been slimed on Nickelodeon. Karma clearly was at play as the child that ended up looking like the not-so-jolly, not-so-giant was the one that sat on the base of the flip chart because he moved halfway across the room to mess about with his buddy. This could easily go on the graph that illustrates how 'the more you f*ck about, the more you find out'. Explaining to a parent why their child will be going home looking like Kermit the Frog may be quite an interesting conversation. Fortunately, the green child's mother was a TA in one of the older classes and found the whole situation far too amusing.

'That'll bloody teach him!' she whispered to the class teacher, who was mortified to be sharing the news that her son looked like Yoda. Clearly Mum was quite used to his inability to sit still and thought the whole calamity was a good learning process for him. She was just glad the paint was washable. The little guy will certainly remember his session of yoga!

One huge tip for teachers modelling any form of stretching: whether yoga in the class or gymnastics in the hall (while trying not to kneel in stray spag Bol), be careful not to stretch too hard. For warm-up stretching activities the hall is usually quiet as the teacher will wish to set the mood for the rest of the lesson. The children will be incredibly receptive to sounds of any description and will notice EVERYTHING!

What did one teacher do? Stretch a little too hard? Yep! Poor Miss Gough let out a little trouser cough that echoed through the empty school hall. Usually, if a child farts mid-lesson and the children hear it, the teacher will declare that it's perfectly natural and to not be silly. Hopefully, this will make the child feel less embarrassed. As admitted in our previous books, both Mr Ps have broken wind in class and let the children take the rap for it; it's almost the perfect crime. Miss Gough didn't have that luxury because as soon as she let off, she made a cartoon face with wide eyes, nostrils flared and her lips in an 'ooh' shape.

There was no way she could blame the children, as it was pretty bloody obvious Miss Gough was the culprit. Giggles came from the back of the class, which were starting to spread. This laughter was infectious and as the children were giggling, the teacher found it impossible not to smirk herself. Problem was, as she giggled, she let out a few more parps, which sent the class into a state of absolute hilarity, including herself.

As they attempted to calm down, one child took it upon themselves to side with the humiliated teacher and in front of the whole class declared:

'Don't worry, Miss, it happens to the best of us!'

In that moment, Miss Gough realised that (despite wanting the ground to open and swallow her up, seconds earlier), the children had no intention of making her feel bad. They are just kids and, unless you're dead inside, farts are still funny. The class had a giggle, sure, but they soon calmed down and had the best PE lesson ever. Probably not the connection Miss Gough wanted to make with her children that day, but at least they showed their respect. Was Miss Gough given the nickname of 'Miss Guff' for the rest of her time at that school? Of course. But it could have been worse, her name might have been Miss Hart, because you only need to change the H to an F then she'd have forever been known as 'Miss Fart'.

So, in this chapter, we have gone from a melancholic state of despair to thinking of nicknames for teachers who pass wind unexpectedly in a gymnastics session. January can definitely make you feel blue, but as long as there are classroom mishaps and teachers who wish they'd had less fruit for breakfast, there's plenty to entertain everyone in primary schools. At least February is an enjoyable month to look forward to.... Or is it?

We've talked about the January Blues and just what a tricky time it will be for everyone's well-being and general health. This next chapter is almost as depressing as we explore the halfway point in the school year, or the 'halfway hump' as it's known. After no major events in January, in February it's not much better. In fact, the most exciting happening is probably Valentine's Day.

Alright... I'll say it, Valentine's Day at primary school is a complete waste of everyone's time and effort.

Seriously, it's the one day in the year when the classes from Year 2 up to Year 6 waste the biggest amount of learning time possible deciding who is going to be girlfriend and boyfriend for all of five minutes. Someone will buy their child a Valentine's card and some heart-shaped chocolates to give to the girl or boy that their child is sweet on. Sounds fun? Not until the playground politics kick in and the kids all start falling out with each other. These kids can be girlfriend and boyfriend to whomever they flipping want, but can you do this sh*t at playtime as I've currently got a spelling test to administer and Kaitlyn is in the corner sobbing her eyes out because she thought she was getting a card from Josh, but his nan forgot to pop to ASDA last night? Not only that but Josh had previously pledged his undying love to Madison and now both girls' parents will probably be having a shouting match after school in the playground.

Damn you, Josh, with your cavalier attitude to romance. You cad!

Now are we on spelling 6 or 7? Ah yes, 7…

… can you spell 'romance'? Oooh, too soon?

Alright, it's quite sweet if you get the little ones to make a heart-shaped card to send to a loved one. It's nice enough until you realise that none of the children have written their names on their near-identical offering, and you'd struggle to read them anyway as they are made of that red card that pencil doesn't show up particularly clearly on.

The concept of sending a Valentine's card to someone you secretly admire is usually lost on the infant classes, but at least they see it as making a card for someone you love, covered in hearts, rather than learning about a Chicago massacre in 1929. If your child comes home with a detailed knowledge of that in Year 1, definitely ring Ofsted.

Speaking of a massacre, what is the point of a Valentine's disco? Yes, it'll probably be a great fundraising event for the PTA, as they can't think of a better event for the gap in the January/February part of the school year, but from the perspective of an eight-year-old, it's just rocking up to a disco wearing your best *Sonic the Hedgehog* T-shirt or a pretty dress and completely ignoring members of the opposite sex.

The only collaborative dancing will be either a conga, the Macarena or, if you're lucky, the Cha Cha Slide! Take it back now, y'all! Other than that, the girls stand with the girls and the boys stand with the boys and pay no attention to each other. I say the boys are standing there on the other side of the room to the girls; chances are they are running around, playing tag, and sliding on their knees until they get a b**locking from the staff member that 'volunteered' to chaperone the event.

At the end of the day, though, as long as the children go home full of crisps, sweets and squash, who gives a crap? The PTA can now afford one new iPad to be shared between eight different classes.

Now, jumping forward in the year but sticking with the dance theme, we were informed of some dance preparations for the late Queen's Platinum Jubilee in 2022. One school was learning iconic dances from one of the seven decades since 1952 and a mixed KS1 class chose the aforementioned DJ Casper's Cha Cha Slide. They would practise every day in the run up to the big performance and it was pretty good fun until one child misheard a few of the lyrics.

One morning in the run up to the Jubilee, the class teacher was approached on the playground by a parent who informed them their son had got into some trouble the night before at the mosque for repeating the words, 'It's time to get F*CKING.' It turns out that the Imam wasn't particularly acquainted with the Cha Cha Slide and thought the lad was yelling expletives for no reason. He didn't realise that it was actually time to get 'funky'. Unless there's an explicit version that DJ Casper secretly released without us knowing. It's safe to say that the lyrics were corrected for the final performance.

Some parents will deal with issues like that when they drop their children off in the morning, but many save them up and wait until parents' evenings. For some reason, parents' evenings can be scheduled for months like February, when it's still cold, dark and everyone is in a grump. Not all schools but I'm aware of plenty that do.

There's no real point doing a parents' evening midway through October as there's not a huge amount to report on other than the kids who have identified themselves as one of the following:

A) An absolute dream
B) A pain in the arse

Or,

C) Erm... are you sure your child is in my class?

Alright, that's a bit unfair, but just over a month is hardly enough time to really know a class and, sadly, in that time most teachers only really manage to get an idea of which pupils aim to please and which children are desperate not to.

Some parents' evenings happen just before the Christmas shenanigans kick in, but each school will carefully (or not so carefully if it's during SATs week) select a date that works best for the school community. February, or some point in the first half term back after Christmas, seems to be a popular time for these parent/teacher conferences, as before February there's potentially not a lot to report; after the end of May and it's too bloody late! By popular, of course, I mean common, because let's be honest, who the bloody hell looks forward to them? Parents dread them as they are either worried that their child is behind their peers academically or behaving like a little sh*t! Most of the time it's just a little chat about how Mollie or Matthew is getting on and what they need to do to get better. Lots of teachers dread it, then when they finish their evening, they realise how much they like their current class. Obviously, this is not always the case but there's usually a huge sigh of relief and a phone call to Just Eat/Deliveroo for when they get home. One teacher even bumped into the parents they had just been sitting opposite in their local chippy, where, funnily enough, they didn't carry on the parents' evening discussions. They just grabbed their battered sausage, chips and mushy peas (not a euphemism) and drove home with a rumbling tummy.

No rumbling tummies in some schools as they will book out half an hour from the evening to congregate in the staffroom as the local pizza place will have dropped off a few boxes of pizza. Sounds good, but after fitting in a visit to the toilet there's not a lot of time to eat. The pizza will be shovelled down the teachers' gobs so quickly that they will be stuffed, bloated and full of wind for the final push with the parents who booked the later slots. It sounds like a nice gesture from the SLT, but trying to hold farts in on a plastic chair can be deadly!

There's always one set of parents that books the last chuffing slot. If you're reading this and it's you – you are a bad person!! Especially if the other appointments finish at 5:50 but yours is booked for 6:50! There's a special place in hell for you if you do this deliberately to p*ss off the teacher!

Joking aside, there are some parents that have difficult hours to factor in when meeting their child's teacher (nurses, shift workers or even other teachers that have parents' evening on the same night). There are only so many slots, and if a child's parents are separated or divorced, there's every chance they won't want to be in the same room or cannot attend the same appointment without having a huge argument. It can make the sessions slightly more entertaining but it's not great for the children involved if they are having to witness it. Booking separate sessions is ideal and most teachers don't mind a few catch-up meetings for those that can't make a slot on the actual night.

I just mentioned booking the sessions. Well, that has definitely changed in the last 15 or so years. Most schools now offer an online booking system, which is great as long as you have access to a computer and some sort of internet connection. Before online booking became commonplace, parents had to – get this – write their name on a piece of paper stuck with Blu Tack to a classroom door! Something that looked like this:

Parents' Evening – Tuesday 6th February

Please use this sheet to book your appointment.

3:40	James S	5:20	Jenny
3:50	Dominic	5:30	Jemma Y
4:00	~~Peter~~ Adam S	5:40	Peter
4:10	~~Peter~~ Heather	5:50	Peter's Dad
4:20		6:00	
4:30	Mrs Bright	6:10	Mr Herbert
4:40	Sarah H	6:20	Alexander
4:50	Susie Cooper	6:30	C. Newman
5:00	Mary O	6:40	Ash
5:10	SARAH B	6:50	Michael's Mum.

If you cannot make parents' evening, please arrange another time to speak with your child's class teacher.

Once the lists went up, parents had to scramble to get the best slots. If you've got three or four kids at the school (I've got triplets), then best of luck scrawling your name in a box. Even trickier if there's no pen supplied or the idiot before you has broken the lead on the pencil. The b**tard! Sadly, there's no undo button when filling these in, so if your husband, wife or partner pings a text asking you to change the selected time, you'd better have an eraser or some Tipp-Ex handy, because everyone can see you messed up!

Handwritten requests for slots are thankfully less common nowadays for primary school parents' evenings and, objectively, they are far more personal than their secondary school counterparts.

Depending on the school, there may be parents' evenings that are still conducted in classrooms where each parent or family gets 10 minutes to hear about their child's progress and behaviour, then the teacher must find a creative way of kicking them out so they can catch their breath, go for a wee or neck a can of Red Bull before the next set come in. Facing the clock is ESSENTIAL!

If parents are taking too long or the teacher is rambling and digging themself a hole, there's the tried-and-tested method of the headteacher (if you've got a supportive one) who will knock on the door and offer the teacher a glass of water or a cup of tea as a sign to the parents to hurry the hell up and b**ger off home!

This method is not needed if the parents' meetings are conducted in the school hall under speed-dating rules. Oh yes! I've genuinely known schools invest in one of those little desk bells that you ping (that wouldn't be out of place in a post office or hotel at the start of the last century) to indicate that it was time up and to let the next family have their turn. Don't worry, if the school doesn't have that type of bell, an alarm on a phone will suffice.

Perhaps 'speed dating' and 'parents' evening' are two things that should never be in the same sentence, but that is what it often feels like, whether looking at it as a parent, a teacher or both!

All that sort of stuff went out of the window during the pandemic when many of these meetings started being conducted over Zoom (or equivalent). Those were some of the most impersonal interactions possible, especially when the English teacher who is also their Drama teacher uses the same diatribe about the same child and forgets that they spoke to the parents 15 minutes earlier. However, the beauty of this approach is that a teacher could conduct the feedback session while sitting at their kitchen table and the parents could dial in from their sofa. It wasn't perfect, but if either side thought the meeting was going particularly badly, they could hang up and blame the crap Wi-Fi. Also, these were brilliant because they cut off bang on the time slot – sometimes mid-chat – which could be good or bad!

Speaking of bad, one teacher on a Zoom parents' evening call was chatting away about a child's progress then spotted the child in the background. They proceeded to compliment the boy on all his hard work and gave him a wave. Young Thomas did not respond, and the parent pointed out that the teacher was, in fact, waving at

an oil painting of the child. Thomas was upstairs playing Roblox on his iPad.

Parents' evenings are full-on, stressful and tiring, but ask any teacher for a funny story (like the one above) from their time in education and plenty will come from parents' evenings. For the most part, they are positive and pleasant, but you do find that that the parents of the children you need to talk about often don't show up. There is also the odd time when you meet a parent for the first time and everything falls into place as to why the child is the way they are. But over the years that we have shared plenty of hilarious mishaps and embarrassing moments from parents' evening, here are some of our favourites:

'Three mice ran into the classroom during a parents' evening and I ended up on top of my chair! The parent had to talk me down and help me out of the classroom!'

'I thought I'd burn a candle in my classroom for ambience before our parents' night started. A parent singed her hair while signing in. Now I'm the teacher who set a parent on fire at parents' night!'

'I'd taught a sibling a few years previously, before being married and changing my name. The dad of the child in my class came to his appointment while mum went to that of the older sibling. Dad was very attentive, listening to everything I said, all went well. Next day, Mum told me that she'd asked Dad what I'd said. "I've no idea," he'd said to her. "I couldn't concentrate on anything she said, all I could think was how much she reminds me of Miss Tully! They look so similar, but they also have the same mannerisms and everything! It's crazy!" Mum had laughed for a solid five minutes before telling him I'm the same person, just with a different surname!'

'I've told this story a few times. Mum was sewing while waiting for an appointment, so I asked what she was doing. I wasn't quite prepared for her response. She made hand-sewn patchwork quilts to stop her looking at internet porn. For Xmas that year I received a beautiful quilt, it would have taken many many hours...'

'I had a dad turn up with his wife to parents' evening and he had tried to pick me up in a nightclub the weekend before. Luckily I'd said no.'

'My husband was teaching Year 5. Parents' evening was due and he asked a particular girl if her mum was making an appointment. The girl mumbled that she didn't know but would ask her. The next day, Mum was waiting to pick her daughter up. She produced a black card from her cleavage, said she was available the next night and that she did discounts for teachers. My husband looked at the card and discovered she was a lap dancer. Needless to say, he flushed bright red and stammered quickly that it wasn't that sort of appointment but one for parents' evening. The daughter smacked her mum on the arm and said, "I told you, mam. He's not like the last one!"'

'In 2002, a mother insisted that her son's relentless poor behaviour was due to his c-section delivery, and not "fighting" his way into the world through the birth canal. She was determined that a morning breaktime should be dedicated to her son being allowed to "fight through" his life frustrations in a pop-up tunnel lined with cushions... we supported this. Funnily enough, it made no difference whatsoever...'

'I had a parent hop up to the desk on her crutches, sit down and put her plastered leg on my desk with the cheesiest-smelling foot under my nose!!'

'On Zoom, the mother wasn't listening to a word I was saying, she was looking somewhere else other than me on the screen, I wasn't sure if she was hearing what I was saying and meanwhile all I could smell was my carrots burning as I'd put them on to boil, but all the Zoom delays meant they'd been on much longer than anticipated. I didn't know whether to tell her and go and turn the hob off, or whether she'd even see or hear me anyway?! Needless to say, they were black when I got them.'

'During one parents' evening the parents had a full-on argument during the meeting, which ended in Mum saying: I don't know why I married you. Dad replied: I know exactly why you married me, it's because I have a big cock! He was actually the local GP back when they existed.'

'At parents' evening at my daughter's high school I watched a quiet couple in front discussing their son with the maths teacher. There were negative comments in buckets about non-existent homework, his attitude, work output, etc. The parents looked totally confused and were visibly sinking into their seats. Finally, they asked if she had the right child. The teacher realised she was talking about the wrong "Steven" and dropped her head onto the top of the desk with such a bang, then waited a few seconds before lifting it and saying with a deadpan expression, "Shall we start again?" My daughter and I were in silent hysterics sat in the queue. I went on to work at the school as an SSA [specialist support assistant] before uni and I reminded her about it in the staffroom. She laughed and said it was the worst parents' evening in her whole career!'

'Had a parents' meeting where the mum sat on the dad's lap, despite there being two chairs. 😖'

'When I worked in Singapore a grandad came to parents' evening wearing shorts and when he crossed his legs a grey wrinkly b**lock fell out of his shorts' leg.'

'I couldn't concentrate on what I was saying as Dad had a piercing in his chin and I spent the whole time wondering how it was done. At the end of the consultation he stood up, pulled down his sweater and I realised it was a high-zipped collar!!🤦'

'It was my second parents' evening ever, but the first at a new school. I got really nervous so I went to freshen up in the staff toilets. I was worried I'd sweated so much and begun to smell, so I grabbed what I thought was the nearest body spray in there. Turns out it was air freshener, and I spent the rest of the evening smelling like fresh pine.'

'It was my first year of teaching, and on my second ever appointment, a young mum and her mum (Nanny) came to talk to me about their little girl. Only they had no interest in listening to what I had to say. I think they misread the situation and thought I was a GP 🤣, as the nan proceeded to tell me about her recent hysterectomy and then pulled down her trousers and exposed her front bottom to show off her infected scar. 😱😱 I screamed and begged her to put it away. Luckily, the female cleaner was mopping the floor behind me and witnessed the whole ordeal and went to my headteacher, who quickly came to my rescue. Needless to say, the nan was banned from the premises. 😊🤮'

'Many years ago our school caretaker found a parent wandering around the school at 7:40 in the morning. When asked why he was there he explained he was there for his child's parents' evening. The caretaker said that there was a bit of a clue in the name! He then replied that he'd thought my other time option of 7:20 was a bit early! He arrived on time, although a bit sheepish, later that night.'

'During a parents' evening quite a few years ago one of my friends (who is a teacher) got locked in her classroom cupboard by a parent who didn't like the fact that her child was struggling! We only realised because the parent told my headteacher to go and save her. After that we all had to have parents' evenings together in the hall. 😂😂 I also had one parent ask if I wanted to get high with him. Obviously I refused but pretty sure I became slightly high from the fumes (he was so chilled though, to be fair).'

'A dad arrived for parents' evening appointment with what looked like a Boots (the chemist) logo T-shirt on. He leant back and it said bollocks all over his considerably large front. He then proceeded to fart – loudly – and said, "Oh, that's a bad one" and wafted it towards me. I didn't really know how to go on from there!'

When it's around the halfway hump of the year, you can hardly rely upon parents' evenings to cheer you up, or the weather for that matter. Many days around this time of year will look so gloomy and overcast that you have no idea if it is going to rain or if it is just... February! February seems to be a crap weather magnet, which usually results in two words: WET PLAY!

I made a few parody videos starting in January 2021, including one about the nightmare experience of rain-drenched break times in school. It wasn't just teachers that recognised the chaos caused by break spent indoors due to bad weather; parents contacted me to say how they remembered what it was like when they went to school. Wet play is a nightmare!

An entire day of teaching and learning can be massacred by wet stuff falling from the clouds and children having to stay in the classroom. It's bad at break time but it's even worse if the rain extends to lunchtime and the children are effectively stuck inside for the entire duration of the day, without fresh air and some time to run around.

It's not even their fault. If I were a primary-school-aged child and I knew rain was on the horizon, I'd be hoping I could make paper airplanes or use the class Lego to make something epic! Problem is, there'd be only a small box of Lego, which one child will trip over while unadvisedly running around. The children can hardly be expected to concentrate during this period, as there's a lot of energy that needs releasing, and colouring in ain't gonna cut it.

Speaking of concentrating, teachers won't expect to have even 50 per cent of the level of concentration from the children that they had before they ended up inside for wet play. It's just not possible, as the younglings haven't been able to burn off their bowl of Chocolate Cheerios from that morning. The maths lesson may suffer because the children are still bouncing off the walls (not literally – that would mean a lot of entries into the accident book). Normal wet break times are obviously tricky, but if the rain that day has decided to have a period where it's absolutely chucking it down to the point where the children can actually hear the rain drumming on the roof, the excitement level will increase exponentially. I mean, they've all seen and felt rain before, sure, but there's something special if it happens outside their classroom and the playground starts to become a swimming pool.

The children will know that it isn't wise to go for a dip in the giant puddle later on at lunchtime, when the rain has stopped. I say it's not wise, but one child will usually end up standing in the puddle to see how deep it is. This is one science experiment that will almost certainly end badly. Another child of equal inquisitiveness will join him or her (let's be honest, it's usually a 'him') in standing up to their ankles in water near the drain blocked with leaves. A further friend may join them, and subsequently one or more of them will fall arse-first into the playground lake and be actively blaming the others. Almost like in the Spider-Man meme where there are three versions of Spider-Man pointing at each other. They all know they did something silly, but they are all trying to blame the others for starting the pushing that resulted in them being soaking wet.

The 'Soggy-Bottom Boys' (two house points if you got that movie reference, although it is a bit niche) will no doubt spend the rest of the day wearing their PE kit and feeling sorry for themselves. Years ago there used to be heaters in the classrooms with wire metal guards on them to prevent children from hurting themselves.

They will still exist in some places but lots of the more modern schools will have underfloor heating. These wire guards were perfect for drying wet clothes. If the school doesn't have them, the puddle-jumpers won't have dry trousers for the end of the day, then at home time, when they are released, they will have to do the walk of shame to their parents, carrying a bag full of still-soggy clothes. It's hilarious to watch, because the lads look like they are about to get whinged at. It's not funny if it's your child and that uniform was supposed to stay clean until Wednesday, though!

One story I have to share about matching children with their parents happened on the day when a photographer was taking pictures for the school prospectus. They took a whole load of photos in different poses and settings, trying to capture the essence of the school in a positive light. There were some cracking pictures taken that day and they looked smashing on the school brochure. One picture in particular that made it to the final print was taken during school pick-up and featured a child opening their book bag to show Mummy what was inside.

It's a lovely picture that captures a nice little moment in time and promotes the importance of positive interactions between parents and children after school has finished for the day... or was it?

Turns out, little Oscar was reaching into his book bag to present his doting mother with a sealed plastic bag. Inside the bag there was a pair of underpants that were previously filled with quite a substantial amount of human excrement. Still, it wasn't until the parent noticed the interaction had been captured on camera that she realised Oscar's sh*tty knickers would be immortalised in the pages of the school promotional booklet. The one that the school would use for seven years!

As we're on Adam's favourite topic of people crapping themselves, one teacher reported that her husband was working as a TA lower down the school, and a young child said that he had a rumbly tummy and needed a number two. The boy was worried that he wouldn't make it in time, so the TA told the little boy to walk carefully and to perhaps 'hold his cheeks together'. Listening surprisingly well to the

advice but completely misunderstanding it, the boy placed his hands on his face and squashed the wrong cheeks together. I've no idea if the kid made it to the loo but I bet it was hilarious to watch him waddling with the facial expression of Kevin from *Home Alone*.

Just a few stories there to lighten the mood and remind parents and teachers that when you reach the halfway hump, whatever trials and tribulations you've managed to overcome, it's important to take stock of how far you've come that school year to feel good about yourself, because the lighter months are on the horizon. It's a very vulnerable time when folks may be feeling at their lowest ebb. From a teacher's perspective, they need to feel that they are doing their best and making a difference; that they are having a positive impact on the young minds they are trying to guide towards a better future.

Halfway hump is so-called for a reason – because it really does give folks the hump. Not even just school staff, parents are equally fed up with this time of year and are craving springtime vibes. For the school staff already feeling under the cosh and pretty grim, they need a boost of positivity and something to help their already fragile self-esteem. If the teachers and TAs look to the children for love and respect, they may be pleasantly surprised by a hand-drawn picture or a lovely compliment. What they do not need is a 'teacher burn', and for the uninitiated, this is where a child says something inadvertently offensive (or downright deliberately soul-destroying but also hilarious in hindsight) to a member of school staff. Think of a child innocently doing a Roy Walker and 'saying what they see'. To a person with visible acne, you may hear, 'Why does your face look like a pizza?' Or to a bald person, 'That man is so tall he's grown right through his hair!'

We share teacher burns on our podcast and there was an entire chapter in our previous book dedicated to them, but because they always go down well, what better time to bring some smiles than by children humiliating already vulnerable school staff.

One good example of this is when a child with Tourette's was struggling to keep his vocal impulses under control and would walk around the school telling grown-ups to f*ck off. It's a condition that obviously the child had no choice in and no ability to keep at bay, but when you're at your lowest ebb, being told to fornicate away by a child is pretty hard to take. He didn't restrict it just to regular teachers, either; the leadership team were fair game as well. The headteacher received a 'f*ck off, baldy' and the deputy head was called a 'fat-arse', which mortified her as she didn't think she had any issues with her weight. The head really liked the lad and secretly confessed to being disappointed when he was put on Ritalin, because his days were a little boring as a result.

Not to be outdone, a little Year 2 child in the north of England bust out a zinger when he came across the door to the staffroom at his primary school. He opened it ever so slowly and stuck his head in. In a strong northern accent, he looked directly at the teachers gathered inside and said, 'And you lot can f*ck off!' before closing the door equally slowly and going back to whatever he was doing. You can't fault his delivery, and apparently the staff inside were struggling to not burst out laughing.

Here are a few that actually happened to me. One seven-year-old boy commented on my facial hair recently – 'Mr P, I really like your beard' –

so I thanked him for his compliment. Sadly, he wasn't done and added, 'I just love how it covers all your chins.' It doesn't stop there, though. When I was covering Year 2, a little girl was strangely fixated on a piece of jewellery.

She politely popped her hand up and asked about my wedding ring.

'What's that on your finger, Mr P?'

'Oh, it's my wedding ring, I'm married.'

I replied to her little question thinking that the short, innocent exchange was over, but the girl piped back up and said:

'Ahh yeah, my mummy says there is someone out there for everyone.'

I was speechless (for a change), but inside I was questioning what made her say such a thing. So in her mind, I'm lucky that one woman on this planet had decided to marry me. She had a point, but it still hurt.

Don't worry, these other teachers didn't get quite off so lightly either.

One trainee teacher received a handmade bookmark at the end of her school-based placement that was beautifully made but had a handwritten message that said:

'I'm so sorry you're living! 😢'

I think we all hope the little girl meant 'leaving', because if she didn't there could be a prospective serial killer that needs an early intervention.

One teacher was playing football with a child in his class at break time and while they clearly had a good time, the little lad had a slightly stern look upon his face.

'I'm still cross cos you keep saving all my goals. It's not fair really, you have big chubby legs like trees!'

He has no filter...

He wasn't wrong...

A Year 6 boy once said to a female teacher, 'All girls think about is their hair, except you, Mrs Glasper. You don't care what yours looks like!'

What a cheek! Horrified by his feedback, the teacher popped to the hairdresser at her earliest convenience and as soon as the same boy spotted the effort that had gone into upgrading the teacher's presentation, he had even more cheek to wink at her and remark, 'Nice try!'

A Year 1 child was drawing her teacher and was very keen that her colour choices needed to be correct. She selected brown for the hair and pink for the teacher's cardigan, but she was scrambling around looking for one particular colour. The teacher was delighted to be immortalised in pencil crayon by her pupil so she asked which colour they were missing. The little girl said, 'I've got a pink for your face but I need a lellow for your teeth!'

The next one is brutal.

Pupil: 'Are you turning into a cat?'

Teacher: 'No, why?'

Pupil: 'Coz you're growing whiskers.'

This was said to a female teacher in her early thirties. Ouch!

I have had plenty of burns sent my way over my long and illustrious(?) teaching career, so I fully recognise younger children have no filter. From getting a new haircut and being called Joey Essex, to constantly being asked why my face is so red when I have an eczema flare-up. I think the reality is that any child any age will happily burn you to the core. Later in the book, I'll go into more detail about the noticeable differences between primary and secondary education as children make the jump, but when it comes to roasting teachers it comes down to the level of intent.

In secondary there's more awareness from the kids as to what they are saying, there's more venom – they will roast you and mean it – whereas in primary there's an innocence. They say the most hurtful insults cut you to the bone, but it's done with love. For example, I was lining my class up recently – or should I say, I was attempting to line my class up – when a child at the front of the line looked at my lanyard with concern. Now, this lanyard picture was taken in my NQT year, 15 years ago, and the kid stared at it for ages, then looked at me and said, 'Are you OK?' To which I replied, 'Yeah, why?' and he said, 'It's just in the picture you look different.' I told him it was a while ago, and he went, 'No no, it's the big bum crack you've got between your eyes, how did you do that?' I couldn't believe it! My instinctive reaction was to say, 'Teaching. Teaching has put this massive indent in my forehead which makes it look like I have a massive arse on my face.' When that child pointed out the bum crack in my forehead he was genuinely concerned for me, whereas I imagine a secondary student would have just called me 'Arse Face' and that would be that. His comment has since given me such a complex, but I can't hide the dent when my teacher stare makes it so prominent. Every time I make a video on my social media I see it, protruding. I just wish that kids had pointed it out a couple of years ago.

Even worse was when I was on playground duty and a child in Year 3 was giggling hysterically behind me – you know, the type of laugh where they are struggling for breath. I said, 'What are you laughing at?', to which she replied, 'Look, my whole body can fit into the shadow of your belly!' Now, I know what you're thinking, it must have been afternoon play, when the shadows are longer – based on the Year 5 science investigation you did. No, this was lunchtime, the sun was at its highest point and this child was giggling at the fact that I looked like a pregnant lady of a seven-year-old baby. Cheers, I'll leave the biscuits today.

But that's not the bad thing, because even when you go the other way it still happens. I'd lost a bit of weight over the summer, and I felt pretty good about myself, and because I had lost a few pounds my trousers were a little loose and I hadn't put a belt on, so every so often during class I'd just pull them up a little. Fast forward to lunch where a child is in tears because they'd got 'the bum touch'! Yes, that's right, my class had invented a highly contagious, deadly disease and basically because I kept pulling my trousers up whoever I would go round to and help with their work would get 'the bum touch'. They'd created a disease worse than Ebola and Covid purely because I'd lost a bit of timber. So I'm trying to console this child while also wiping away the tears myself, and this child, by the way, is the same one who, when a classmate in Reception filled his shoes with diarrhoea and walked around the classroom, he was making patterns with the toy sand trucks in the trail behind him.

The final burn of this chapter is about when I was the recipient of some rinsing by my class after I inadvertently shaved off my beard. If you have hair clippers at home you'll know that there's usually a set of different heads you can put on the clippers to determine whether it's going to be a grade 3 or a grade 0. I trim my facial growth all the time, but on this occasion I completely forgot to put the guard on the clippers and took a monumental chunk out of my beard. Nightmare! I had the option of turning it into a Hulk Hogan Handlebar moustache, but it was well past Movember and I couldn't go in front of my class or deliver teacher training around the UK looking like I was about to enter the Royal

Rumble. So I made the decision to remove the entire beard and just start all over again. Would anyone notice? Of course they bloody would!

My wife couldn't even look at me. My kids thought I was a completely different person. It was a tough few days, I can tell you. There was a collective 'ooh' when the children at school saw me for the first time (and not in a good way), so I decided to turn it into a learning exercise. The children were each given a Post-it note and asked to complete the sentence: 'Mr P without a beard looks...'

– like a hairless cat
– awful
– new but weird
– like a knee
– terrible
– like my gran
– like an overgrown toddler
– like a tall, funny baby and a bull combined

I was mildly impressed with this one:
... like his teacher picture on his lanyard from 12 years ago.
But the one that hurt the most was: like...

Ouch! Thanks, kids.

Just as you enter March and start getting your head around the fact that winter may be on its way out, parents will be thinking to themselves there could be a little calm as the evenings get (only slightly) lighter. At least, there are a few normal weeks where they don't need to make special arrangements, and then... BOOM!... World Book Day.

First held in 1995 in the UK, World Book Day usually falls on the first Thursday in March, and its purpose is to make reading fun for children and more accessible to all. Some schools will have some reading-themed events, some ask staff and children to dress up as a character from their favourite book, and some do as little as possible. If you're the English/Reading Coordinator at a school it usually falls upon you to organise the damn thing, and as long as your head-teacher is happy with what you've planned, you can either go all in, or go a different way where you invite in a storyteller to do an assembly rather than a cosplay event.

Most schools will do something in the middle and will have a lot of fun with it. Some schools are mindful of the level of the dressing up, as they know their families can barely afford food and heating, let alone a highly flammable Willy Wonka outfit that they'll only ever wear once. It's nice to have some donated outfits from the previous years that you can pass on so those children don't feel left out. If you're one of the sort of people that donates theirs, or you're a teacher that facilitates this sort of scheme, you're a legend and the children are very lucky to have you.

Depending on the patience levels of the staff, a school may do a parade or an assembly if the children are all decked out as book characters. This... may... take... ages! Whoever is at the front of the assembly will usually start by saying how wonderful everyone looks and bring to the attention of the school which teachers look like twits. Not the book *The Twits*, mind, just the teachers who are unrecognisable under their face paint yet have just finished teaching improper fractions to Year 5.

These assemblies start at a nice, plodding tempo, but by the time they are an hour in and are only halfway through Year 2, they usually have to speed it up a bit.

There are some really classy costumes, like a pair of brothers dressed as Frodo and Sam from J.R.R. Tolkien's *The Lord of the Rings*, which were quite sweet. One child may come as Emmeline Pankhurst because she's been reading about the Suffragettes. If a Year 1 comes as Jean Valjean from Victor Hugo's *Les Misérables*, then you know the parents are more interested in projecting that they are well read than actually encouraging their son's enjoyment of reading. Now we've got the classy ones out the way, let's talk about the crap ones.

There will be children that come to school on World Book Day as folks that technically appear in printed books but are kind of a disappointment or miss the spirit of the event. This one is acceptable...

Teacher to child wearing a full Man Utd kit:

'Who are you today, Jimmy?'

'Marcus Rashford,' he replies, holding up his *Little People, BIG DREAMS* and *You Are a Champion* books (by Marcus Rashford). Despite being very much Caucasian, little Jimmy at least chose someone who encourages reading and has done a lot for school-aged children.

One from a few years ago that is the opposite is a child dressed in full Liverpool kit. When asked who he was, he replied 'Luis Suárez' and held up a Liverpool annual. Ffs.

There'll be loads of children dressed as Batman, Superman, Iron Man and Spider-Man, and while there are lots of books published about these characters, it would be more impressive if they had chosen these due to their love of graphic novels, but it's more likely it's because they still have that costume from Halloween. I certainly regretted my Incredible Hulk outfit when, after three showers, the paint wouldn't shift. Speaking of graphic novels, one child may come as Rorschach from Alan Moore's graphic novel *Watchmen*, so you know that their parents are comic book fans. It would be impressive, but it's completely glossing over the fact that *Watchmen* is totally inappropriate for primary-aged children.

It can be funny when a child is dressed as their favourite character from a book that the teacher has never heard of, and yet the child will look them in their eyes expecting them to know exactly who they are supposed to be.

'I'm Farley Drexel Hatcher from Judy Blume's *Tales of a Fourth Grade Nothing*,' they will say, and the teacher will look at a child in regular jeans and a T-shirt and have to feign knowledge of the book they've never heard of. (Side note, Judy Blume books are amazing, so everyone should check them out, especially those featuring Farley Drexel Hatcher.)

The teacher will have to do that plenty of times as they may not have heard of all the books that the cool kids are reading. The children that choose a character from Michael Morpurgo's *Private Peaceful* or Diana Wynne Jones's *Howl's Moving Castle* will usually be those that already love reading, so this day is as much about them as it is trying to engage more reticent readers.

For many school staff across the country, one sight we often see that kind of turns World Book Day into a bit of a joke is outfits for Where's Wally, or, as they call him on the other side of the Atlantic, Waldo, hanging up in supermarkets. Yes, it's a bit of fun, but ideally you don't want children celebrating reading by dressing up as characters from books where there are HARDLY ANY BLOODY WORDS! And even then, they're just telling you about another character, scroll or dog that you need to find. A bit harsh, but the Wally books are hardly promoting reading even if they are a lot of fun.

Speaking of fun, some teachers will go nuts on World Book Day with their own costumes. You could have an entire set of cards from *Alice in Wonderland*, an Elmer elephant, a Stick Man, plus huge kudos to any staff that go full Oompa Loompa and are still cleaning orange face paint out of their ears a week later. We salute you!

Special mention to headteachers who don't take themselves too seriously and dress up as Miss Trunchbull from *Matilda*. The commitment to the monobrow is impressive, but please don't get carried away and start swinging children around by their pigtails... even if they deserve it.

(Me as the fairest of them all and my heavily pregnant wife)

We've mentioned it on our podcast before, but I think there can't be many things funnier than watching kids play football while dressed up on World Book Day. If you're the teacher on break duty that day, then you are in for a treat. You can even do your own commentary while watching them in action.

'Here comes Cruella de Vil... she pulls back and hits the top bin! It's an absolute finish!'

'He squares it to the Gruffalo...'

'Thing 1 passes to Thing 2, they're really building up a great partnership...'

It's the bit where the Cat in the Hat does a two-footed lunge on the Lorax. Some nasty Dr.-Seuss-on-Dr.-Seuss violence is not ideal, but what's hilarious is trying to maintain a straight face when the Cat in the Hat's face paint is running because he has tears in his eyes and is claiming that the Lorax hurt him first. Annoyingly, the BFG and the Very Hungry Caterpillar are sticking their noses in, but then, in possibly the strangest turn of events ever, Draco Malfoy is being the voice of reason and trying to get everyone to be friends so they don't ban football.

How you're supposed to act as VAR and deal with the on-pitch fracas while dressed as Dorothy from *The Wizard of Oz* is anyone's guess.

(My mate Cockney John and I enjoyed this far too much!)

Not quite from the sublime to the ridiculous, but the funny business in the month of March doesn't stop there.

Another staple of the school calendar for well over 30 years in the UK is the fundraising event known as Comic Relief. It used to happen every other year until the introduction of Sport Relief in 2002, with which it then alternated, which meant that in every subsequent year there was some form of crazy fundraising in mid-March. Much of what I'm detailing here may apply to Children in Need in November, too, but Comic Relief comes with slightly more opportunities for classroom shenanigans. Waxing the legs of male members of staff is funny all year round... unless it's your legs that are getting waxed, of course.

They do have Red Nose Day/Comic Relief in the US as well, but it's done differently, even if the message and purpose are similar. So we're talking about the British version here, and how it affects schools; the day where pretty much everything curriculum-based goes out of the window because the children are too hyped up, covered in red hair spray and full of cakes to focus. If Ofsted came that day for a no-warning visit, they may find that there's not a huge amount planned that will tick all their boxes. Plenty of learning is still going on, of course, but it is done in a way where the children have a better understanding of causes abroad and at home that need urgent help/fundraising. If the Ofsted inspector tries to be too strict while the children are covered head to toe in red and are sporting clown noses, he deserves to be shoved in a gunge tank or put into a bath of baked beans. Do people even still do that? A bath of baked beans?

When you were younger, Red Nose Day could be the greatest day of your life because you'd be glued to CBBC as they started talking about all the fantastic things that were going on. Lenny Henry would be making guest appearances on *Top of the Pops* and *Blue Peter.* There was usually a theme like 'Say Pants to Poverty', where people would all come dressed with pants over their normal clothes. 'Big Hair and Beyond' meant that people wore wigs and did cool stuff with their hair; 1991 had 'The Stonker'; 1997's tagline was 'Small Change – Big Difference', but the overarching theme over the years has been to 'do something funny for money'.

There's a serious message as well, and as they still do now, they used to have lots of comedy skits on the main programme interspersed with serious films from Africa and closer to home, showing people in dire need of funding because they were suffering such hardships. Plenty of generations grew up knowing more about the world and where money was needed because of Comic Relief, and it's great that schools still carry on the traditions and sentiments. It's still brilliant fun if it's a Comic Relief year, and the children embrace it wholeheartedly.

On Red Nose Day in schools, the children could wear their own clothes for a day while the teachers had to wear something silly, usually in exchange for a donation to the charity. Some schools still do it where the teachers all come dressed in school uniform for a bit of a laugh. This is all good and fun, as most teachers still have their old school tie or blazer, although no promises it still fits! However, there's a limit to how far the teachers can go, because the last thing you need is some of the Year 6 lads getting a little hot under the collar because one of the younger, more attractive teachers looks like she's been expelled from St Trinian's. This also works for the male staff and their chosen attires, but there's less chance of being risqué and more chance of them looking like Angus Young (the lead guitarist from AC/DC).

Comic Relief days are sometimes the ones where the children have a little free licence to be a bit cheeky and the teachers can be rather silly too. It's one of those days where the spirit is right and teachers prank the children by surprising them with an impossible spelling test. It started by featuring easy ones at the beginning:

1. house
2. sandwich

Slightly trickier ones as they progress...

3. ambulance
4. restaurant

Increasingly harder ones...

5. serendipitously
6. questionnaire

Then ridiculous spellings for the final efforts...

7. antidisestablishmentarianism
8. floccinaucinihilipilification

For those wondering and who can't be bothered to google it, the f-word (no, not that one) means the action or habit of estimating something as worthless. Just like that fake spelling test.

It's worth mentioning that this is a perfectly acceptable joke to play from about Year 3 upwards (although school staff should perhaps let children with learning difficulties know that there's a prank on the horizon, so they are in on the joke rather than getting upset). Probably not a great idea to pull this on Year 1 children, as there may be a few complaints from parents!

While we're on the topic of teacher pranks, I learned of a brilliant one where a teacher had promised his class some brownies if they worked hard enough and managed not to fall out with each other every lunchtime. The promise of brownies was the catalyst for some fantastic behaviour and real focus when approaching their work. Clearly the teacher had created a culture in the class of collective responsibility for their common goal because in the build-up to the potential treat the children worked their socks off and were immaculately behaved. They'd earned their reward a few times over and they knew they deserved it. What they ended up with were plates full of letter Es made out of brown paper.

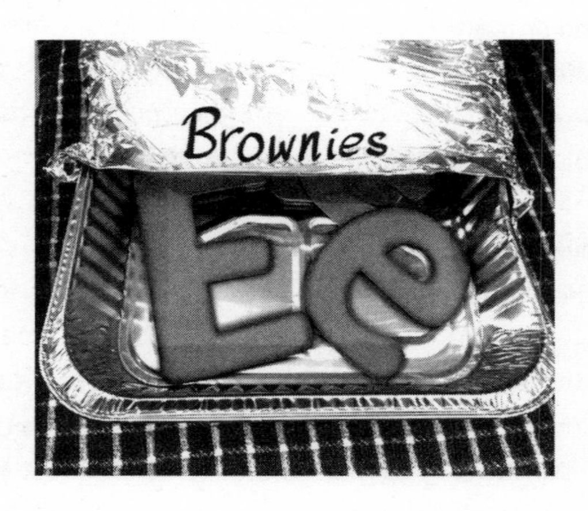

Teachers over the years will build up a bank of genius ideas like this, and when enough time has passed, they'll dip into their greatest hits and give the children a good laugh. The bank of ideas can also be dipped into when teachers want to prank each other. With all the time they spend among children, teachers like to have fun with each other – a funny drawing on their whiteboard ('Mr Hayden woz ere') or a fake dog poo on their desk. It doesn't half make the day go quicker when you're smiling a little. The children notice it and it's often infectious. If they know the teacher is happy to be at work, it goes a long way to making the children's enjoyment of the day.

So we're going to end this chapter with a few stories about teachers being a little bit cheeky, to prove that, however professional a teacher may attempt to come across as when dealing with parents, they are, deep down, potentially as bad as the kids!

Here's a wonderful example of mistaken identity. In most schools, every second of the day counts, and planning when to grab maths resources, mark books or even go for a wee can make the difference between a decent lesson and doing a funny piddle dance because the teacher or TA didn't make time to empty their bladder. During assembly times, teachers and TAs often work with groups of children or prepare resources. In one school there were some TAs that had a morning ritual of meeting at the photocopier during assembly time to get some sheets printed. It had been a crazy morning and when it reached photocopying time, the TA plodded towards the printer (still in a daze after trying to teach money recognition to Year 1 children who had barely used physical coins in real life). She spotted that her printing buddy was already there, wearing her outdoor coat because the school was bloody freezing. For a laugh, the TA decided to sneak up behind her friend and whisper in her ear, 'I dunno about you but I seriously cannot be arsed today!' Expecting her mate to turn around and agree with a smile on her face, the TA realised she'd made a giant boo-boo. It wasn't her pal after all, it was a tall Year 6 girl who just so happened to have a similar coat. Yikes.

I bet that kid was given an extra packet of Haribo at the school disco to keep quiet.

This next story features something not being kept quiet at all!

A teacher used to work at a school within walking distance of her home. She'd walk to school and sign in via the iPad in the reception. She had really decent banter with the office staff, and would often say goodbye to them and wave through the window if she was leaving before they were. When she turned the corner, the office staff could still see her through the large, mirrored windows. It's great to have work colleagues you can banter with, as they make the day so much more enjoyable.

One day, the headteacher was out so the teacher made plans to do her allocated preparation, planning and assessment (PPA) time from home. The usual Wednesday staff meeting was cancelled that afternoon, so the teacher thought she'd take advantage and clear off at lunchtime. This particular day came after she'd had some Tex-Mex food the night before. This type of food was something she enjoyed, but it didn't always sit well with her the following day. Her class was doing assessments all week in the mornings, so her classroom was pretty much silent during these times. Her TA had taken a group out to a different room, which meant she was on her own in class for most of the day. With no TA present and no lavatory nearby, she had no chance to pop to the toilet and settle her increasingly bloated and spicy tummy. Her dishes the previous evening had been mostly meat and cheese, so not only were her enchiladas repeating on her, but she was fairly bunged as well.

This poor lady was suffering with a case of the meat sweats and was building up a big bank of burrito-based blowoffs. She couldn't wait to finish for the day, so rather than mark books and prepare lessons, she had every intention of spending the ensuing hours lying on her sofa with some peppermint Rennies or Wind-eze. Before she could reach the sofa, she had to grab her bags and walk out through the reception area. Normal banter wasn't on the cards with her ladies in the school office, sadly. She'd just about managed to walk down the corridor, only letting out a solitary nervous toot on her way. The exit was in sight, and she was almost ready to explode.

Bidding a very quick farewell to her office pals, she signed herself out with great haste and shuffled out of the automatic doors. It was at this point that she saw the coast was clear and let out a huge fart that a rhinoceros would have been proud of. It lasted about 20 seconds and sounded like a chainsaw. Just when she thought it was done, there was a second, slightly more tuneful addition to her performance which lasted a further five seconds. And with that our teacher felt significantly less bloated.

The problem with passing such an epic guffaw was that she was so focused on the release and relief but paid no attention to what was around the corner. Fortunately (or so she thought) there was nothing around the corner... but her relief turned to dismay when she spotted that one of the office windows was wide open and she realised that her office chums had heard EVERYTHING!

A voice came from inside the window,

'Bloody 'ell Lisa, that one was on the Richter scale!'

'Sounds like you exorcised four daemons at once there, girl!'

She was mortified!

Still hearing her colleagues giggling away, she did the walk (or waddle, as she still had a dicky tum) of shame back to her house knowing she had disgraced herself in front of her colleagues. She messaged her colleagues to explain and, rather than further take the p*ss, they both sympathised, including the one lady who said she could 'Fart for England' following her hysterectomy. Poor Lisa told them both that it was the Tex-Mex food that caused the issues, and they both could relate. After that reassurance, she felt she could show her face the following day with only minor embarrassment.

The next morning she arrived at work and walked past the large, mirrored windows, stepped through the automatic doors and went to sign in on the iPad in the reception area. It was strangely quiet in the office, and she could see neither of her friends. Oh well, she thought to herself, I'll catch them later and we'll probably have a giggle about it then. She continued to tap away on the iPad when two humans popped up from behind the reception desk, wearing sombreros and fake moustaches and yelling 'ARRIBA!'

The pair of b*stards!!! She vowed out loud never to trust those gringos again, but unfortunately they were all laughing too much to hear.

Spring, spring, what a good thing!

I'm not sure if that's from the famous *Come and Praise* hymn book but it's a spring song that many have heard of but only remember the first line.

After February half term there's the big countdown that is ENTIRELY dependent on the consistency (or lack of) provided by the great British weather.

Can you guess what it is?

Is it the countdown to SATs? Nope, Year 6 and Year 2 can worry about that. If you're a teacher or child in those year groups... erm, sorry about that! It is potentially THE biggest decision of the year.

Headteachers come under HUGE external pressures from parents, Ofsted, teaching unions and even politicians (who may be excellent in some cases, but who also may struggle with arses and elbows). Of all the pressures, this may be the most significant. The decision I'm talking about is the answer to this important question:

'CAN WE GO ON THE FIELD YET?'

After months of being confined to the tarmac, the children are starting to experience the sun regularly and yearn for the days where if they fall over it's not an instant graze, fractured limb or concussion. Could it finally be time to go back onto the school field?!?! What a conundrum!

Pros:

- More energy out of the children's system so they can focus when in the classrooms.
- Great exercise for the pupils.
- Fewer head bumps as the children aren't smacking into each other on a cramped playground.

Cons:

- Mud.
- Grass stains.
- P**sed-off parents having to supply fresh clothes every single day of the week.
- More mud.
- Field gets ripped to shreds and is cut up for the summer.
- Even more mud and plenty of it walked through the classrooms.
- Did I mention mud?
- Muck magnet revisited.

Oooooh, what to do? What to do?

If the head makes the call too early, there's an army of complaints on the school Facebook page or WhatsApp group, and shares in Ariel and Lenor will increase in value significantly. Make the call too late after Easter and the ground is concrete!

If your local school was originally a Victorian building with a playground the size of a postage stamp, you'll want the younglings out on the field as soon as is reasonably possible. And before we get growled at (not sure how you do that reading a book), some modern schools have lovely areas with mud kitchens, etc., where the children bring wellies and waterproofs for all weather conditions.

Teacher hat on: What lovely and enriching experiences for the little learners. It's just a little bit of mess.

Parent hat on: FFS, why have they only got one sock (wet), a pair of muddy underpants and, for some reason, another child's shoe!

Not all schools are blessed with nor can afford wellies and waterproofs for all, but despite the quibbles about messy clothes, it's great if the children can enjoy some time outside of the classroom to explore their environments.

Speaking of outdoor learning, in the last 20 years there has been a huge uptick in schools with 'forest school' sites. Obviously, schools in the countryside stand a better chance of having these facilities, but it's nice that more and more schools are getting to push outdoor learning. If your school has the facilities, forest school days are the ones that children look forward to the most. Children are quite happy to do their maths in charcoal on a log or go pond-dipping.

Usually, the Year 6 classes will get the forest school slots in September and July; September because then they can tick a box to say they've done it, and July because SATs are out of the way and they can d*ck around as much as they like in the brambles. Also, from the teacher's perspective, in about eight weeks' time they will be someone else's problem! Sorry to any secondary school teachers reading this, but after SATs week, we don't care what or if they learn.

As the terms progress there are little wins. Yes, maybe the field may be a bit more available, the nights are starting to draw in later, the temperature could potentially hit the teens and, before you know it, Mother's Day is on the cards. I mean, literally, there will be Mother's Day cards in production, and you can guarantee that some teachers will be more prepared than others.

You can usually tell if the children have had plenty of time to make the cards that they bring home. The organised teachers will have a tried-and-tested go-to card that gets made every year. I'm sorry to say that if that teacher moves year groups and your child or a sibling has them again, be prepared for the same design you received previously (although the quality will depend on whether they've gone up year groups or down). Funnily enough, intricate little flowers are harder to create when your mini artists were nine or ten years old last time and now they are only five or six!

Some teachers are always on the lookout for a new and impressive idea, so they'll be scrolling Instagram and Pinterest, looking for a showstopper of epic proportions. There may be moving parts, there may be intricate petals and some actual sewn material with lace and a doily (ask your nan) incorporated – a craft extravaganza that will be a symphony for the eyes and take pride of place on the mantelpiece.

For most teachers, however, it's a 'Sh*t it's Mother's Day on Sunday, cancel this afternoon's RE and let's quickly make any old tat' effort.

It's the thought that counts... and literally zero thought has gone into this one. There's not even enough time to check whether the possessive apostrophe is in the right place (Mothers'/Mother's), even less time for checking the spelling and sentiment on the personalised message inside. They range from:

'Mummy, you mean the world to me and I'm so grateful for everything that you do!'

to:

'Cheers for wiping my bum!'

I think I even saw that on a greetings card in a shop the other year.

The different events and traditions that exist in the UK, which are celebrated inside and outside of school, are all good fun, but if you had to describe Easter traditions to a visiting alien, where would you start? Comedian Mitch Benn created a song about the randomness of Easter called 'Zombie Jesus Chocolate Day', but as children raised as Catholics, you can imagine me getting a ruler across the bum cheeks for such blasphemy (if it was still the 1950s). Joking aside, how on earth did it go from the death and resurrection of Christ to a strange rabbit bringing chocolate eggs to children that are well behaved (or, more often than not, little b*stards as well). We can't blame British culture entirely for this, but it's strange how traditions around Easter have developed over the years.

An easy answer relates to eggs as new life and the rabbits and chicks as springtime creatures. To prove the point about how confusing, yet accepted, it all is, a Year 2 child once made an Easter card of Jesus popping out of an egg. I never saw that mentioned in the Bible!

There's some maths you can do if you fancy it, where the children work out the cost of an Easter egg, calculate exactly how much chocolate you are getting in the egg and in the bars/packets of the sweets. Chances are it's a revelation that they've paid £3.50 for an egg and two bars of chocolate, which bought separately will cost about £1.75. This means you've spent half of the price of the egg on packaging! Granted, any business studies students would point out the cost of the packaging, the design, the distribution, manufacturing costs and marketing add up, but still... Alright, I'm being a killjoy with the last bit, and even I remember the excitement of having about nine Easter eggs of differing size and quality stacked up on the living-room table, thinking to myself, where do I start?

Another staple of British primary schools at Easter is egg hunts, egg decorating and egg-rolling. Let's start with the Easter egg hunt. This is a fun little game that can be enjoyed by Reception children seeking little chocolate eggs and popping them into their little baskets, all the way up to mega-competitive Year 6 children scouring the school grounds and potentially putting themselves in danger to see if a very poor-quality chocolate egg is on top of a cupboard. It never is, but that doesn't stop the class daredevil clambering up the bookcase to check. It's an activity that never loses its appeal, whatever age the participants may be.

Some schools have egg-rolling, where there's a ramp set up in the school playground or hall and children take it in turns to roll a boiled egg as far as it can go. It's a bit of a waste of food, if you think about it, but children do get excited about activities like this. Some children take it very seriously and give their eggs a bit of a push. Get the speed right and you could have a winner, get it wrong and it's a cracked mess at the bottom of the ramp before you've even got going. Eggs, by their very nature, are not ideal for rolling on a hard surface as they are thinner at the top than they are at the bottom and tend to skew to the left or right depending on their starting position. The biggest tip I can give any school attempting this activity is... do it outside! Chances are the eggs will break, and the last thing you need is an eggy pong in the school hall. Yuck!

Egg decorating can be fun, but if the children do this at home, it's just like the pumpkin carving and parents may take over, so judging the best ones that did or didn't have help can be tricky. At least with egg decorating the parents can make a hole at the top and the bottom and blow out the contents before any painting goes on. No point wasting a perfectly good egg.

Lots of schools will get involved with the previously mentioned Easter activities, and they seem to be popular as they are back every year to the point where children will look forward to them. As soon as they see a pair of bunny ears in a shop (as we all know, it can be as early as 2 January), they start to get excited for a potential upcoming visit from the Easter Bunny.

Traditions come and traditions go, and new ones are invented every year that probably won't catch on, but kudos for trying. There may even be some schools where traditions seem to be more important than the actual curriculum. Usually, but not always, it will be those

little village schools that hold such activities dear, and it's ingrained in the culture of the people who love to live there that they must continue these for generations to come.

I'm almost trying to paint a picture of a place like the fictional village of Sandford, Gloucestershire, from *Hot Fuzz*. I'm using a pretend village to illustrate so as to not offend any place in particular, but it's the sort of place where everybody knows each other and the community is very tight-knit. They don't like outsiders and the SATNAV won't work past Northleach.

These are the places where they adore a bit of the old-school activities, and you can bet their Easter traditions date back hundreds of years. You'll still have the egg-painting, egg-rolling contests and a sponsored bounce where children wear cardboard bunny ears. They'll also still have competitions in the village hall where they make miniature Easter gardens. If you've never seen them before, they are lovely little activities but also totally pointless. A child (or possibly their parent) will get a foil baking tray or biscuit tin and use earth, stones, grass and twigs to create a little mini garden where, for some reason, it's part English village but also part Garden Tomb in Jerusalem. 🤷▒♂

It makes no sense at all, but families from certain places in the countryside do them every year. I've never come across Christmas, Halloween or Pancake Day gardens, so there may be a reason why they are made specifically at Easter. They are definitely less common in areas that are further from the countryside, which makes sense. You'll maybe not find them regularly in Moss Side, Manchester (although I'm happy to be proved wrong), but it's another Easter tradition that schools and communities like to keep alive.

While we are still talking about rural traditions, I know a teacher from a school situated out in the sticks (Forest of Dean, not Center Parcs) who can confirm that they genuinely have an Easter Bunny, like in *The Vicar of Dibley*. Someone, every year, will dress as the Easter Bunny and be captured on the Ring doorbells and personal CCTV dropping eggs off around the village. A kind and fun gesture for the people that live there, yet nobody has a proper idea who it is (it's not Dawn French). The only clues they really have are that it is not very tall (about 5 foot, taller with ears) and it is female. I'll let you work out for yourself how they know it's female, if you get what you mean. It's also definitely someone who has sponsors or a bit of money themselves, as the eggs they deliver are of pretty decent quality – none of your '100 chocolate eggs for £1' that you may find in a pound shop. You know the ones, where they legally must be fit for human consumption but you're not entirely convinced that they are. Not in this teacher's village, though; the fluffy springtime Santa was delivering Cadbury, Galaxy and even a few Lindt ones. Good work, Mrs Easter Bunny!

One more Easter tradition that seems to be less prevalent in many of the schools I know is the Easter bonnet parade. I don't really know much about the history of Easter bonnets but the general gist is about renewal and redemption (yes, I googled it). I'm sure the origin story on Wikipedia is true, but there's every possibility that someone was running activities at a spring fayre and just thought...

'Sod it... I'm bored, I'll decorate me hat!'

If a headteacher decides that the whole school should join in with an activity, you can bet that the children from Reception to about

Year 3 will be well up for it. KS2? Mixed responses. Still, if the school or PTA managed to bulk buy or get some plain hats donated, then I don't care if you're 11 and taller than your teacher, you're making an Easter bonnet, tough guy! The making of the hats isn't the issue – it's standing up in front of the whole school, looking like a prize fool. They are decorated with plastic flowers, brightly coloured polystyrene eggs and, most importantly, these poor creatures...

... yep, the distressed-looking, fluffy Easter chicks.

What kind of human decided to create these monstrosities? There's a TikTok channel dedicated to these terrified-looking pom-poms with legs. From afar, you can look at them and think that they are quite cute and they add a bit of colour.

Up close? Holy sh*t! These poor things look like background characters from a horror film.

So there we have it, we've had a little exploration of a few of the common and slightly less common aspects of Easter time in schools. I've joked about the weirdness of some of the traditions and the examples of the places where they happen, but it really is quite a nice time of year for the children – and also an excellent excuse to eat a sh*t load of chocolate!

Let's get this out of the way. For the children taking them, the SATs (Standard Assessment Tests) mean absolutely sweet FA. No child has ever taken a SATs test to benefit themselves or their educational well-being. Nope!

SATs tests have been around since May 1991, when the first cohort of Year 2 children sat down and began the tradition of kids being stressed out for no reason. Don't get me wrong, assessments do have a place in schools, as you need to know what the children can and can't do. Sure. But at what point did someone think:

'These teachers look far too happy in their chosen vocation... let's stress them out with a week of strangely worded testing to make their children feel completely inadequate'?

It's been said many times that the children learn, or are at least taught, so much that has no bearing on their lives as a grown-up. Food Tech (or Home Economics, as it was known for many years) is very relevant. Playing the recorder? Not so much! If money is tight, you can try to feed a family of five for a fiver at Aldi, but can you provide sustenance for your children with the first eight notes of 'London's Burning'? 'Three Blind Mice' isn't much help either.

Yes, I'm being incredibly facetious, but my point remains that stressing children out by testing things that they will not need to use in adulthood is a waste of teachers' energy and the children's learning time. The leading maths brains that create the curriculum mostly get it right, but there's definitely plenty in there that children may not ever use again. Well, unless you end up working at GCHQ or MI6, and even then it's only to write the Christmas codebreakers.

It's not just maths; if a child struggles to recognise if the active or passive voice is used in a sentence, don't worry, so do the parents! As for the teachers, they've been using past participles, gerunds and coordinating conjunctions for years in the correct context, but now they have to teach them and get children to remember the specific name for what they are using. Who does this benefit? It's certainly not the confused children!

Do you remember the SATs letter that went viral about a decade ago? They are incredibly common now but at the time this idea was pretty sweet in its sentiment.

It read something like:

Dear Year 6

This week you will be sitting your SATs tests in English and maths...

They do not test your skills in drama, music, art and languages...

Your job this weekend is to go and have lots of fun with your friends and family...

And then it ended with an inspirational quote. This one's by Aristotle:

'Educating the mind without educating the heart is no education at all.'

I believe in you!

Yours sincerely
Mr/Miss/Mrs Headteacher

They are quite lovely for the children to read, and if they put their minds slightly at ease then they have achieved their purpose, but some of them are starting to get pretty cringey – especially the ones that have been 85 per cent plagiarised from another school's website and shared with the local press as a marketing exercise. Every year a school will create one that goes viral, despite something similar being done the year before, and the year before that... and... You get the picture.

I'm not even against the sending of them, but it's starting to get a bit like overkill and feels like the letters aren't even for the children's benefit. That's where it becomes a problem. The sentiment of not testing children for the sake of it is an important one. There was a brief movement in the mid-2010s arguing to 'Let Kids be Kids', as some parents were planning to boycott the Year 2 SATs tests. More recently the More Than a Score campaign has done the same in relation to the new EYFS (Early Years Foundation Stage) baseline assessment tests. These tests in England are designed to assess the skills and abilities of children when they first start school at the age of four or five. The idea behind these assessments is to provide a starting point or 'baseline' for measuring a child's progress throughout their time in primary school, specifically until the end of Key Stage 2 when they are 11 years old. The tests are intended to cover early literacy, communication, language and mathematics.

Many educators and early childhood experts see these baseline assessments as problematic for several reasons:

Developmental appropriateness: critics argue that formal testing at such an early age is not developmentally appropriate. Young children develop at different rates, and their abilities can vary significantly from day to day. As a result, a one-off test may not accurately capture a child's abilities or potential.

Impact on well-being: there are concerns about the impact of formal testing on young children's well-being and anxiety levels. Starting school is a significant transition, and introducing tests may add unnecessary stress.

Narrow focus: the tests have a narrow focus on literacy and numeracy. Critics argue that this could lead to a narrowing of the curriculum, with schools possibly spending more time on these areas to the detriment of other important aspects of early education, such as play, social skills and creativity.

Teacher–pupil relationship: the early days of school are crucial for building relationships between teachers and pupils. Some educators feel that conducting baseline assessments could detract from this important bonding time and the establishment of a nurturing learning environment.

Accuracy and reliability: there are questions about the accuracy and reliability of such assessments. Young children's performance can be influenced by many factors, including their comfort with the test environment and the tester, making it difficult to ensure that the assessments provide a reliable baseline.

Educational equity: there are concerns that baseline assessments could exacerbate educational inequalities. Children from disadvantaged backgrounds may have had less exposure to educational opportunities before starting school.

I don't really see the point of assessments that teachers will not see the results for and therefore cannot act upon immediately. Again they will just be compared to the end of KS1 tests to further judge the school.

However primary schools approach the 'testing times' each May, it's important that the children are at the centre of any concerns. The increasingly cheesy letters do still have a place if they are sent for the right reasons. One major positive was that they brought to many people's attention the pointlessness of SATs, reaffirming that these tests have no bearing on the children's overall academic development other than an understanding that life's not fair and most of the important things in your existence will be decided by idiots like Michael Gove.

The 'Govester' wishes he had power like that, and although SATs weren't even his invention, that oleaginous (yes, I found a thesaurus) berk (and I've learned some rhyming slang) was on a mission since he became Education Secretary in May 2010 to p*ss off as many teachers as possible and, in turn, the parents and children. I'll whinge about him properly later, but from a SATs perspective, it went from being a bit of a whole-school challenge to overcomplicating things so much that they were no longer using SATs to find out what the children COULD do, and instead focusing on what they COULDN'T. SATs weren't perfect before Gove, but they definitely became worse as a result of his badly thought-out reforms.

Using your time machine (if you have one), you could go back and speak to a Year 6 teacher in 2008 and have a conversation about what they'd focus on during the year. Everything on the three maths papers should've been covered in the years before. Greater depth would hopefully be achieved over their final year, plus the topics of early algebra, ratio and proportion would be shoehorned in as well. Yes, children arrived in Year 6 with lots of gaps, but filling in what was missing was a positive challenge and teachers' jobs weren't particularly on the line.

Some teachers used to play Sherlock Holmes with the mental maths tests and try to guess which questions would pop up. They practised plenty of times with the children and tried to anticipate what would be on the test. They knew there'd be a question where the answer was one-fifth, 20 per cent or 0.2, and they would train their eagle-eyed mathematicians to spot it. There was a calculator paper (and the school would always lose three calculators between May and late April the following year). Nobody ever knew where they would go – was there a secret black market among school maths coordinators?

Were they the good old days? Probably not, but fast forward to the current SATs set-up where children are literally in tears before they go in. Not every child in every school, but the whole SATs process has become pretty vile. They insisted that children use certain methodology in their calculations (apparently the 'bus stop' and 'grid multiplication' weren't Victorian enough for Mr Gove) and he scrapped the mental maths paper in favour of one focused on arithmetic. They wanted a return to the 3 Rs of Reading, (W)

Riting and (A)Rithmetic from years gone by. Don't get me started on bloody SPAG (Spelling, Punctuation and Grammar).

This part of the book isn't meant to scare parents about when it's their children's turn to sit the bloody things. It's not meant to deter teachers lower down the school from stepping into the Year 6 role. This little part exists to remind everyone that SATs tests mean absolutely bugger all in a child's life and if you speak to the secondary teachers, they'll confirm that they don't believe the validity of the results anyway and will carry out their own assessments of the children when they join their schools in Year 7.

Once the ridiculous hyperbole of the Year 6 SATs is out of the way the school lets out a collective sigh and returns to normal. Do spare a thought, however, for the poor Year 2 teachers that have all of that to come but with none of the respect from the rest of the school. Alright, I say none, but it's fair to say the rest of the school don't take Year 2 SATs quite as seriously as the Year 6 ones. Mostly because they are usually completed over a two-week period so as not to stress out the little ones.

I have said this plenty of times on my social media and in print, but Year 3 and Year 5 are the only primary years where there isn't some type of formal assessment. There's EYFS baselines, Year 1 phonics check, Year 4 times tables and Year 2 and 6 have their SATs. It's really important from a teaching and parental standpoint that the children aren't stressed out so early in their primary school careers that they develop stress-related anxiety before they've even started secondary school. I have HUGE admiration for those amazing Year 2 teachers who manage to make the two weeks fly by without the children realising they are being assessed. These real-life Hermione and Harry folk deserve a gold star.

While not a fan of SATs, I appreciate that it's important to know where the children are academically. About a decade ago they weren't using 'age-related expectations' or 'expected standard' to judge children by, they were just called levels. Lots of teachers had and still have issues with the term 'expected standard'. Not only are they fairly off the mark as far as the accuracy of where children should be in their learning, but the language suggests that children are deemed simply not clever enough for their age group. Fancy telling a child in front of their parents that they are failing to reach where they are expected to be? By all means, tell a child and their parents which times tables to focus on or how to use a semi-colon in the correct context, just don't tell them they are an academic disappointment. For the previous decade and a little bit more, the Department for Education has definitely been 'working below the expected standard' – and my expectations were fairly low to start with!

For those that remember them, levels weren't perfect but at least lots of teachers and families knew where they stood with them. The Year 2 SATs were used as a bar to judge the Year 6 SATs. If the children were a Level 2 at the end of KS1, they would be expected to have progressed to Level 4 by the end of KS2. Sounds pretty straightforward, and some children might struggle a bit whereas others may make better than expected progress, perhaps jumping from Level 2 to Level 5. Big pats on the back for any teachers that helped them make that jump, although there was often some unspoken hatred between the Year 2 and Year 6 teachers. The Year 2 SATs were teacher assessments and when the Year 6 teachers would look at their incoming class for the new year, they would think:

'How the hell did Terence Hesketh get a Level 3 in writing? He can't even use full stops!'

This could cause a tricky conversation between the Year 2 and Year 6 teacher in the same school, and if the head-teacher finds they are at loggerheads, they can just threaten to switch the year groups that the teachers are in next time. I guess it's not so bad if there are separate infant and junior schools. If Ofsted pop into the junior school and question the poor progress, they can blame the other school for over-inflating the grades.

Some schools (not all) have a culture where if the SATs results were good the Year 6 teacher would have to share the plaudits with all the teachers before them. However, if the SATs were crap, it was the Year 6 teacher's fault. I've only heard of the latter happening in one school and, sensibly, the Year 6 teacher didn't stick around for long!

Onto one last test-based story.

One day in a one-form-entry primary school, a teacher was overseeing the administration of a reading paper. With only one class in the year group, they were able to fit the whole class in the school hall. There were a few children with SEN (Special Educational Needs), who had allocated members to take them somewhere else to complete their papers. No matter how stressful it can be, schools will do their utmost to make the children as comfortable as possible and usually with a trusted adult.

One girl was nervous about SATs but she didn't have too many issues with the maths papers. Her biggest fear was the reading comprehension test. I don't know quite what was causing her such anxiety but when her mum brought her to school she looked very pale. The poor child was such a trooper and didn't want to think she was letting her teacher down. The teacher put her near the front and kept reassuring her that they'd be proud of her, no matter what.

The test started and five minutes passed before the girl started to feel unwell again. While walking around the hall, the teacher was monitoring the whole class and picking up dropped pencils, if required. The poor girl clearly had nerves that were getting the better of her and she started convulsing in a way where she looked like she was gagging.

The teacher had to act fast, and without making too much of a sound he zipped past a few tables, getting to the girl just as she turned to the side and was about to decorate the floor with a load of phlegm. Fearing the entire SATs test would be disrupted, the teacher went down on one knee and managed to catch... yes, catch, the projectile before it hit the wooden floor. Thinking fast, the teacher took his handful of slime into the adjoining school kitchen and, like Spider-Man, 'THWIPPPP!' – he launched the mess into the sink and quickly washed his hands. Fortunately, the queasy youngster was given a glass of water and helped to settle herself by the lovely TA that was present. She finished her paper and, amazingly, reached a Level 5 (which at that time was a decent achievement). The teacher, however, had at least three years of being called 'Spewy' by his colleagues. It was a pretty grim experience, obviously, but those ninja-level reactions were something that teacher should be very proud of indeed!

When the weather is deemed passable, schools will be flocking to places like PGL, Robinwood and Blackwell (other adventure parks are available) for their class residential trips. If your local school is lucky enough to be situated close to one of these places, a stay for a few nights can be the highlight of many children's school lives and a place where many memories can be made. Obviously, there's no guarantee it won't rain for the entire duration of the trip, but that's the gamble of booking somewhere in a forest in the UK.

First of all, let's talk about the cost. Teachers completely understand how expensive things are and sadly we have no control over how much the venue, the coach and specialist staffing cost. It can be amazing for the vast majority of the children in a year group, but for some families it's a huge expense. I've known schools actively fundraise through cake sales and mufti days to try to make a class trip slightly more affordable so as to not price any family out of joining in. There are some children that just don't fancy it, and that's absolutely fine, especially if the school brings in another teacher for a mega class project with lots of art, PE and cooking. The kids staying in class while the others are away deserve to have fun as well. Not everyone has the same experience; one lad who is now in his 20s still hasn't forgiven the teacher that covered his class for making him learn (for an entire bloody week) about... CLOUDS! That's right, he can look in the sky and identify a cirrus, cumulonimbus or an alto-stratus, but, to be fair, he couldn't give a sh*t. He and his friend were given a chart to fill in each day to say which clouds were in the sky and then draw them. I think it's safe to say that they all looked like sheep without legs and the boys just picked random combinations because they knew the teacher wasn't going to check as he was as bored of the topic as the children were.

Back to how pricey it can be, there's no point in paying the full whack for a child to go on a trip where they don't want to do anything. Perhaps the climbing wall and zip wire may be a bit much, but the laser tag and the team building could be fun. If the child refuses to even put on a harness for the reasonably low tree trek (think Go Ape but closer to the ground), then it may be a bit of a waste of money.

Some mardy-arse parents, to prove it's too expensive, will take their child to the same site the weekend before for a fraction of the price. The parent will be smug that they didn't have to fork out megabucks, but they are kind of missing the point of a residential and the almost 'rite of passage' experience that it presents.

For some children it will be their first time staying away from their parents. Or, at least, the first time other than staying with grandparents while Mum and Dad get drunk at a wedding and either fall out big time or accidentally conceive a baby brother or sister. Not all parents do this, but if you're a child reading this (and we're glad we starred out the worst swear words) and you're staying with Granny and Grandad, it's because your parents (or at least your dad) is hoping to perform the no pants dance. While you're eating popcorn, watching *Toy Story 4* and looking forward to a McDelivery, your mum and dad are probably having a few sherbets and deciding if they still fancy each other. Sorry… where was I? Oh yeah. Staying overnight somewhere without your parents.

A school I'm aware of has a lovely little introduction to staying overnight with school friends, as they have an evening camping on the school field. To mark their transition from KS1 to KS2, the Year 2 children get to spend the night in shared tents with their pals. Where the tradition came from is unknown, but what a smart way to prepare the children for a potential residential down the track. If children find their courage to be away from their parents for a single night, they might be far more comfortable spending a few nights apart down the line. It's a nice way for parents to test the water to see if their young people are ready to go away with school.

All schools are very different in how they approach residential visits. Some do a couple of nights at a scout camp and some children go to France, which is quite a big step up for a primary-aged child. We know loads of teachers that are residential veterans, and some that have been once and vow never to go again. It all depends on their experiences.

Now when it hits the summer months, there are staple activities like the residential trips I've just mentioned, plus rounders matches and sports days, but for years, schools would wait until the final terms to teach their statutory SRE (sex and relationships education). It's now taught throughout the year in many schools, but if you ask a Year 6 teacher from 15 years ago when was the best time to teach the stuff, they would always have said the final term. To tickle your fancy (ooh-er), here are a few rather cheeky stories about this theme.

Teachers do not enjoy being observed, even during their favourite lessons. The teacher in charge of English will still dread their lessons being watched, even if they are king or queen of co-ordinating conjunctions. Find a teacher that says they find the experience useful and constructive, and I will call bullsh*t! What could be worse than being watched by senior members of staff whose purpose is to provide a judgement on how well an experienced teacher is doing their job? The answer is being observed in your first year of teaching, but the topic is puberty and the class contains Year 5 children.

One poor soul had her mentor and headteacher watching such a lesson and obviously wanted to take preparations seriously to avoid grief. A key feature in lessons like these is the anonymous question box where children are given pieces of paper to write questions to ask the grown-ups about a topic that could be rather embarrassing at times. A smart move in the situation, and the teacher took time to give the class a heads-up about the lesson beforehand. Fail to prepare and prepare to fail. Clearly this teacher was taking the necessary precautions to get the best out of her class during the session.

The lesson went ahead pretty well with the input and activity, so when it came time for the Q&A, the teacher was starting to feel more confident and lots of the children's misconceptions were addressed. Trying not to look too smug in front of the adult audience, they selected a few of the children's submitted questions, only to be greeted with a piece of paper that read 'Why does my mum's front bum have a beard?' From being on the cusp of smugness, they went to having to calm the giggles of an entire class of Year 5 children. The teacher explained the actual scientific words for pubic hair and vagina before explaining how adults' choice of length is a personal thing (the head and the mentor were smirking away at this point). Funnily enough, the teacher recognised the handwriting of the girl that submitted the question, which made the interaction with the mother at pick-up time slightly awkward. It's hard to make eye contact with old 'Hairy Mary' and wish her a pleasant evening knowing full well that she has an ample lady garden.

Don't worry, it's not just the girls that cause hilarity in Sex Ed sessions. One school had a nurse come in to do the session, including the aforementioned Q&A. The questions were fairly tame, and mostly about feelings and hygiene, but one lad had written on his piece of paper 'clitarus' (his spelling) and the teacher was interested as to who submitted it. A boy raised his hand and the nurse politely asked, 'What do you already know about that word?'

'Nothing,' he replied. 'But me dad says it's the only bit that counts!'

Lucky mum!

Plenty of parental interactions after school following these sessions can be cringy as hell, especially if the child being handed over is a bit of a character, and many of the telephone calls between school and home start with 'Do you have five minutes for quick chat?' It's never a good sign if the staff member is clearly at the point of giggling when making the call.

One podcast listener had a child like that, and during his time in Year 2, it was not uncommon for multiple 'quick chats' to take place during the term about their child's interesting behaviour. On this particular day, the child had brought in some items from Mummy and Daddy's special drawer. The young scamp had not only brought in some 'balloons' but he had blown them up and was swinging them around his head and bopping them towards his classmates. That's right, condoms in Year 2! The teacher recalled him saying, 'They are fantastic balloons that get soooooo big and never pop!!!' He was absolutely gutted when they were removed from the class and the remaining sheaths were passed to Mum at home time. Not many children go home at the end of a school day with a reading journal, an empty lunchbox and half a packet of rubber johnnies. Cringe time indeed.

Now, what's worse than a one packet of condoms in school? Twenty-three packets of condoms! Seriously, a teacher discovered that many packets in the class role-play-area kettle. I'd attempt to explain how they got there and why they were there, but I think the mystery of the entire situation is far more fascinating.

I'm relieved to say that that is the last of the sex and relationships education stories because in the summer months there is a far higher purpose that puts SRE in the shade. No more SRE, because I'm all about S.E.R:

SUMMER EQUALS ROUNDERS

Ffs, Adam! Did you think that up all by yourself?

Yeah, was it a seamless link?

No, it was crap. Now get on with your rounders stories!

Will do!

Now one of the biggest flexes of being in Year 6 is the legendary 'Staff vs Kids' rounders game. This event may still take place in certain schools, but some may have retired it due to the copious injuries suffered by grown adults who fail to warm up and still think they can smash a ball 30 yards and outrun an 11-year-old fielder.

As I said before, sport at primary school was my life. And the prospect of facing the staff when I hit my final year of primary school filled me with such excitement. I remember being a spectator in Year 3 and planning my batting stance and field positions for when I finally made it to summertime in Year 6.

I was so passionate during my support that my school chair would dig into the hallowed turf as I jumped enthusiastically throughout the game, cheering on the Year 6 pupils. Mr Marciniak was the teacher in charge of all sport and PE at my school, and I was desperate to get in his head and get one over on him. I'm being polite in saying that he wasn't much of a fitness fanatic, but he definitely rated his skills against the kids (even though he would become short of breath picking up a pen lid from the classroom floor). What he lacked in stamina, he more than made up for in enthusiasm.

To his credit, he made sure that the school was an active place, but his inter-school team selections could sometimes be quite bizarre. He would pick certain football players who weren't interested in football – this would confuse the main core of the team, especially when a lad called Joe came out with a cut-up cereal box as his shin pads. It surely had nothing to do with the fact that Joe's mum was incredibly attractive. In fact, come to think of it, all the random picks had good-looking mums. That dirty dawg!

Marciniak would start his teasing about the Staff vs Kids rounders game once SATs were done and dusted. To be fair to him, in the games that I watched he had a fairly decent batting record, plus he could bowl and catch surprisingly well. The year we played, Marciniak knew he was in for a game. Mr Tyrell (our headteacher) was a towering, athletic figure, and a fearsome adversary, so having him on the Marciniak Allstar team made it an extra challenge.

Our primary school was a two-form-entry one, meaning the size of the crowd was epic and so was the atmosphere. I'd never heard noise like it for a school rounders game. Our Year 6 team had a few butterflies but were ready to rise to the occasion, whereas during the whole game the staff remained cool, calm and collected. After some quality batting and fielding, it was a close-run thing. Towards the end, the children had set the staff a solid target of six rounders for victory. In a short space of time, not unlike a Hollywood movie, the grown-ups had achieved five and a half of those rounders going into the last batter. Who could that possibly be? You guessed it... Mr Marciniak. He stepped up, in his glasses (with strap for athletic comfort), ready to take his hit. I remember it as clear as day, it's almost like time stood still. The ball was pitched and Marciniak watched it the whole way, his arm pulled back ready, and with the full force of his monstrous girth his bat made contact with the ball. As it flew over my teammates' heads, the game looked like it was over.

Clearly delighted with the contact, Marciniak set off, running far too close to the animated crowd. As he sprinted (if you can call it that), his glasses were wobbling on the bridge of his nose, but he made it past the first post. Stage one complete. He then had to change his footing to turn in time and make a beeline for the next base. With a quick glance, Marciniak saw that the ball was still in the outfield and clearly thought his luck was in, but just as he reached second post, he unbelievably caught his foot on the black rubber base, sending him hurtling towards the ground like a sack of spuds. In the battle of gravity vs Marciniak, there was only ever going to be one winner, and down he went. The crowd were completely losing it with the drama of this insane game, but that wasn't the only thing being lost, as Marciniak's blue Adidas tracksuit bottoms had been pulled down by the momentum of the fall (and, sadly for him, none of the yummy mummies were there to witness his manliness on display). Not to be defeated, he limped with his arse hanging out in front of some clearly traumatised Year 3 children. Unfortunately, in the time it took Marciniak to pull his pants up and stumble to third base, the ball had already been stumped at last post and the Year 6 team were the champions. With his head in his hands and what remained of his jogging bottoms also in his hands, Mr Marciniak's dreams of being the staff rounders hero were in tatters, just like his trousers.

Like Mr Marciniak, school sport is a real passion of mine. I genuinely have such fond memories from my school days and I'm lucky enough to share that passion with the children I work with. Speaking of passion, one thing I sometimes have to be careful of when acting as team manager is that I am quite loud. I'm always trying to use my volume in a positive manner, but I care about the children I work with and want them to reach their potential and succeed as best they can.

Honestly, I know what sport can do for many children, whether that's teaching sportsmanship, working in a team or just having fun and exercising. Since I started working in schools over 10 years ago, I have been to literally hundreds of competitions with a wide range of children from all age groups and I simply love to see them in action. I'm a competitive guy, but I just want the children to have the same passion and energy for playing as I do.

One funny story involving my passion and energy was at my first ever rounders tournament in 2013. I love rounders and it was the first time I'd been involved in a competition of any capacity since the year 1999, when I'd captained my primary school team and had a reputation of being a bit of a big hitter. You know, where the opposition sees you coming into bat and starts taking steps backwards because they know you're going to blast it for miles. That was me!

The excitement was in the air as I took a group of Year 6 children to a large tournament of 11 other schools. I had done some training sessions with my children to give them the best opportunity to familiarise themselves with the many changing rules of the great game. At this time in my early career, I worked alongside my mate, a PE specialist from Newcastle who is affectionately known on our podcast as... 'The Geordie PE teacher'.

While I was the team manager/coach for the day, he took on an advisory role. He would arrange all the competitions but would leave the squad selection to me. This wasn't because he enjoyed organising the events, he just liked afternoons out of school. When we arrived at this rounders competition, Geordie PE teacher saw the lead organiser, whose name was Martin, a guy who he had known for many years. I was quickly warned that he was a very serious individual and to make sure I was on my best behaviour.

The usual pre-competition chat was fairly standard, about showing sportsmanship and having fun. One of the big messages was that the high school children would be refereeing the event, so to please be respectful. Obviously, fun is what it's all about, but when you have a competitive Year 6 crew, primed and ready to go, knowing this could be the last time they pick up a rounders bat, you want them to give it their best go to try to bring home gold.

In the first game I quickly knew something wasn't quite right in the application of the rules. We were fielding and the other team were in bat. The agreed rules for the tournament (for those who are rusty on their rounders knowledge) is that when you hit the ball, you are supposed to keep hold of the bat and run around the bases tapping the base as you run past, and if you stop on a base, you have to have your bat in contact with the base. I'm clearing this up now so you, dear reader, can appreciate my frustrations.

I'd say it's a pointless, silly rule, but who am I to question them?

The opposition school were batting and they were not touching the bases as they ran. I thought, no problem, they may not be playing this rule. It wasn't a huge issue initially, as long as the same rule applied for my team. They finished their innings, we did quite well, and it was now our turn to bat. Our strongest batter stepped up first and smashed a beauty over the fielders. He began running around the bases, and when he went past first base, the high school referee blew her whistle and called out my batter for not touching the base.

I always demand my children show respect to the umpires and accept their decisions, but this felt terribly unfair. I did my best Elsa from *Frozen* impersonation and 'let it go'. I reminded our children of this touching-the-base 'rule', but as our third batter smashed the ball and made their way around the bases, it wasn't clear that they touched the final one. Instead of awarding us the rounder, they called them out. At this point, I calmly made my way over to the umpire and very softly pointed out that it was slightly unfair as the opposition team were not pulled up when they did it. The umpire – who was roughly 14 to 15 years of age, apologised and said they'd try to be more consistent. Fast forward to the end of the game; we had been narrowly defeated and I was delivering a positive team talk to keep up my players' spirits. Martin (the boss) came to speak to Geordie PE teacher to complain about me supposedly 'going mad at an umpire'. I was appalled at such a BS accusation but old Geordie PE teacher was not happy with me (despite the fact that he was beside me during the game and knew I'd been very sensible). He said:

'Howay, man, Martin is not 'appy! You need to keep quiet during the next game, pal.'

That was me told! I had been firmly put in my place. As the next game approached, I felt like I was on the naughty step and only allowed to support my team with marshmallow claps and a soft cheer at any positive play. After a competitive performance by the kids, it came to the last ball, and we needed a rounder to win. You could allow me to get a little animated at the prospect of winning the game on the final hit, but I stayed in my box due to fear of getting the Martin treatment again. Fortunately, our final batter hit a fantastic ball through the fielders and made their way around the pitch. I knew it would be tight but as the ball was making its way to the fourth base, our batter clearly ran past the base (making sure they touched it with their bat). Surely, a guaranteed rounder...

... nope! Unbelievably, the umpire gave our batter out and we lost by one. I was quiet and composed but secretly fuming. I had no intention of feeling Martin's wrath so I managed to hold it together until I heard a commotion. An irate Geordie PE Teacher started braying:

'HOWAY! HOW ON EARTH IS THAT OUT, MAN?!? THIS HAS GOTTA BE A FIX!'

Don't worry, good old Martin was standing closely behind. I presumed he was there to keep a close eye on yours truly, but in the end, he had to calm his old pal down instead!

Howay, man!

The summer months should ideally bring warm weather (rounders weather, if you will), and while there'll be times when a teacher will look outside and see rainclouds and wonder if it's still February, a few days later the country could be in the middle of a heatwave.

Speaking of heatwaves, we have no intention here of getting too deeply into the climate change emergency. It's 100 per cent very serious and Greta Thunberg will say things far better than we ever could, but there have been periods in the UK, during term time, when the weather has been dangerously hot. Absolutely roasting. In the last decade, we have experienced some temperatures in the UK that have broken records. I don't remember such heat at school as a child, but that's probably because I wasn't paying attention.

In the last 30 to 40 years, humans have taken far more notice of the sun and just how dangerous it can be. Once there's a yellow, amber or red weather warning on the cards, there'll be an alert sent to parents about sending their children in with sun hats and slathering them in suncream. Some children will bring in sunglasses but the headteacher will make clear that trendy eyewear will be brought in at their own risk. The school insurance won't cover any damage to Jemma's Ray-Bans or Matilda's Guccis.

How the hell do the kids have better sunglasses than I do? I grew up in a generation where we became incredibly brand-conscious with regards to our footwear, jeans and jackets. There was a time during the late 90s/early 2000s when I was obsessed with dressing like a gangsta; I was properly into my FUBU clobber. Looking back, I clearly looked a lot less like Warren G and a lot more like Ali G. In fact, I'm very glad I'm not wearing a FUBU puffer jacket during the new British summer heatwaves. The jacket would melt onto me!

Back to the kids' designer outfits, I saw a girl at school the other day with a Michael Kors coat and a Christian Dior rucksack. Either her parents are loaded or she'd picked up some counterfeit stuff in Lanzarote in the summer. It looked decent quality and she was strutting around like it was real, but when did primary schools become Paris Fashion Week? No amount of 'drip', as the cool kids call it these days, is going to cool them down when there's a heatwave and the only dripping is off my forehead as I sweat buckets. Other countries are totally prepared for such temperatures, but it seems that in the UK we never learn our lessons from previous years.

At least in primary schools they can wear short sleeves and shorts/skirts or summer dresses. If it gets too hot, they may even tell children to wear their PE kit for a couple of days. Another time when PE kit is on the menu is when it's around sports day. Sports day is something we've talked about a lot on our podcast or in previous books, but it can be the gift that keeps on giving. We have some grainy footage of our six foot four dad, Big Mike, absolutely dominating the dads' race in the 90s. We were hugely proud at the time, and he still remembers the day fondly, but not all sports days had such media coverage.

The rise of camcorders in the late 80s and early 90s meant that there may be some footage out there of your sports day. Sadly, it's probably on an old video in your parents' attic and you don't even have a VCR player so it's difficult to watch the damn thing. No such issues exist now, as the invention of smartphones means that everything is captured, and in HD. Big Mike would love to relive his glory days as Urmston's sprint king in HD, but for every amazing success there are some supreme calamities. Children falling over on sports day is obviously something that will always happen. If they bounce back up, the parents will cheer vociferously to will them on to the end of the race. They'll receive a bigger round of applause for overcoming adversity and still going the distance. If a child falls over and gets p*ssed off because they swear they were tripped up, then the last thing they need during their meltdown is 50 iPhones capturing their tumble and subsequent tantrum.

For the next two stories, I'm pretty sure we were all glad that there are neither pictures nor footage available, as you'll find out shortly.

There are high expectations for appropriate school attire worn by teachers during sports events. Yes, some of the teachers can wear their gym kits, especially if they are competing in the teachers' race, but sadly the school has no control over what the parents wear. One dad turned up wearing some 1970s-style running shorts and clearly the netting used to keep his undercarriage intact had either been worn away or ripped, because while he was running, one then both of his testicles became loose and were on display to all and sundry. He paused to pop them back in but once the 'boys were back in the barracks' it was too late. What he thought he was doing wearing his Sebastian Coe shorts to a school event we'll never know, but there was definitely a letter sent home the following day and hopefully his wife gave him an appropriate 'b**locking'.

Not to be outdone, one mum was equally hideous in a moment that was witnessed many, many years ago in the 1970s by a teacher doing work experience.

'I was once asked by the head to walk down the field just before sports day started and move two parents. When I reached them, one was the mum of one child and one was the dad of another child and they were semi-clothed and having sex. I don't know who moved faster, me or them!

During a Reception class race, one child tripped and fell, then had a massive tantrum on the track. His mum walked onto the field to help him but, weirdly, as she ran towards him, her knickers (yes, you read that correctly) started falling down.

You would expect some sort of embarrassment, but no, she just stepped out of her drawers, picked them up, then continued towards her little one having a meltdown. To make the situation even more weird, the mum used her tighty-whities to dry her child's tears. Such behaviour would certainly be logged as incredibly concerning nowadays, but considering the time that has passed, the mum would probably be about 75 now and the child could be a middle-aged chartered accountant. Still weird, though!

Continuing the theme of inappropriate dress for sports day, one teacher definitely made her own faux pas when she borrowed her husband's T-shirt and hoodie of the same colour to wear at the event. It was overcast first thing in the morning, but by the time sports day hit, it was a lot hotter as the sun had made an appearance. The teacher started the event wearing her coloured hoodie but as the temperature increased, she decided to remove her top layer. What she didn't realise was that the T-shirt underneath (despite being the perfect colour) was actually from a stag do that her husband had attended. Printed on the back were the words '2-Thrusts Dean', and whether the children realised what it meant or not, the overwhelming majority of the parents and staff did. The biggest problem was that she didn't notice for about half an hour, and in that time the parents were all discussing how poor old Dean must have been gutted that his wife was advertising his inability to last more than two thrusts.

Now onto someone with far more perseverance that Dean. There's a video posted a few years back of former professional footballer and England star Gary Cahill taking his kids' sports day sack race VERY seriously. At six foot four he could barely hold the handles of the tiny little sack he had his giant feet stuffed into, but he was going hell for leather on the track. Roughly neck and neck with another competitive dad, it got to the closing stages of the race and his elite-level sportsperson instincts kicked in, so he leapt like a salmon to cross the finish line with his head. He won it by a noggin! Proof that it doesn't matter how famous you are, sports day is a serious event for competitive parents. There's even footage of Princess Diana absolutely smashing it during a 1991 sports day. The other mums running also took it very seriously, but from the outfits on display you could see that they weren't expecting to run that day. There was a huge selection of long skirts, big cardigans, blazers and giant earrings.

This brings us seamlessly from famous to infamous. And the outfit choice in this next story is very much part of why it's so comical. The best viral clip of a sports day in recent years can be found on YouTube, and if you start typing 'parent sports day...' it will give you the auto-fill option to add the word 'thong'. So famous is this viral video that YouTube already knows which clip you need to see to brighten your day. It was a regular mums' race at a regular sports day, but this one stood out because of a stumble, a fall and 'wardrobe issues'.

First of all, huge respect to any of the parents that compete in these races. You might become a hero in your child's eyes, but you also might get shared multiple times over on the *2 Mr Ps in a Podcast* Facebook group because you fell over. This poor parent was running barefoot in a perfectly lovely blue dress and still sporting sunglasses. She started with all the other parents and was running fine until she lost her footing and face-planted the grass. Not only did she end up chewing the ground, but as she fell her dress flew up and over her bottom, revealing a black thong. It was only a second or two, but for the poor mum it must have felt like she had her rear end on display for ages. This is not helped online where someone has slowed the clip down and put the old 'Hello darkness, my old friend...' piece of music by Simon & Garfunkel as she hits the turf, and the mooning begins.

If you are reading this book and you are the parent in the video, we salute you and think you are a legend! Your short moment of utter humiliation has brought great joy to everyone. If it makes you feel any better, there's a video of a dad falling over with his full arse (no thong) hanging out and he inexplicably did this ON CONCRETE! Seriously, the fella's trousers were down so far you could see what he'd eaten for breakfast.

If you have children, whatever age they may be, there's a common sentence starter that you'll see on social media, and it's a phrase that definitely gets used routinely between parents and school staff:

'I'm not sure I'm ready for (insert child's name) to be in (insert child's year group).'

Of course you're not ready! Nobody is!

When the little humans were brought into the world (and let's be honest, it's the mums who do all the hard work in that process), you have an idea about who they may become, what they'd like to be and whether they'll have Grandad Paul's nose or Granny Maggie's eyes. God forbid they get Uncle Nick's ability to fart, but as long as they are a happy and mostly healthy child, you're very lucky.

There will be some families that have everything mapped out before the child even gets to Reception class, but if you have kids and you're one of those parents that make bold statements and declare that your child will never visit McDonald's for ethical reasons, then I applaud you. I also call bullsh*t because as soon as little Rupert goes to a friend's bowling party, your house will be full of plastic Happy Meal toys and the taste of McNuggets will be one they're unable to forget.

By all means be vegan, be excellent at recycling and only have wooden toys, because ultimately, it's probably great for the environment. Stick to your principles, and as long as you're doing your best, that's already good enough. As previously mentioned, Adam and I don't claim to be perfect parents and we definitely make a sh*tload of mistakes on a daily basis, but we're not grandstanding about our children's upbringing either.

If decisions are made from birth about how a child will think and act before they've had a chance to discover the world for themselves, it may backfire and the child might rebel. I'd never tell my kids how they should think, except that *Die Hard* IS a Christmas movie, *Mrs Brown's Boys* is sh*te and if any of my kids supported Man City they'd be disowned!!!

In fact, ignore what I just said... bring your kids up however you want!

Another phrase that is often heard among parents of Year 6 (and sometimes Year 5, if people are super-keen) is...

'I'm not sure I'm ready to start looking around secondary schools!'

And that one is 100 per cent scary... well, scary to begin with. From baby human to pre-teen is a huge jump, but the step after that is incredibly nerve-racking for parents everywhere. How can they go from rocking up to school in a *Paw*

Patrol jacket with light-up trainers to being nearly as tall as their nan and knowing far more swear words? Where has the time gone?

I get messages from parents all the time about their anxieties for their children taking the step up to secondary school. This chapter will hopefully go some way to explain what happens, but I assure you I'm no expert, despite my triplets having already made the jump. I certainly don't want to scare anyone who's about to reach this stage with their kids, because actually it's a pretty amazing and exciting time as they start maturing into little grown-ups. I'm more putting it on people's radars, because while nothing can prepare you for the big step, there's every chance the children are even more anxious than their parents. Amazingly, once they're settled at their new secondary schools and all the lies about Year 7s getting 'bog-flushed' (heads flushed down the loo by the bigger kids) have been completely dispelled, parents of 11-year-olds realise how jealous they are that they aren't getting to start secondary school all over again.

This becomes apparent during tours of the secondary schools; you know, the ones folks were dreading when they pointed out how unprepared they are for their child to be old enough to be making those visits. What was once a feeling of fear turns into...

... Holy sh*t, look at the computer lab!
... You can pay for your lunch with a fingerprint?
... That artwork was done by a Year 9!?!
... They've got a 3D printer?!?
... I remember setting Stuart Weaver's blazer alight with a Bunsen burner in 1995!

Not all secondary schools are perfect, and some may be better than others (hence the tours), but once a child has managed to bumble their way through their first term of Year 7 – you know, getting lost, losing their timetable, accidentally farting in the science lesson (hopefully not too near the aforementioned Bunsen burner) – it becomes clear that they may not be your baby (or babies... as I may possibly have said before, I have triplets 😬) for too much longer. You'd be amazed how quickly the overwhelming experience of a child starting secondary school soon dissipates once they find their groove.

Not all children will make the perfect start to their secondary school careers (I know I never did), and plenty will fall foul of the uber-strict rules on punctuality and dress code. If the school is part of a MAT (multi-academy trust) or a learning 'federation', it may be that half of the schools within a certain radius operate under the same executive head with the same school ethos and rules, so it's not a great idea for a child to get permanently excluded from one place as it's quite possible that they could end up at a near-identical school in a different location.

Before the children can make their jump from Year 6 to secondary school, they need to have their moving-up day.

The jump to secondary school, as we've already mentioned, can be huge for the children and huge for the parents, especially if it's their first/only child. A detention for missed homework in Year 7 will be such a huge blow for a child that has never missed a deadline in their life. They'll feel like the world has ended, and just like the boy that brought a pin into an inflatable school with inflatable staff and inflatable children (joke incoming... sorry), they'll feel that they've let the school down, the teachers down and themselves down. Yeah, that joke wasn't worth it, was it? Sorry. 😬

Seriously, though. A missed piece of homework can be devastating for a Year 7 trying to find their way in their new school. What the children need to do is learn from their mistakes and know that it's part of the process of having further responsibilities about their own organisation. That said, most homework is online in modern education, and if your child gets a detention because the online platform wouldn't save the homework properly... kick off! Children also need to challenge bullsh*t, and if a secondary teacher decides to take the side of a learning platform over the word of a child, the child may need their parents' backing. Otherwise, the character-building life lesson is, 'Life's not fair, get over it!' Life may not be fair, but nor is getting a detention despite doing your homework.

There's a lot of pressure in your first year and the children are only supposed to bumble through Year 7 anyway. By the time the same kids are in Year 9, they'll be full of hormones and may have already factored a Wednesday detention into their week because they can't be arsed to do that homework at the weekend.

We're both primary school-based but we do know plenty of secondary school staff. There's a mutual respect and disrespect between primary and secondary teachers; respect from the secondary teachers, as they'll openly admit:

'I couldn't teach Reception kids, it's like herding cats.'

But scorn from others when they say:

'It's not really teaching, though, it's just colouring in, isn't it?'

It's only usually w*nkers that say the last one and it's mostly to elicit a reaction before smiling because they know they've wound up their primary friends. Teacher banter. I don't know if you have ever seen a secondary school teacher in a primary school, but it is literally like they've been dropped into the *I'm a Celebrity* jungle doing a bushtucker trial with all these creepy crawlies around them.

Equally, primary teachers will express their fear at teaching secondary-aged students. It is so weird because for me as a primary school teacher, teaching secondary kids would intimidate me but I also know a lot of high school teachers that like the smell of their own farts and only know enough about one subject to teach it. Seriously, some of the secondary teachers today are complete dweebs. Gone are the old-school, slightly alcoholic woodwork teachers that wore brown corduroys and smelled of fags. They were all retired about 20 years ago, leaving a bunch of David Brent figures that know a lot about slogans, plus plenty of quotes from philosophers whose names they can't even spell.

You see, primary school staff can trash talk as well! Perhaps we'll leave that fight there, as at the end of the day, they are all teachers and should be united against their common enemy... THE PHOTOCOPIER!

So while there's a mutual respect (and disrespect) there, under the current system we've almost been conditioned to hate each other. Secondary schools hate primaries because, unwittingly and unknowingly, we seem to be setting them up for failure due to the SATs scores we mentioned in a previous chapter. Progress measured is obsessed over and the results are a stick to beat the staff with because of league tables. In years gone by, secondary staff would briefly look at primary school SATs results and scoff because they'd test the children in September to get a baseline assessment of their own. Due to Progress 8 metrics, it seems that primary schools are now sending up inflated SATs results (as they are equally under pressure to hit targets) that actually have some bearing on secondary attainment. Secondary teachers will get the false impression that their new cohort will be a doddle. Then they meet the students, and these kids can just about write their own name. Progress 8 means the primary results are now used to predict GCSE grades, putting even more pressure on the students at such a key stage of their development. My 19-year-old stepson did OK in his GCSEs but he was under so much pressure because he was being predicted a 9 in French, based on his English SATs score. Sitting a SPAG test that does f**k all (said in the present progressive tense, I believe) to help them be better writers, kids at 11 tested on whether something is in the active and passive voice is completely pointless. Even someone on Gove's curriculum design team came out and admitted it was all made up – fronted adverbials was just something someone said and it sounded all right so it got added in.

And if anyone is reading this part wondering where the alphabet grades for GCSEs (A*, A, B, C, D, E, U) have gone, some genius decided that turning them into numbers would raise standards. I'm as confused as you are!

Unattainable goals and unachievable expectations mean that there's currently a HUGE shortfall in maths and science teachers in secondary schools, and lots of primary maths specialists or teachers with science degrees are often very welcome to apply for jobs there. There are always vacancies. You'd also be surprised how many make the transition between the two. Secondary school teachers who are fed up with hormonal monsters and marking essays may wish to work with younger folk that don't answer back as frequently. Primary teachers who are sick of toilets that look like there's been a dirty protest and celebration assemblies that feel like they last about 80 years may wish to take the step up to big school. I've joked a little about some secondary teachers, but there really are some absolutely amazing ones. While lots of high schools have been turned into uber-strict Trunchbull academies in the last 14 years, we are lucky to have some truly phenomenal folk out there inspiring young minds in a very restricted system. Whether primary or secondary, it's the current system that eventually forces teaching staff to rethink their life choices and embark upon new adventures, wherever they may be.

As for new adventures, whether moving up to secondary school or just moving up a class, the children will take it all in their stride. Some will rise to the occasion and some may take a little longer to settle. If there are any young people reading this or hearing the audiobook in their parents' car, and you're a bit worried about moving up, try not to fret. Your parents are just as anxious as you are and they've already survived their secondary school experiences!

If Adam can do it, you can too!

There comes a time in the school year when there's an unwritten agreement between staff, parents and children that the rules that have strictly been in place since the start of September aren't necessarily adhered to. So as the final term starts, you could forgive the children, the school staff and the parents for not taking every second of every hour too seriously in their quest for educational excellence.

You'll see the children's uniform looking less pristine as the jumper that was crumpled into the bottom of their bag because it was too hot the previous day has been quickly shoved on the following morning with no time to iron it. Trainers that were once definitely banned start to make their way in without teachers taking much notice. Air Jordans might not be ideal for athletics, though, especially if it's the long jump or hurdles – there's more chance of tripping over into a face full of sand or clattering every hurdle in the name of fashion.

Hoodies... let's talk about hoodies. Many schools nowadays will let their Year 6 leavers sport a custom-printed hoodie with the school logo and the children's name or initials on the front. On the back, it will say 'Leavers 24' (or whatever the year is). It's really a nice touch and definitely a positive memory for the children as they depart primary school.

It may be the school or the PTA that organises this, but sometimes it's just one or two lovely parents that take the initiative. If you are that parent, we salute you. It's a thankless task but we feel we should thank you in this book for taking on such a mammoth job. First of all, you need to gauge interest, then find a company that prints personalised hoodies in a decent range of colours. Messages will be sent out to the entire year group and some parents will sign up immediately, whereas others will wait until the last minute on the final possible day to place their order. Once they've got a list, they need to check that the spellings submitted are correct because not only will the child's name be printed on the front, it will also be inside the two big numbers on the back listing everyone else's name. If you've got a year group with four Jacobs then it's important to make sure that every Jacob has the first letter of their surname on there as well. Even more annoying is when you have two children called Jacob B and their surnames are Brand and Brown, so you end up with Jacob Bro, which sounds pretty cool, but spare a thought for poor Jacob Bra!

Some schools will let the Year 6 crew wear them for the rest of the year instead of branded school jumpers, which is a flex and a half, but, as cool as they look, they may be less required if it's sweltering hot in July!

It's not just the children that dress differently in the last few weeks of the school year. Rather than wearing professional attire from Monday to Friday and only wearing sports clothes on a designated PE day, you can bet that the staff are following 'Active Mum' and wearing their sports kit every day or switching from suit and tie to shorts and polo tops. Female staff will potentially have a summer wardrobe that they know how to utilise, but as this book is written by male staff, we bow to their ability to look snazzy in the summer term. Footwear certainly is adapted as it gets warmer. You may even see flip-flops sported by a teacher that has no business showing his hairy toes in public. He must be careful, however, that he doesn't end up with the nickname 'Bilbo'.

Clothing is less strict and so are the staff/pupil engagements. Mr Statham would definitely insist on being called Mr Statham for the majority of the year, but after the May/June half term, 'Mr S' is perfectly acceptable. It gives the departing Year 6 crew a bit of status for their final few weeks, and when they bump into Mr S in a few years' time they are dishing out fist-bumps rather than calling him a w*nker.

It's not just the children being slightly less formal, either. Mr Hill will fear no repercussions if he calls Jordan a wazzock during this time, as he knows that Jordan's parents agree that he is, indeed, a wazzock. The bond has been formed early enough that they think he should be called far worse, so Mr Hill's choice of words are completely accepted. The curriculum is still going ahead, apparently, but on some days it really doesn't. At one school in the mid-2000s, it was the day that most children went for their secondary school moving-up day but as there were children attending completely different schools locally, one Year 6 teacher was left with a grand total of... four children. Yep, that's right, not even enough pupils for a game of cricket. Well, I say that. You'd have a batter, a bowler, a wicket-keeper, and let's just say that little Anthony has got a hell of a lot of fielding to do. Especially when the teacher is batting!

On this day, the teacher (who was the deputy head) thought he'd use the children to clean out his cupboard... BAD IDEA!

We've talked in our previous book and on the podcast about some of the junk found in a teacher's cupboard. You can add some of the below items to the list of infamy:

- SATs tests (from the 90s).
- Old cooking ingredients that expired in the late 80s.

- Tarantula skin in a plastic box (child excluded permanently before they could show, or indeed tell).
- Four tape players.
- A letter signed by the then education secretary Estelle Morris approving the South African qualification of a previous teacher to work in the UK (the teacher lasted six months and clearly didn't take his stuff with him when he was unceremoniously sacked for teaching only lessons that he made up on the spot).
- Two fake dog poos (save them for later use).
- Global Hypercolour T-shirt from 1993 that changed colour when you got hot.
- A bag of 1991 red noses for Comic Relief that were unsold. The ones with the little hands and a face.

While it was clearly an excellent use of the children's time and a chance for that deputy head to exorcise the daemons of whatever evil existed in the school before he arrived, I'm not sure the activity met the health and safety standards and requirements even back then.

As for standards at a healthy school, you can bet that all goes out the window as well, especially if the PTA want to try to introduce 'Ice Lolly Friday' to raise extra funds and justify the portable cooling fridges that they purchased for the school fête. We touched upon it earlier, but in recent years in the UK there is usually a week or a few days where the temperature is unbearably hot, and if the school doesn't have air conditioning (could they afford to have it on anyway?) the class is reliant on a non-existent breeze coming through the small windows that barely open. There are also doors that often let more heat in, so you wonder if it's safe for children to be at school in the first place.

This usually sparks a rush on the local supermarket for ice lollies to keep the children cool when the sun is at its hottest (yes, I know that's not scientific, but you know what I mean). This is when you get supermarkets limiting the purchases as one school has emptied their entire freezer stock of the cheapest lollies available and walked them back to the school of 400-plus children. It's wonderful for the store's profits but a bloody nightmare on their stock reordering levels (as well as annoying for the other customers). If things aren't getting heated enough already (see what I did there?), they try to get the local press involved and they come to interview the headteacher about the ice lolly embargo.

After the free publicity, the supermarket will donate some free stuff to the school and they are best friends again. No more ice lollies, though, as the weather has changed by Thursday and it is now p*ssing it down.

Back to trying to survive in the heat. As previously stated, schools in the summer when it's REALLY hot are pretty horrible, and if a headteacher manages to find something in their budget for a few extra fans it can make or break whether or not the school can properly function. Classrooms, at the best of times, are rather smelly and humid during the summer months, but one TA decided to add to this

atmosphere – and not in a good way. She was in charge of a Year 1 class while the teacher was attending a transition meeting. The children were on task and completing their activities reasonably well when the TA felt something wasn't right in her stomach. Tummy rumbling away, she was starting to feel the delayed effects of Taco Tuesday from the night before.

The TA managed to manoeuvre herself to the back of the class and unleash a silent trump to hopefully calm the Mexican monster in her guts without too much fuss. Mission accomplished... or so she thought. Silent farting is quite a skill, but one must not forget the 'silent' may also be accompanied by the famous 'but violent' or even worse, SBD (silent but deadly). Top tip: never release an SBD in front of a fan, and for goodness' sakes don't do it with two fans in the class. The dual fans will create what could easily be described as a 'toot tornado' and as soon as the horrendous gust had been released, polo shirts were being pulled in front of noses and poor innocent children were retching at the pong. What had she done?

The windows were already wide open but the smell had no intention of departing. Shortly afterwards, the teacher re-entered the class and was smacked full in the face by the grievous honk. Responding as all school staff do, the teacher asked, 'Is there anyone that needs the toilet?'

Yeah... THE TA!

A decision was made to do story time outside on the grass that day, and when asked if there was a possibility that one of the Year 1 children had potentially soiled themselves, the TA pretended that she had already checked, rather than admitting that she had caused a major disturbance with her mighty wind. Perhaps she should avoid the tacos next Tuesday. What is it with school staff and Mexican/Tex-Mex food? I'm not saying they should lay off the fajitas, but perhaps restrict them to Friday and Saturday nights when they're not in class the next day.

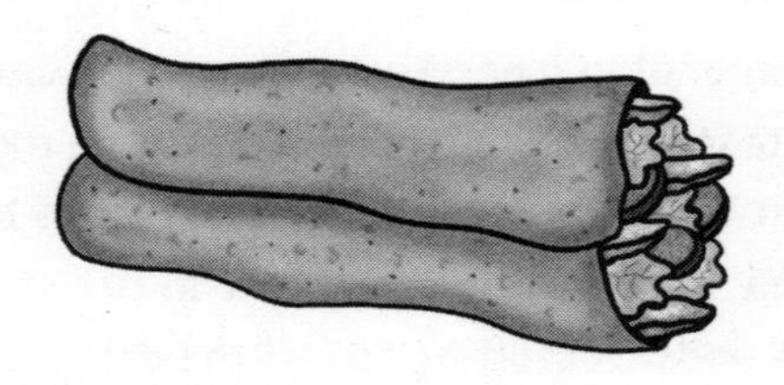

Now, seamlessly we go from letting things out...

... to letting things in (see what I did there?).

In a perfect example of trying to do something positive that will backfire, I present the case of the fly in the classroom.

Bloody annoying by anyone's standards, but it's really hard to get the children to carry out some quiet reading or a long piece of writing in silence with a particularly loud flying insect disturbing the peace. If schools are still waiting to see if they will receive a visit from the 'Big O' (Ofsted), then they will need to ensure that they have not given up on monitoring what everyone in school is doing, including teacher observations.

One teacher was being observed by her headteacher towards the end of the school year, when a fly started causing mayhem. Telling it to BUZZ OFF would make no difference, but it was fortunate it was only a fly. If it had been either a wasp or a giant bumblebee, you can be sure that the majority of the class would have lost their sh*t. Really, however, I'm not sure it was that fortunate after all. Using their initiative to ensure that the class was not disrupted by the buzzing annoyance, the teacher opened a window and the fly made its merry way back into the world outside.

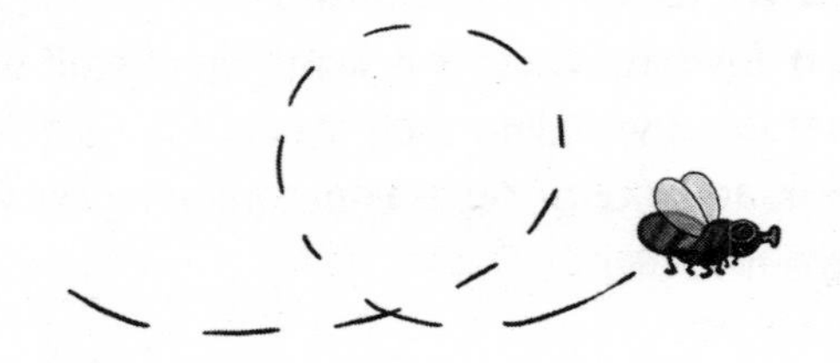

Nice work! Now the observed maths lesson could go ahead as planned and the teacher was deservedly chuffed with her handling of the situation and the co-operation of the fly. Teamwork makes the dream work.

Problem was that the window was left wide open and in flew...

... a flipping PIGEON!

Our feathered friend immediately realised they had made a mistake and started flapping frantically while headbutting the ceiling, sending the entire class into a frenzy, resulting in a postponement of the observation and an evacuation of the classroom.

I'm not sure dealing with insect and avian invaders is in the teaching standards, and it is certainly not on the Ofsted ticklist. If the school is outside of an Ofsted window and effectively in the clear until the SATs results are announced (which may trigger another visit), then the need to maintain standards in books has definitely lessened. With massive budgetary constraints on schools, more and more classes are simply passing up the previous year's books to the next class, sticking in a page that says Year 4 2023–24, then continuing to use the rest of the book.

If the book only has a page or two left (including the ones at the back where they do their spelling tests), then there's no point, but if there's 90 per cent of the pages left, it's a good shout. There will certainly be a lot more maths quizzes on whiteboards or games on Kahoot. If you've never heard of Kahoot, it's like a kid-friendly quiz app similar to *Who Wants to Be a Millionaire*'s 'fastest finger first'. The children love it, they are easy to create, and from a teacher's perspective there's no marking, as it's difficult to use your pink and green pens and highlighters on 30 iPads! You can try, but the ICT/Computing lead at school may be sending you a bill.

Teachers may insist that the children continue to behave, as they can still influence the content of their school reports. This is probably complete b*llocks, since the sort of teacher that does that will have written them all in May anyway. Speaking of school reports, they are pretty much worthless nowadays; in many schools they are a tickbox exercise with just a few general comments. Some schools still go all in and

WITHYFIELD PRIMARY SCHOOL.

REPORT FOR THE YEAR ENDING 1991.

NAME: Richard Turner CLASS: Mr L Wadhams

AGE: 9 NATIONAL CURRICULUM YEAR: 4

ENGLISH	Richard demonstrates a keen sense of humour both verbally and in his written work. Sadly he can regularly cross the boundary between good and bad taste. There is far too much toilet humour in his very scruffy and untidy written work. Perhaps he should read far more Tolkien and far less Viz!
MATHEMATICS	Richard's work can be erratic. He is mechanically sound but makes the odd error due to badly set out workings. If he spent more time setting out his calculations and less time doodling Bart Simpson he may be able to spot his mistakes. Sound times tables.
SCIENCE	Clearly Richard is very interested in Science and he explains his investigations well verbally. Sadly his written work does not reflect his ideas and this really lets him down. He MUST concentrate!!!
OTHER SUBJECTS	Richard thinks quickly and has a good general knowledge which he is keen to extend. A very competent and lively artist.
P. E.	Richard does not make enough effort in P.E. and can be very LAZY!
GENERAL COMMENTS	Richard is a smart child but needs to stop messing about and concentrate. His written work is untidy and he seams more interested in doing Harry Enfield impressions than pulling his finger out and getting on with his work!

Richard is a lively and likeable lad with a sharp and intelligent mind. He now needs to concentrate on improving the presentation and accuracy of his work. ☺

L.B.Wadhams Class Teacher

G. Capeling Head Teacher

have pages of printed words with a general comment from the headteacher at the end. For the teachers reading this that need help with theirs, I'll talk a little more in the next chapter about how the report-writing game has completely changed with AI tools like TeachMate. The reports we see nowadays are very different from the soul-destroying ones of yesteryear.

If you were a beautifully behaved child in years gone by, then your handwritten (yes, that's right, handwritten) report would still have all the clichés about the child being a pleasure to teach and words like 'kind and conscientious' in there to boot. These are all lovely and perfect little memories for the children that had teachers that liked and respected them. Something to look back upon with great pride.

I'm not talking about those children, I'm talking about the reports written by an old-school battleaxe or... or... (what's the male equivalent of a battleaxe?) a grumpy old b*stard about the children they did not care for. Reading them now, you know there's no way these teachers would get away with telling a child just how bloody useless they are on a daily basis, and neither should they. But that's what happened. Ask your parents if they had good or bad school reports.

If they had good ones... boring! If they had a teacher that mostly disliked them, then the scornful nature of the report is quite a sight to behold:

'When they bother to grace us with their presence, Richard is a disruptive nuisance and incredibly lazy.'

This sort of comment would not be acceptable now, even if Richard is a lazy, disruptive nuisance. It would have to be worded far more diplomatically. You can't just write, 'Penny gets bugger all done because she never shuts her gob!' It's shocking to read now but you can't rule out that being on someone's report from 50 or 60 years ago.

Anyway, the threat of a bad report is still utilised nowadays into the final weeks of term, even if there's zero chance the teacher will make any effort to change it.

In further evidence that the end of the school year is fast approaching, the incredibly tight timetable from September will be completely ignored. This happens as the school will throw themselves into class or year group productions. School productions can be such a doss around for some children. They can also be the best time of year for any budding actors or actresses.

The most musical and dramatic teachers (even if by default) will usually be in charge of the auditions, selecting the performance, writing or adapting the script and choosing the music. It's potentially a thankless task, but if you get it sorted over a day or so, there might well be no planning and marking for the rest of the year. By agreeing to oversee or direct the school performance, the teacher(s) will be taking one for the team. As a result, they will know the children's lines inside out and back to front after witnessing hours of practice in a boiling-hot school hall.

If the school's big enough you can have teachers practising with the children that enjoy acting while the children that don't enjoy it stay in the class with a particularly creative team teacher or TA and do set design or make props. One or two particularly techie children can be put in charge of creating a PowerPoint to display in the background or add sound effects. The children that have no interest in any of it can have an iPad or laptop passed to them and they can help design a programme or posters for the event. As long as everybody's busy in a positive way, who's kicking up a fuss?

The end-of-term production is a way to kill a lot of time, but there's also the possibility of a Year 6 leavers' assembly. These can range from half-arsed to Broadway level. In some schools, the leavers' assembly can be just children reading out a few memories from their time at school and getting a certificate from the headteacher, who reads out an analogy while holding a pot plant and talking about how the children are outgrowing their current school and are ready to move on. It's quite a sweet speech but most children heard it a few years back when their older sibling left.

Other schools go all in and we learned about one that did a variety show with singing, gymnastics, cheerleading, football skills, comedians (debatable) and... synchronised swimming!

Obviously not actual swimming, as they didn't have the budget for a pool to be transported into the school hall for a three-minute skit. This 'swimming' involved a large piece of blue material being stretched and waved to make a water effect at the front of the stage while a group of lads pranced about (surprisingly elegantly) in unison and looked hilarious in the process.

Whatever the leavers' assembly looks like at the school you either went to, teach at or your own children attend, there will be a huge range of ways that the children are given a send-off from their primary years. The one thing that is universal is that the parents and grandparents (plus some of the teachers that can't help themselves) all bloody cry!

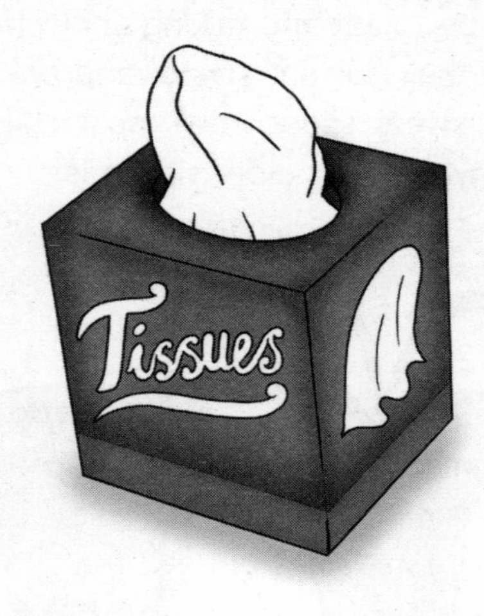

As Alice Cooper famously declared in 1975, school would be out for summer. Summer is a time during which parents, kids and teachers get a chance to take a step back from life and try to relax, chill out and compose themselves. Switching off is definitely hard to do for some, and if you work in education, it's harder than many realise. Ideally, if you can afford it, you can get out of the country (but let's be honest, the cost of living makes it increasingly unlikely that everyone will be able to have breaks away during the six weeks' holiday).

The 'six-week holiday' sounds long, doesn't it? And for parents, it will feel ridiculously long. Seriously, having to entertain your own children is hard enough two days out of seven during term time, but for 42 days straight while also juggling work or other commitments (unless you ship your darling little cherubs off to a holiday club or grandparents), it can be truly soul-destroying. Don't get me wrong, there is nothing better than spending time with your own children, but I guarantee there will be a moment during the summer holidays, as a parent, where teachers or school staff are secretly pumped for the September return to school. School staff with children may claim that they yearn for structure and a better routine, but we all know it's so they can attempt to actually have a tidy house, go to work and do their job. Actually, let's be honest, I just want to be able to go for a dump in peace.

Alternatively, for the school staff that dread returning to the mundane daily routine, the summer break will disappear as quick as a flash (see, Lee, I've been working on my similes). On the rare day when you have the opportunity, you may decide to do a bottomless brunch and you quickly find out the hard way that you can't handle your booze anymore. The repercussions are that it swiftly wipes away a full week with a hangover. Perhaps you may have arranged a lovely getaway with your family, and if that's the case, make sure you are aware of the destination, because I found out the hard way on my summer break one year. In the summer of 2022, I took the initiative (for once) to book a holiday to thank my wife (a teacher) for putting up with me being on the road so much with our live podcast tour. We did 50 dates, so that's a lot of time where she was flying solo with our little ones, Max and Isla. When the tour ended in July 2022, I thought I should surprise her with a lovely, relaxing and romantic getaway for just the two of us. She said on a few occasions that she found our little wrecking machines harder to manage than her Year 6 class at times, so she deserved the break. Uncharacteristically, I tried to think of everything to make the trip as smooth as possible. I sorted sitters, splitting it between the grandparents – obviously – then I went online and booked a week in Corfu. I know, husband goals, right? Well, not exactly...

We flew to Corfu, as promised, and I was telling Kim that we would be staying at a very lovely resort called Island Beach. I was expecting to be in the heart of the island eating gyros and smashing frozen cocktails all day, loving life with a little bit of tranquillity and gorgeous sunshine, before returning to reality. Upon landing in Corfu, we grabbed our bags and hopped onto our transport; the bus to the hotel had mixed clientele, as there was us, two families and a group of 20-plus-year-old lads and a group of 20-plus-year-old lasses. Not to worry, I thought, Corfu has plenty to offer for all ages. The bus set off, dropping each group at lovely hotels in really nice areas of Corfu. At this point I began to feel nervous – why are we not getting out at these lovely areas of the island? Seriously?! When was the driver going to call out 'Island Beach Hotel?' Fast forward to Kim and me being the last two on the bus. Where was the guy taking us? I was ready to go full Liam Neeson with my particular set of skills if we ended up 'Taken' by the driver, but then I remembered that I wasn't in a movie and that my main 'skills' were watching movies and eating ice-pops. I wondered if I hadn't remembered the name of the resort correctly, but there, clear as day, on the holiday documents that I definitely didn't print off at school, it said 'Island Beach'. I had bugger all signal on my phone so I couldn't google the details. Further examination of the documentation revealed that we weren't travelling to the central part of Corfu, but down south. As soon as Kim saw the 'WELCOME TO KAVOS' sign, I knew I'd f**ked up.

Yep, I had accidentally booked our romantic getaway to the piss-up capital of the island. I know what you may all be thinking, how am I still married? Funnily enough, as two members of school staff, with young children, you could have dropped us in a barn in the middle of nowhere and we would have appreciated the break. I won't lie, it was rather 'interesting' strolling down the Kavos strip and seeing which dive bar had the best offer of free drinks upon arrival, but we made the most of it. So, the moral of the story is, by all means book a well-earned break with your partner, but do make

sure you read the small print as you could accidently be lounging next to 18-year-olds doing laughing gas at 10am!

Like Adam on his Club 18–30 holiday, if you're lucky enough to get away somewhere hot, then you may be aware of the sun-lounger wars. Some of the behaviour is a sight, and it's not impossible to equate it to a playground squabble between two headstrong children that refuse to back down.

For years there's been this cliché that on your summer break in a foreign (hot) country there's a war between the English and the Germans to reserve sun loungers at 6am. In fact, there's an advert from about 25 years ago where a British guy throws his towel across a pool and it lands perfectly, stopping some suntanned wobbly Germans from getting the last lounger. Well, this is still true, but the fact is, us Brits are even worse. I know teachers that have witnessed rows over towels and sun loungers that escalated from a lack of courtesy to full-blown verbals in front of their kids, which begs the question – what sort of PSHCE/Citizenship lessons did they have back in the day?

Obviously none, as Phil Mitchell's cousin and leather-faced Linda are now calling each other an arsehole in front of their respective families. Where in the curriculum does it state not to be a douchebag over sun loungers on holiday?

It's not as if the hotel staff can make them sit on the friendship bench until they've learned to calm down. There's only so much schools can do to help create the next generation of world citizens, but at the end of the day there are plenty of learned behaviours that the children will absorb, so rather than teach the current primary school cohorts how to argue, it may be better to get them to be more tactical. Plan out a route to the loungers in the small window of opportunity between the hotel cleaning staff mopping the floor and when the loungers are available for claiming. Perhaps practise towel-throwing so it lands perfectly well enough to 'officially' claim the loungers.

If you're a teacher who refuses to switch off, you can give a blanket punishment by chucking everyone's towels in the pool and giving the whole resort a time out. Although, I wouldn't recommend it unless you can run in flip flops and can hide from an angry mob of pissed-off Brits, Germans and other assorted Europeans.

I'm obviously jesting, but it does prove the point that the more things change, the more they stay the same. For every kid properly wearing a swim shirt and smothered in suncream (unlike in the 70s and 80s when kids just strolled around in their swimwear getting their noses and shoulders burnt by day two) there will be a dad who's eight pints in by 11:30am and struggling to stay on the inflatable doughnut he bought for the kids but is now using to keep himself afloat as he's too drunk to swim.

Once school is officially out for summer, many people will think that teachers and school staff just put their feet up and laze about for the next month and a half. Some do, and that's their prerogative, but most teachers will finish for the term and either leave the school site and not think about it for at least a month, or they will be back in on the first Monday of the holidays sorting sh*t out. Not all teachers will do one or the other, in fact, most teachers will be somewhere in the middle, but you definitely have some keen beans and plenty of last-minute folks too. The keen beans will spend hours putting up amazing displays ready for

September. I wasn't and never will be one of those teachers but I kind of respect the ones that genuinely enjoy it. If the resources on the walls help the children, great! Just please don't ask me to come in and join them. I've got Netflix to binge and biscuits to eat.

One display some teachers spend far too long preparing are birthday charts, which will appear in many classrooms (mostly Early Years and KS1). Within reason, the birthdays will be evenly spread out across the year. You may have a few birthdays in late July or during August that deserve to be celebrated as soon as the school year begins (which means a child may come home with a stack of Maoams and a fair few packets of Haribo on their first day. Cue the disappointment when they receive nothing the following day).

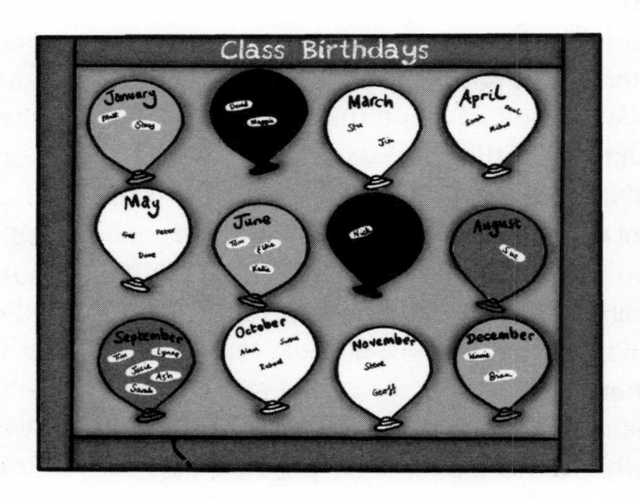

When did this come in? Bringing sweets in for the whole class? Back when families regularly took children out of school during term time to avoid 'Center Parcs prices' there were often some truly dreadful hard-boiled monstrosities that would require dental work after consumption or some Fruitella-style sweets where the packaging was so blurred that you had no idea whether you'd be getting orange, peach, lemon or bacon. But as a kid, you'd eat it anyway. In some schools (especially those chasing 'healthy schools' status), the giving and receiving of birthday sweets is banned. Or if a child brings them in, they are asked to hand them out once they leave the classroom.

One teacher reported that they had an abundance of September birthdays for a class they had, where the children were born nine months after Millennium Eve! Clearly a few folks decided to celebrate the new century with quite a few sparkling vinos and a fair bit of horizontal hula, if you get what I mean. 😉

The school site can be a hive of activity at different points but also dead silent. Some schools will run summer camps, and these can be great, especially if working parents can't get the time off or don't have grandparents locally that can lend a hand. If the summer camp is in full flow, you can bet there will be plenty of noise and lots of laughter. Being at school when there are fewer rules and routines can be loads of fun and it's a great time for children to hang out with schoolmates from different year groups. If there's not a summer holiday club, the school can feel like a ghost town. Teachers with children may pop in and get their offspring to help sort the PE shed or tidy the bookcase, but it's pretty dull when a member of staff is in the building on their own.

In one school, it was usually quiet as hell during the summer holidays. It was a one-form-entry school, which meant that there were seven classrooms in total. With a school this size, the caretaker and cleaner were the same person. No site managers here, just a lady with seasonal staff that would be employed for short stints to help clean. This meant that teachers each had their own set of keys, and they would be in charge of opening and locking the school if they needed to get in out of hours.

The teacher in this story was married, but his partner was an accountant, so they didn't share the same holidays. The partner was also a huge Disney fan and would drag him to Florida to visit Mickey and Minnie. He liked visiting Florida (who wouldn't?), but he didn't quite share her love of the House of Mouse. After two weeks staying in a villa in Kissimmee, he realised his holiday was over and he should pop into school and label some glue sticks. He still had all his planning to do and seating plans to arrange. Plenty to keep him busy for the rest of the summer break.

The main issue for this teacher was that he was still pretty jet-lagged. He arrived reasonably bright and early on the Tuesday morning and unlocked the school so he could crack on with things. After a very productive morning he popped to the local supermarket and grabbed far too much food from the hot counter. Clearly craving British grub, he filled his boots, but this made him rather bloated and less prepared to keep up with the preparations for next year. There were a few brand-new beanbags in his reading corner, so he thought he'd remove the cellophane and have a quiet sit-down on them. That quiet sit-down turned into a little snooze, and so full was he from his mini banquet from over the road, combined with his jetlag, that he went into a deep sleep. A few hours passed and when he woke up, he found himself covered over with a blanket and with a cup of tea on the little table next to where he was kipping.

'Where on earth did the blanket come from and why have I got a cup of tea?' he wondered to himself.

It was at this moment that he looked up and saw his head and deputy head smiling away at him in the doorway.

'Morning, Mr B! I trust you slept well. How was Florida?'

He felt like a prize buffoon, but he was grateful for the cup of tea (which was still pretty warm). He knew that he wasn't in any trouble, but he also knew he'd never live it down.

'Rip Van Winkle' became his new nickname, which was later shortened to 'Winkle', so if any new staff joined the school and questioned his moniker, he'd have to explain the story of being caught kipping in the book corner.

I don't know what the moral of this story is. Perhaps it's 'leave the cellophane on the new beanbags and don't buy too much food at lunchtime', but that's hardly catchy enough to appear in *Aesop's Fables*. It's probably more about not being afraid to make time to relax. Whether you work in schools or not, there needs to be a period where you can let your hair down and catch your breath. Where you can make time to catch up with your sleep. Snoozy MacDougall in the previous story may have taken it a little bit too literally, but bless his little cotton socks for trying.

With all the talk in previous chapters about holidaying with random 18-year-olds and children going off to secondary school, there comes the moment you really start to feel old. Surely my teenage years weren't that long ago? Sadly, a quick bit of maths and it turns out they were! Surviving the school year is hard enough; it's even harder when you realise that you're not as young as you once were. Even though I'm still in my thirties, I'm actually one of the oldest members of teaching staff at my school. You know that you're no longer considered to be in the cool-kid gang when there's a staff night out and there's pre-drinks... but you're not invited.

Have you seen the film *Grown Ups*? It's the Adam Sandler movie featuring all his mates, where a school basketball team from the late 70s and early 80s reunites following the passing of their beloved coach. The group decide to rent a big house near a lake for the Fourth of July celebrations to rekindle their friendship over a long weekend. The whole premise is that they've all 'grown up' (see what I did there?) but they now have families and slightly different outlooks on life, yet are still the same people (sort of). It's a fun (if flawed) film, but if you were to watch it your response may be... 'But the 80s were only 20 years ago!?!?'

Sorry, folks, they really weren't!

The *Grown Ups* film was hardly going to win any awards, but it definitely ticked all the Sandler boxes:

- Reasonably good at the box office
- Feel-good story
- Slightly offensive
- Rob Schneider

It's a nostalgia film with lots of flashbacks, but what really hits home is that the main cast, who were in their twenties during the 90s, are now turning to their own kids and grumbling that they don't know how to have good old-fashioned American fun. They are now the parents whingeing at their kids about not knowing they are born.

This is not OK! That's the job of old people, so when did Sandler and co. become the old geezers? What's also upsetting is that the film came out in 2010! So it's been well over a decade since even then.

I'm not sure the generations that grew up with Barbie Girl, Tamagotchis and downloading Crazy Frog ringtones are ready to be the voices of reason and the adults that make proper decisions about the world going forward. From our perspective, we're nowhere near ready to be adulting and certainly not happy to no longer be considered 'cool'.

For anyone over a certain age reading this book, there's the scary realisation that you are no longer young enough to still be (or at least consider yourself) cool! The fact that a lot of us still use 'cool' rather than 'peng' or 'sick' shows we're not ready to be considered as past it. If you're still a young whippersnapper, I don't hate you but... well... shut up! And when I say 'certain age', I'm not specifying a number, but if you're referred to as being a Millennial or Generation X, there's a short period of realisation that has either happened or is on its way that hurts like a gut punch. It's called: 'F*ck me, I'm old!'

When the hell did we become the grown-ups? For some of us, it's debatable if we've ever really grown up, but technically both the Mr Ps are legally classed as adults. Don't get me wrong, plenty of adults strive each day to prove otherwise, but adulthood is here and it has been for a while. There's a really sweet part in the latest *Bill & Ted* movie (which very few people saw or cared about, as it came out during the pandemic in about seven cinemas worldwide) where the eponymous heroes realise (spoiler alert) that their life's mission was about their children and their future. The Bill and Ted that were supposed to unite the universe were Billie/Thea, aka Little Bill and Little Ted. The OG B&T were part of their backing band. Potentially weird to use a film that nobody saw as a reference, but the sentiment is highly relevant.

As amazing as the glory years of my teaching career were, the buzz I get when I'm in front of groups delivering my training sessions, or the pop that Adam and I receive doing our live shows, nothing beats seeing my own kids reaching goals and growing into the little legends I know they will be – in life and on the sports pitch. I'm so lucky in so many ways that I get to see them make the big jump to secondary school and beyond. Lots of adults my age (I'm not even THAT old) will get to that point and realise it's our children's time to shine in whatever way they choose to. Teachers and parents realise this but it's really hard to wean yourself off being the main event in your own life. It's even harder to be seen as no longer the main character in your own movie or TV show.

Our heroes are ageing too. Hulk Hogan is in his 70s, the Karate Kid is in his 60s, Zack Morris and Kelly Kapowski are both now over 50, and I'm sorry to report that Kenan & Kel are officially middle-aged. If you're reading this and are too young to know who these people are... LUCKY YOU! Well, lucky that you have your youth, not lucky you didn't experience arguably the best decade or two of pop-culture awesomeness.

With the availability of streaming services, adults can share their childhood favourites with their children. It's amazing to watch some of your favourite TV shows 20, 30, even nearly 40 years later and realise they are still awesome, but some of the comedy has aged REALLY badly. I'm not talking about the dodgy stuff from the 60s and 70s, where it was perfectly fine to hear some pretty offensive views about minorities that would be deemed hideously inappropriate today. I'm talking about the Fresh Prince objectifying women and fat-shaming Uncle Phil. Don't get me started on *Saved by the Bell* and just what a piece of sh*t Zack Morris is. There's even a YouTube series dedicated to why he's a complete b*stard, called *Zack Morris is Trash*, and it's worrying the sorts of things he used to do to make money or annoy Mr Belding.

However you choose to corrupt your children, or if you're just watching *Pokémon* from the early 2000s and playing the guessing game where it's an insult to guess Pikachu, it's a nice bit of family time (if you can call it that).

If you watch a Netflix show like *The Toys That Made Us*, it pulls back the curtain on the toys so many people loved as children. It was amazing to see how these toys that were produced and adored were created.

Watching shows about how the plastic tat you loved as a child came to be is fascinating and a lovely slice of nostalgia. What is slightly upsetting, however, is the absolute disdain that the toy makers had for their target market. We believed in the folklore of *He-Man, Care Bears* and *Teenage Mutant Ninja Turtles*. We didn't realise the makers of the toys just wanted to flood the market with any old shite because the kids will buy it. The *He-Man* cartoon (and I realise some people will never have seen it) was just an advert for the next figure that was coming out.

'We need a new character.'

'What haven't we done yet?'

'Erm... we could do one that smells!'

'Great! What'll we call it?'

'I don't bloody know... Stinkor?!?'

'Perfect!'

I'm not exaggerating when I say that this is not too dissimilar to what went down. Google the *Masters of the Universe* toys and you'll see that the majority of them had exactly the same physique, save a modification or two. There was a character with a massive fist and, I kid you not, his name was... 'FISTO!' 😳 What some of the big companies did back then was keep the action figures relatively cheap (which our parents were grateful for), then reused the moulds. Some of the WWF Hasbro toys have identical bodies with different heads. Most of you reading this will have no idea who the Texas Tornado and Tatanka are, but wrestling fans of the early 90s knew they were buying the same figure with a different head... and still did it. That's how much it meant to the kids buying the toys.

Every generation will have their favourite toys: a jumping Evel Knievel (this pre-dates even me and Adam) and *Star Wars* in the 70s to *Ghostbusters* and *Transformers* in the 80s. From *Power Rangers* and WWF wrestling in the 90s to *Pokémon* and beyond, if you are hit by the nostalgia bug, you may need to pop on a pair of rose-tinted spectacles when rewatching some of your classic shows, because you'll realise how crappy the plots are. Look how popular the *Barbie* movie was, and before that the *Lego* movies (including ear worm soundtracks). There's money to be made here, as the children from the 70s, 80s and 90s are now the parents of today. And we're still desperate to live vicariously through our younglings. Just like my Lily entering a talent show reciting Smithy's Indian takeaway order from *Gavin and Stacey*, there's a lad in America on a viral video performing the dance from *Napoleon Dynamite* to Jamiroquai, wearing a Vote for Pedro T-shirt. Clearly the parental influence is strong in the pop culture field with that one.

Some references in the last few paragraphs may be spot on and resonate hugely with you, or if you're slightly younger, then you probably had, erm... *Johnny Bravo, Cow and Chicken* and *Hey Arnold*! on your Cartoon Network and Nickelodeon. Everyone, however, will usually cling on to the idea that their formative years were the best. Their toys and music were top-notch and anyone who disagrees is a giant poo-head.

Just like the glory years for many of us (mine are the 90s and 2000s), we assumed that what we listened to was amazing as well. Your parents will mostly have thought it was bloody rubbish! Catch a retro *Top of the Pops* on BBC4 (funnily enough, the ones with certain DJs don't get aired anymore... I wonder why?!?) and you'll automatically cry that 'Here Comes the Hotstepper' is nearly 30... that's right... 30 years old. What the actual f*ck?!

Another sign of getting old is the realisation that you and your peers are starting to pass certain milestone ages from pop culture. Adam is now older that Stacy's Mom (33) from the Fountains of Wayne song, and I am now the same age as Stifler's Mom (38) in *American Pie*! For goodness sakes, Danny Glover was only 41 when he uttered the immortal line from the *Lethal Weapon* films: 'I'm too old for this sh*t!' 41!

Another thing that has really knocked me for six is that there are some songs that turn 20 in 2024, such as 'This Love' by Maroon 5, Snoop Dogg's 'Drop It Like It's Hot' and, unbelievably, Natasha Bedingfield's 'Unwritten'. Feel free to pause reading this book and stick 'Unwritten' on in the car; I challenge you to not sing along with gusto to this absolute classic. What is also worrying is that on some music-streaming services there are playlists of 'oldies' that contain Blink-182! Say it ain't so...

Weirdly, parents of school-age children are a lot more up with the times, and it's perfectly possibly to attend an Ed Sheeran or Katy Perry concert together because both the parents and the young people like the same music. I don't know if that's down to the longevity of some artists or the fact that the grown-ups refuse to... well, grow up.

For teachers, it's a sign that you've definitely been teaching for quite a while when you run into an ex-pupil or two dressed to the nines on a night out. The rules aren't fair with this, because if they get so drunk that they break their heels, punch a bouncer or fall down the stairs, it's all part of a great night out. If the teacher does the same, then their professionalism is called into question. It's perfectly legal to randomly bump into an ex-pupil on a night out and, as long as they are of drinking age, buy each other a pint for a laugh. Doing Jägerbombs at 1am, however, may be a bit much.

On a night out, one teacher was so drunk that she was performing some delightfully named 'sl*t-drops' on the dance floor at her local club. Clearly, she was having the time of her life with her girlies, and she threw some significant shapes that evening, drunk enough to have lowered her inhibitions but not so drunk to not see that she had caught the attention of some young gentlemen. Content that she still had 'IT', she continued to bust out her greatest hits of sexy moves until it dawned upon her that the men looked familiar. It was only then that she realised who they were and why they were staring; the dapper young dudes on the other side of the club were in fact boys who had been in her Year 5 class about a decade before... AWKWARD!

Speaking of awkward, one male teacher was in a supermarket and stocking up on condoms as his favourite brand of Durex Extra Thin Feel were a lot cheaper if he used his Clubcard. What he didn't realise was that the person on the till serving him was actually an ex-pupil. Cringe!

'Oh hello there, Jamie...' or words to that effect were muttered as young Jamie made full eye-contact after scanning the box of rubber johnnies. Blip! An eyebrow was raised as the pupil passed it down to the bagging area and the teacher rapidly shoved the box of prophylactics into his bag for life. The shopping was paid for but the embarrassment was still there, and the conversation ended like this:

'Thanks, Jamie, nice to see you!'

'Happy shagging, Sir!'

What a nightmare! A nightmare made even worse by the fact that the teacher (overcome by embarrassment) had forgotten to scan his Clubcard after all that, so he'd paid full whack for all his shopping, including his Durex Extra Thin Feel condoms.

Lots of teachers are genuinely curious to know how some of their pupils are getting on once they leave school, especially when they turn out to be wonderful humans. If an ex-pupil plays rugby for an England national U16 or U18 team, then they can jokingly brag that they 'taught them everything they know'. What is more entertaining, however, is when a teacher learns that a child that didn't always make the right choices... is still not making the right choices after leaving primary school.

If you've read our first book or listened to our podcast, you'll know about David (not his real name). He's the child that couldn't stop lying and told his entire class that he had a donkey in his garden... which he didn't. Perfectly normal behaviour, I'm sure. Well, a colleague of mine caught up with young David many years later on a local bus and informed me that he tried to pay for his ticket using a... get this... Blockbuster Video Card. Blockbuster? They went out of business nearly twenty years ago, so where the hell did he swipe that from? Good old David, keeping his legacy alive, purely for our entertainment.

You can get a wake-up call of how quickly time passes by occasionally looking back at your Facebook memories. You'll have a friendship anniversary with someone that you probably hate or only met once at a wedding, yet they still wish you a happy birthday every year. You'll have a few pictures you're tagged in where you think, 'I remember when I still had a jaw line and all my own hair.'

But for those reading this that are parents, you'll notice a stark contrast between you in 2019 and your online self in 2009.

Your Facebook timeline in 2009 may say:

'Great result today Rovers, a well-deserved 3 points!'

'Just watched *Avatar*. AMAZING!'

'I just bought a giant bag of Monster Munch. Lol!'

Not quite as cringey as my terrible social media posts from yesteryear full of song lyrics, film quotes and embarrassing haircuts. Also, who the hell laughs out loud at crisps?!?

The 2009/2019 comparison is just plucked out of somewhere. By all means, compare your Facebook timelines a decade apart and laugh at the stark difference between the stuff you share now and the tripe you posted then (and probably need to delete 😬).

Parents, fast forward from back then to now and your timeline is full of days out to farm parks, a cinema trip to the latest animated movie and, for about five minutes until you got bored of doing them, Wordle scores.

The nights out that you enjoy are fewer and further between, and while make-up skills and selfie filters have improved your appearance, you definitely can't handle your sambuca like you used to. It's quite a shock when you have to plan your hangover for the following day. Also, in a shock to many of us that still consider ourselves young, plenty of children that were still at primary school in 2009 are now qualified teachers and, with any luck, reading this book! If you're one of those and I taught you, I'd like apologise for the wonderful world of the future that I promised you'd grow up in. Nostradamus, I am not!

If you've already been through the depressing transition into being considered a proper grown-up, perhaps even a similar age to our parents, then this won't have been a shock in the last 15 to 20 years like it has been for us. You had your realisation years ago. Question is, do we want your advice on how to do it gracefully? Nope! Of course not.

Also, if you're reading this book and you are a lot younger than a teacher and a TA in their mid- to late 30s, I'm sorry to have painted such a bleak picture. But it's OK, because you can lip-sync Squidward quotes on TikTok and dance to 'Blinding Lights' by the Weeknd. If you're even younger than that and you're still a 'free reader', as they call children that have read everything in the school reading scheme, you've got all of this ahead of you. In fact, one of my proudest moments came when a colleague spotted a Year 5 reading our first book (*Put a Wet Paper Towel on It*) during a quiet reading session, and giggling away about the crazy classroom stories and jokes about children breaking wind. It was amazing to hear that. It was also a big relief when I remembered that we starred out most of the really f**king bad swear words!!

Another sign that we're not cool is that people will look back on our style choices and laugh. I'm not talking about laughing at your mum and dad's 70s flares or 80s mullets, I'm sorry to report that TikTokers are referring to the 90s and early 2000s fashion as retro! RETRO!?! Oh crap, I'm not ready to be retro. If you've seen videos like Sophie 'Tired'n'Tested' McCartney's about getting ready for a night out in the 2000s, there are hairstyles with very dark colours in the lower part of the hair, yet blonde on top, pencil-thin eyebrows that were a nightmare to pluck and blotchy fake tan with clumpy mascara. That was just the girls; the lads were no better. I think there are a few guys that got married back then sporting their mop top who will look back on their photos and question:

a) Why did I choose to look like Paul Weller's nan in my wedding photos?

and...

b) Who the hell is that in the background? Did my wife used to work with them?

It's great that we no longer wear chains on our ripped jeans, dog tags round our necks and bandanas on our arms. Also, it's fantastic that Adam no longer straightens his hair to look like Chris Tarrant.

There was a period in the early 2000s where the haircuts were inexplicably weird but worryingly accepted. Kind of at the tail end of Busted and into McFly. Don't know what I'm talking about? You can still see these hairstyles sported by the employees of Complete Entertainment eXchange on the high street, or as we all call it, CEX. One of the greatest memes ever came out a few years ago with a picture of the Great Yarmouth branch of CEX, where sadly the building was ablaze.

Fortunately nobody was hurt and they managed to put it out, which means I feel no guilt in doing this joke because... (clears throat)...

> Whooooooaaaaaaahhhh that CEX was on fireeee!
> (Kings of Leon, 2008)

Sorry, I couldn't resist. It's almost as bad as the Facebook post from my mate during the 2011 London riots where he wrote:

'Well, the Kaiser Chiefs saw this coming!'

As in, 'I predict a riot'... OK, sorry. I'll stop doing these and go back to slagging off the fashion that we loved 20 years ago, the stuff that we thought was cool at the time but actually made most lads look like Lee from Steps and most girls look like they'd missed the audition for Atomic Kitten.

Just like old Facebook posts make us cringe, I guess the items people wore just felt right at the time. This was the era where Primark stores started popping up on the high street and people could grab a brand-new clubbing outfit for less than £15. Clearly, we were all indoctrinated, as 'Primarni' is still going strong and one of the only stores on the high street still heaving with people most weekends. I'm not throwing shade on Primark, although all three Parkinson Bros were Next employees anyway. Admittedly, some of us lasted longer than others.

Staying on the high street but going back to CEX, can you believe that your once-loved items are now seen as 'classics'? If you remember the original PlayStation, then you'll remember the futuristic sound as you pressed the power button. It was pretty loud and distinctive, and you'd better have muted your TV if you were planning on playing *WWF Smackdown! 2: Know Your Role* late at night. Also, you'd have to make sure you didn't accidentally lean on the volume button of your remote control, otherwise your parents might have heard the commentators Jim Ross and Jerry 'The King' Lawler screaming about 'stone-cold stunners' and 'tombstone piledrivers' at 3am. Be prepared for a b*llocking if that was the case.

To make me feel really old, I saw a dance mat in the window of a charity shop the other day. Those bad boys got plenty of use in the early 2000s. If you were really good, you could anticipate the next steps as you busted a move to 'Wannabe' by the Spice Girls on *Dancing Stage Fever.* Although, I'm convinced there's an unfair advantage for people with smaller feet, rather than my complete lack of coordination and ankles made of glass!

Sadly, advancing years is something we can't fight, but I think that all the Parkinson brothers and our peers were lucky enough to grow up (jury is still out on whether Adam has done this) when we did and experience all the amazing pop culture of the time, which we will no doubt keep holding in high regard and share with our kids.

I'd like to end this chapter with a tweet I discussed on our podcast from user John Penniman @historiographos, who tweeted a screenshot of an email sent from a student which read:

'Good afternoon Professor Penniman,

Hope you had a great break! I was wondering if it would be acceptable to use sources from the late 1900s for our final paper (I found an interesting paper from 1994). Is there a cut-off date for publication? See you tomorrow.'

Ah, the late 1900s! I can't wait to tell of a time when connecting to the internet required a phone line for dial-up, and the way to find a number was to pick up an ancient relic, a book called Yellow Pages, and search through. If only my own children went to my old secondary school, they may still be able to see the old carvings I left engraved on a desk, usually of a Wu-Tang Clan symbol for an authentic primary source of the late 1900s.

The bloody cheek of it!

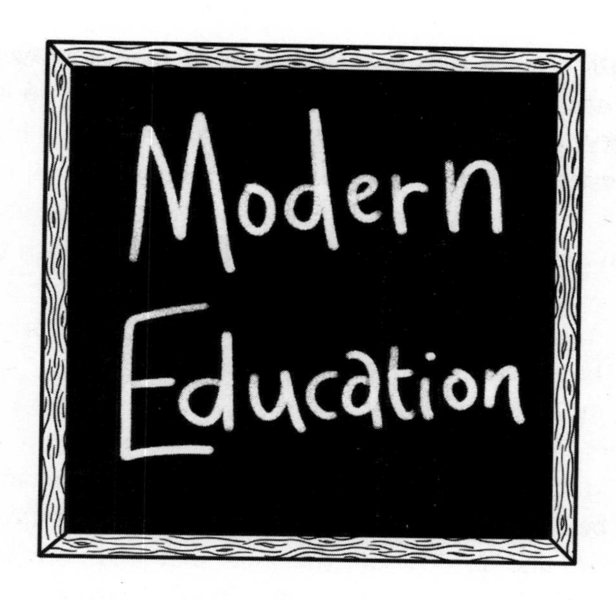

First of all, well done for making it this far into the book.

In our previous two offerings, we basically had silly school-based observations, funny stories and fart jokes. I'm sure you'll agree that there have been plenty of those, but near the end of the books we usually let Lee (Mr P) have a big bloody whinge about the state of education.

I'm not whingeing, I'm ranting, and for good reason.

Well, you'll be delighted to hear (possibly) that we've reached this point of the book, so strap yourselves in as Lee goes off on one (although most of his points are very valid) and puts the world of education to rights.

I'm not sure I appreciate the introduction, bro, but I probably will have my usual rant in this chapter. After 17 years as a teacher, I have seen far too many amazing staff members leaving the profession and I know of so many families that have been pulling their hair out for years trying to do what's best for their children. Their hands have been tied by budgetary constraints and a system that is set up to fail them.

I'm sure I'll be accused of Tory-bashing, but who else has been in government for the last 14+ years? So much that is wrong with our education system in the UK stems from poorly thought-out decisions by people that clearly care more about headlines than helping families.

On my social media channels, I've built a following of teachers, parents and anyone that finds my stuff mildly amusing because I wanted to celebrate what's amazing about being a teacher, take a light-hearted look at life in the classroom and also call out the sh*te that stops our schools from giving the youth of the nation the best start in life.

Anyone reading this book (and thanks for purchasing it) will have some sort of link to school life. Everyone went to school and remembers the good and bad aspects of it, and while much is still the same, plenty has changed beyond all recognition.

We tried to poke a bit of fun at the different types of parents in the Types of Parents chapter, but we want to make it clear that we recognise that the vast majority of parents are doing their absolute best, and I would argue that in today's climate it is harder being a parent than ever before. We are facing so many more challenges and there seems to have been a really seismic shift in workplace culture, meaning that many parents are being told that to be a good parent you have to work. However, with the change of workers' rights, zero-hour contracts and the like, most jobs are no longer 9 to 5. We all have our phones with our work emails connected, knowing that if we aren't pulling our weight, we can easily be replaced with someone else who will. Therefore, it is almost as if to be a successful parent you have to spend the least amount of time with your own children.

And that time is precious, hence the constant discussion about taking children out of school to go on holiday during term time. I should state at this point that fines and other measures were not brought in by schools and teachers. We didn't decide to think, I tell you what we can do to bring in more budget for glue sticks, let's charge parents for taking their kids out of school and we'll charge based on where you are going. Butlins? That'll be £50. Mauritius? That'll be £200. If you're a parent who has been stung by these fines, please don't take that frustration out on the school. That was government policy, and like most things parents get annoyed with, it is the clueless politicians deflecting from addressing the root cause of these problems. Just as I write this, in February 2024, the two political parties are talking about investment in childcare and breakfast clubs for every child. Why is there no discussion about more flexible working for parents? Schools are not the answer to every issue, but due to austerity measures over the past 10 to 15 years they have had to pick up the pieces. When I first started teaching we had Sure Start centres, also known as Sure Start Children's Centres, which were introduced in the UK by the Labour government in 1998. The initiative aimed to support families with young children under the age of four living in the most disadvantaged areas. Sure Start centres were designed to improve the health, education and emotional development of babies and young children so that they could flourish at home and when they started school.

The services offered by Sure Start centres varied, but they typically included early education and childcare, parenting advice, health services (such as health visitor services and speech therapy) and support for parents, including advice on employment and parenting. The overarching goal was to give children the best possible start in life by providing a holistic approach to support, encompassing not just the child's education but also their health and broader family well-being.

The approach to Sure Start centres and their funding changed significantly after the Conservative-led coalition government came to power in 2010. Facing austerity measures, the government reduced funding for local authorities, which in turn impacted the funding available for Sure Start centres. While there wasn't a direct policy to close Sure Start centres, the reduction in funding led to a significant number of closures and a shift in how services were provided. Many centres were merged, and services were centralised to cover larger areas, potentially making them less accessible to the families that needed them most.

The consequences of these closures of Sure Start centres have been felt by schools with the reduction in Early Years support. It has led to increased pressure on schools, which are now more frequently the first point of contact for families needing support. Schools may have had to step in to fill the gaps in Early Years education and support for families, potentially without the additional resources or specialist expertise that Sure Start centres provided. This shift can affect the readiness of children entering formal education and can place additional burdens on educational settings to provide broader support to families.

Just recently it has been reported that over half of children starting school are not school-ready. One in four children start Reception and are not yet potty trained. Ask any Early Years staff member and they will tell you the difference they have seen. With dwindling budgets and so many more challenges that schools are facing, they are unable to fix this problem.

At the same time, there have been reports around attendance in school in the press recently, as persistent absenteeism has risen dramatically post-pandemic, with nearly a third of secondary school pupils missing over 10 per cent of lessons. The reaction to this online had a lot of parents saying that if they want to take their children out of school for holidays they will, as precious family time is more important. Now while I completely agree with that sentiment, I also recognise the impact that absence from school can have. But again, fining parents isn't the solution. There needs to be a policy that puts a cap on how much holiday companies can charge during school breaks; you limit that, problem solved.

Take Center Parcs, which my family have loved going to. We have spent a weekend at the end of November at Center Parcs as a way to kick off the Christmas season. The kids would see Father Christmas and we'd have a lovely time. But the difference in price is extortionate. Take a cabin for a week for a family of four – two adults, two children. If I were to book that from 4 March 2024 for a week slap bang in the middle of the spring term, it would cost £1,128. Just a month later, 1 April, during the Easter break, the cost for the same cabin would be £2,198 – nearly double. That's the issue, so cap the amount that can be charged. Ultimately, teachers and parents want the exact same thing – the best for their students. We are on the same page. While there might be differing opinions on different aspects of school life, teachers are always doing things based on the intention of it being the best for the students.

So much policy is out of our hands as educators. I very rarely agree with government policy; in fact, I have said numerous times that I don't think the Tory government has implemented anything that has improved education over the past 14 years. For every boast from the government about how they've improved education, there are 10 other ways in which they have ruined it.

Take a recent tweet from our current Secretary of State for Education (at the time of writing) – Gillian Keegan:

> *Under the @Conservatives, we have rocketed up the international education rankings. Whenever Labour run education, standards plummet.*
>
> *There's nothing more dangerous to children's education than the Labour Party.*

And I couldn't help but quote tweet it with the following:

> *– Unhappiest kids in Europe*
> *– Fewer children than ever reading for pleasure*
> *– School buildings crumbling*
> *– Less than half the target of teacher trainees*
> *– Biggest retention crisis*
> *– Morale in the profession the lowest ever*
> *– Ofsted...*
> *The list goes on.*

They're delusional.

Take the idea that the UK is now fourth in the world for reading; this will go down as one of the Tory's biggest wins in education, and when Nick Gibb, Schools Minister, stood down this was seen as his greatest achievement, and that his rollout of the phonics programme was the main reason for this. Now while I know phonics has a place and helps the majority of children, I don't think it works for everyone. I think other strategies should also be used for students who are dyslexic, like my son, yet he was still being forced to do phonics interventions in Year 6. Here's the thing they don't mention about being fourth in the world at reading: we have now got fewer children reading for pleasure than ever before – kids hate reading, they don't want to do it. Again, I am not saying this is directly down to phonics, but I don't think it has helped engage children in the wonderful world of stories.

So as teachers and parents we are on the same page, but there are so many things outside our control. The system means we have to teach an outdated, boring, dull and often pointless curriculum. We share the same frustrations with the lack of funding and support for SEND children. I definitely feel the bond between parents and teachers has been fraught over the past decade due to the political narrative of deflection and division. But I will tell every parent this: you have so much more in common with the student's teachers than the politicians making the decisions, and remember that some of the media demean schools and teachers because they like to stoke hatred because it gets more clicks.

But there's a reason why teachers still love their jobs (when they get a chance to) and children see their primary school years as the best of their lives. Whatever level of perfection we see on Instagram, Facebook, Twitter and TikTok, I think we can all agree that it's far more entertaining to laugh at the craziness, pitfalls and epic fails related to being a parent with school-age children in the 2020s, and laugh along with everyone else making it up as they go along. You've seen the videos from TeacherTommyT and SammyGray, etc., and it's heartening to see that everyone is trying to function in the modern world and is failing miserably. Honesty about the struggles makes us all realise that we're human.

That doesn't excuse crap parenting, and there are plenty of people that should up their game in that regard, including a number of grifters that make money from getting angry about teacher strikes before they've bothered to listen to the reasoning. Most teachers haven't had a real-terms pay increase since austerity began in 2010, but the majority of teachers were striking because of how they want to improve things for their children. We're losing teachers in their droves, and ultimately it's the children that suffer. Think of your favourite teacher from your childhood. Who inspired you? Who made you want to come to school? What was it about them that helped you to access learning?

Now think about them in today's climate and how most of them would be put on a support plan or formal capabilities (basically a way of getting an 'underperforming' teacher constructively dismissed). This goes for secondary teachers too. Mr Andrews, the incredibly charismatic and flamboyant languages teacher that could inspire an entire class to engage in conversational Spanish through role play, body language and facial expressions, wouldn't last five minutes in the modern classroom as he's too busy tracking data and evidencing progress in the children's use of past participles. Back in 1999, he could have the class eating out of the palm of his hand (not literally, because that would be weird) as he acted out verbs and why they would be reflexive, yet nowadays he'd have his hands tied with the amount that must be covered by a very prescriptive curriculum.

Sadly, there are a lot of aspiring teachers that will complete their teacher training, rack up £30k of debt and leave within the first year of teaching. There's something very wrong with that.

There are no obvious answers that could completely stop the exodus of good teachers so early in their careers, but it would make a hell of a lot of difference if the profession was respected more in the media (yeah, right) and not simplified to the point of the old clichés pumped out by parents like Daddy Big B**locks and his ilk. Of course, there are some dreadful teachers out there, and parents have every right to complain about the odd crap one, but sadly it's quite often the ones with potential that leave their vocation in the early stage of their careers, and lots of the bad ones remain because they can't afford to do anything else.

I'm at the point where I've seen my own kids go through primary education and are now part-way through secondary school. If you met Adam at secondary school, you'd be very surprised to learn that he is now working as an educator, or even that he is employed at all.

I'd argue with him, but it's a fair point!

The penultimate chapter will have a slightly futuristic theme and we'll be looking at some elements of the schooling of the future. This could include fingerprint scans instead of registers as children enter the school. What about parents' evenings using holograms? Something that's less sh*t than Microsoft Teams in case there's another pandemic and we're back to remote teaching and virtual learning? With plenty of schools still full of dodgy concrete, that may be more common than we realise. What would be nice in the future is where we evolve to a point where MPs have to wear a band that sends an electric shock around their body if they start lying. I still can't believe an Education Secretary (Silly Gilly Keegan) claimed that lots of children prefer being taught in Portakabins, then got cross because nobody praised her for doing a 'f*cking good job'. That would definitely warrant a ZAP!

While we're on the topic of Education Secretaries, between 2010 and 2024 there have been 10 Secretaries of State for Education. Potentially more by the time this book comes out...

Let's do a quick Top 10 of Ed Secs from least-worst to Gavin Williamson (I wonder who'll get the top spot!):

10.
Michelle Donelan – Technically the best on this list because she was only in post for two days, but also because she worked previously for World Wrestling Entertainment and therefore must be mates with Triple H and the Undertaker!

9.
Justine Greening – Don't remember much that she did that was terrible, but I can't remember what she looks like.

8.
Damien Hinds – Same as above. I don't remember him doing a lot that was too dreadful, so he gets a free pass.

7.
Nicky Morgan – 'Continuity Gove'. The teaching profession was delighted when Michael Gove was moved from Education Secretary to the Department for Justice after being deemed 'too toxic' in 2014. I only really remember her for carrying on pretty much most of Gove's drivel.

6.
Kit Malthouse – No idea.

5.
Nadhim Zahawi – I forgot he held that role. Usually brought out to defend terrible government decisions on BBC and Sky, he ended up changing the subject most of the time in these interviews like a child that hadn't remembered to do his homework.

4.
'The ironically named' James 'Cleverly' – I forgot he held the post as well. Does the same BS routine as Mr Zahawi but looks grumpier in the process.

3.
Gillian Keegan – Seemed to be alright initially, but telling A-level students that nobody cares about their results, the 'f*cking good job' comment and the thing she said about Portakabins put her higher up (or technically lower down, based upon crapness) the list.

2.
Michael Gove – How this man missed the No.1 slot for the damage he caused to our education relies entirely on Gavlar's ability to be even worse.

When Gove arrived as Education Secretary in 2010, he went out of his way with his disingenuous politeness, claiming to be on the side of the teachers then overcomplicating everything and making sweeping reforms to reflect the 1950s-style of education system. Which was quite strange because the man was born in 1967 and didn't start primary school until the 1970s.

He p*ssed off the teachers, complicated the teaching of English by insisting children should be able to identify a past participle in a sentence rather than focus on the vocabulary used. He brought in maths methodology that made it as hard as possible for children to learn how to calculate. For many years the 'grid method' had worked brilliantly for children multiplying using double digits and above, but he tried to almost outlaw the thing because it didn't fit in with his plans to turn children into robots to improve our standing on the international PISA results.

Sadly, sensible former Tories like Rory Stewart still quote PISA results as a way of pretending that standards improved under Michael Gove, when the only thing that went up was the number of teachers leaving the profession early and the need to teach to the test. Don't be fooled, this man damaged education for the long term and deserves every bit of scorn directed at him.

1.
Gavin 'Gavlar' Williamson – From confusing Maro Itoje with Marcus Rashford, to releasing anti-bullying campaign videos despite being found by a committee to be a hideous bully behind the scenes himself, Gavlar manages to make Michael Gove look slightly less sh*t.

Many compared Gavlar, due to his voice, demeanour and facial expressions, to Frank Spencer, the calamitous and naive main character from *Some Mothers Do 'Ave 'Em*. The man with the reverse Midas touch, as everything he came into contact with turned into a disaster. Ooh, Betty! The difference being that Michael Crawford's hapless buffoon was quite loveable and entertaining, and Gavlar is anything but loveable.

He'd lecture educators on raising standards yet couldn't be bothered to pronounce words like 'them' and 'those', choosing 'vem' and 'vose' instead, as well as the number 'free'. Make no mistake, this is no speech impediment, it's just lazy pronunciation, the sort of thing that teachers would be picked up on during an Ofsted inspection as poor modelling for the children in the lesson.

Speaking of Ofsted, this dweeb (a month or so into the pandemic) told parents to report their child's school to Ofsted for not providing adequate home learning. I even made a video about the ridiculousness of Gavlar sending an inspector to my house to rate my home-schooling provision (sadly, I achieved the result of 'inadequate').

The pandemic was tricky for everyone, so you'd forgive most people for occasionally getting things wrong, but it's hard to forgive Gavlar for buggering up the A-level and GCSE results with a dodgy algorithm for calculating results and doubling down when it all went to sh*t. Some students ended up with results about two grades below what they were predicted, yet lots of the children in the posh schools seemed to be fine. He even thought it was a good idea to force school children to write a faux-patriotic song called 'One Britain, One Nation'. 'Strong Britain, great nation' was the chorus. This jingoistic tripe was every bit as bad as people thought it would be, a crap Brexit anthem for primary children to become indoctrinated by. Good job most schools paid no attention to it. I'm not having a pop at the children and teachers that helped to create it, but it was unbearably bad and I doubt the children involved knew they were spouting Farage-friendly lyrics to tick a false patriotism box.

He's really going off on him, isn't he, readers?!

After the Salisbury nerve-agent attacks, Gavlar solved the issue by telling the entire nation of Russia to, and I quote: 'Go away and shut up!' But don't worry, folks, there's no way this level of mediocrity would be rewarded. Wait? He was rewarded? With a knighthood?!?

Sir Gavin Williamson?

You won't be hearing that name from me again and certainly not with the title of 'Sir' at the front. Where's the sick bucket?

Yes, I've just had a rant and I'm sure being Education Secretary isn't easy (despite the list above suggesting that competence and integrity are not essential in many cases) but schools can and should be much better. There's something very wrong with turning our schools into exam factories to the detriment of the children's and staff's well-being. Something that I get asked a lot on social media is about well-being. A perfectly awesome teacher may pop me a message that says:

'Hi Mr P, I've been tasked with leading a well-being staff meeting. Is there anything you can recommend?'

My answer is always the same... 'CANCEL THE MEETING!' Honestly, because I can guarantee whatever the teacher had planned or whatever tick-box exercise they were going to do will not compare to giving teachers time to get themselves up straight and leave at a sensible hour. Now I've said for a number of years that the best, most important way in which you can improve a teacher's well-being is to trust them to do the job that they are very capable of doing, and therefore reduce workload. But giving them trust is incredibly difficult for some school leaders, and we are so limited because of our education system where we've had a government who do not fund or even care about education (and of course there's the existence of Ofsted). There are so many things schools can be doing internally to try to give that trust, reduce that workload and therefore give teachers time.

Half of the time, well-being is only focused upon in case Ofsted ask about it. I've made a number of social media videos for some recent research projects, in which I've made it clear that well-being is completely and utterly subjective anyway. What works for me isn't going to work for someone else. Personally, what's great for my well-being and what brings me the most amount of joy in my life is watching my children play sport. I spend most Sundays watching my kids on the sports field. I leave the house at 8am then get back at gone 4pm. It brings me so much joy to see them step up and try their best at something. I genuinely think the life skills and lessons they learn through competing in sports are the most important thing they can do as a kid.

I know there are some people who are going, 'Are you joking? Standing out in the cold watching your kids? I can't think of anything worse!' And to that I say, get a heated gilet (thanks, Mrs P, for my Christmas present) as it will change your life!

While I'm on the subject of school sport, I started talking about the way school sport has been affected for nearly 15 years when we looked at the pitch-side legend in the types of parent section. While I'm often pitch-side and I certainly don't consider myself to be a legend, I have seen it from the perspective of a teacher and a parent.

I'm undeniably proud to say that two years in a row my school won the Trafford Sports School of the Year award, in one of which I also won 'school sports practitioner of the year'. There's no way I'd be able to do it now if I was full time in class. It's no exaggeration to say that teachers are drowning in paperwork and marking, and are suffering with general exhaustion. Plenty of teachers still run sports clubs, but it's more common for schools to buy into specialist sports coaches for extra-curricular activities. The turning point for me was following the 2012 Olympic games, when the government cut so much of the school sports funding as part of their awful austerity measures. Funding was disappearing, and this was the first occasion I realised things were changing – and not for the better. My concerns were detailed in my first article published online in the *Guardian*. Many of the key points that I raised at the time are relevant now and go some way to explaining the stagnation of sport in our school.

I can't help but think that former Prime Minister David Cameron had the issue on school sports totally wrong. The government at the time were too focused on competition between schools rather than enjoyment and participation. At this point, I must state that I fully support competition in sport and feel that children experiencing competition is vital in building essential life skills such as determination, courage and willpower that they can apply in many different areas as they get older. The complete change in culture was my issue. I'm the eldest of three incredibly competitive brothers, so I totally get the importance of a winning mentality.

I work at a primary school that has a flourishing sports programme due to the dedication of members of staff devoting so much of their own time running clubs, hosting events and coaching children outside the school day. This has been happening for many years, on top of their other responsibilities. We have been very successful in numerous local and national competitions, but our main achievement is that every child represents the school in some sort of competition before they leave. I don't feel my colleagues or I could do any more to provide the children with opportunities to excel in sport.

So why do we do it? Well, personally, I feel my duty as a teacher is to provide children with as many opportunities to excel and find talent in a subject. What sport does more than a lot of other subjects is that it provides children with a healthy lifestyle and the right values to live by. It also gives children personal lifelong memories. What subsequent politicians have been blinded by is the fact that one of the main reasons Team GB were so high up the medal tables at the 2012 Olympics was down to the previous government providing opportunities for all children to play, enjoy and love sport, whatever their ability. I joke about Adam being a child that didn't always make the right choices, but he was able to excel and show the best version of himself through rugby and football. Adam was in his element on the sports field, and no ADD diagnosis was going to stop him.

Funding cuts made it incredibly difficult to provide excellent opportunities for everyone in schools and employ the specialist coaches that would introduce youngsters to new activities and then run competition to maximise participation. Hockey, lacrosse and athletics may have been outside of some children's 'comfort zones' initially, but once introduced more regularly, many children were joining clubs to pursue them further.

From my perspective, what I wrote in 2012 is still incredibly relevant in 2024. When I'm on the sidelines at my children's sports fixtures, I will regularly have the same conversations with fellow parents about the lack of opportunities, competitions and sports offered at their schools. I must explain that my teaching colleagues are too snowed under to even help breed the love of sport that needs to exist.

As you can tell, I'm so passionate about school sport and how it links to so much about our children's development of key skills. It still smarts that it has been treated with such disrespect in the last decade or more. For the education of the future to really thrive, I'd focus on making it a priority. It's not the only priority but I truly believe that it can open the door to all children regardless of their ability or potential learning difficulties. I briefly mentioned before about Adam and his own barriers to learning at school, but regular podcast listeners will be shocked to hear that the next part is a surprisingly sensible section from him about SEND.

He's right, most of my contributions in this book are fairly light-hearted, jovial and (let's be honest) downright silly, but I'm actually going to be slightly more serious in this section as I think it's important to share part of my son's journey into school. Something you'll hopefully know if you're a parent is to trust your own instincts. You'll see loads of Facebook and Instagram posts about children reaching certain ages (although anything over twelve months baffles me) and celebrating certain developmental milestones such as rolling, crawling, walking and speaking. They are fantastic to celebrate, but when you think your own child may not be reaching certain milestones, it causes concern, worry and eventually some distress. This happened to us with our son, Max.

Max was born in 2019, and as far as my wife (Kim) and I were concerned, he was developing well. The poor little lad had a serious case of bronchiolitis and pneumonia at six months old, which was pretty scary, but we thought he was ticking along OK otherwise. When Max reached his first birthday, we did start to notice a few concerning behaviours, and as we both work in education we thought we'd use our wealth of knowledge (mostly Kim's) to look a little closer. I work with a lot of children with additional needs, and as someone with an ADD (Attention Deficit Disorder) diagnosis I can appreciate how it feels to struggle to access learning. We definitely had concerns and, I admit, we googled (yes, we are those parents) 'autism'.

Of the developing behaviours, the most obvious was probably a delay in Max's speech, as he hadn't uttered the typical first words most children do, yet he could weirdly request that Alexa play Jason Derulo. We put it down to lots of things but one huge factor at the time was the first Covid lockdown. During the pandemic, I qualified for the 'extremely clinically vulnerable' list due to my type 1 diabetes and asthma. The doctor also recognised that Max would be in that bracket as he had been so poorly as a baby. As a result of our medical statuses, we didn't see or interact with people in the flesh for many months. By the time we were able to, it took him a while to settle back at nursery and even get to know family members again. Max's key worker at his nursery asked my wife to observe him as they had noticed he wasn't interacting with his peers as he typically should. Another quirk involved spinning, and while we thought he was just a good dancer (his big sister, Isla, would always love joining in), we read more about children using repetitive movements to regulate themselves, which included spinning.

When Max turned two, he still hadn't said many words and mostly communicated through pointing or guiding our hands to what he wanted, yet he was amazing at recognising the alphabet and counting. Like me, he has a huge affinity for anything physical, so we took him to mini-rugby and football sessions, but it started to become clear that he had issues following instructions. In fact, he spent most of the sessions trying to escape or climbing up the wall bars (in his £40 kit). I think we really knew that Max probably had additional needs when we saw him next to other children his age. For us, the realisation was difficult, but Max was loving life and we tried to focus on doing what made him happy, which was mostly eating (again, like me) and playing outside.

Between the ages of three and four were probably the most difficult times for Max, and during this period he was biting – a lot – most days. We share plenty of stories in our books and on our podcast about children with interesting behaviours, but no parent wants their child to be hurting other children and adults (on purpose or otherwise). We hoped this was just a phase, as we all remember children that were 'biters' from our own childhoods, but on top of this his sleep pattern became incredibly erratic. For a long period, he would be awake from 1am to 5am, most nights, which required both of us parents to sleep almost in shifts. It was like his body didn't know when day and night were. Late-night repeats of ITV's *Tipping Point* (he still loves it now) would actually provide some reasonable distraction in the wee hours of the night, but waking him at 7am the following day would become a nightmare. The vicious cycle of tiredness and dysregulated behaviour was in full swing by then, and obviously incredibly hard to break.

The nursery staff that worked with Max deserved medals, as they went over and above to help him. It was almost as if they felt terrible reporting to us when Max had a bad day. The Special Educational Needs Coordinator (SENDCo) asked if they could refer Max to a Speech and Language Therapist (SaLT) and start to gather evidence for an Education Health Care Plan (EHCP). This was great – or so we thought... Max was going to move to a school nursery in Trafford, which was a different Local Authority (LA). As Kim and I both work in education, we had some understanding of the potentially huge waiting times involved in these processes, so we were incredibly grateful when the SENDCo arranged a thorough handover to Max's new setting, including all of the reports and observations made by the staff.

They prepared us well for the September transition, and we were up front and honest with the new staff about what Max could do and the aspects he found difficult in his development, such as his language, toileting and interacting with his peers. Another of Max's traits was his tendency to run off (we found out the correct term for this is 'elope' but it just makes me think of Max in a little tux on his way to Gretna Green). The initial meetings at the new place concluded with us feeling hopeful, and promises about help with toileting habits and day-to-day interactions were made (we were hoping the biting would at least reduce a little). Sadly, by the third day we were contacted to inform us that Max would not be allowed to return the next day and a decision had been made that a reduced timetable would be introduced with immediate effect. Both Kim and I work in schools that are really inclusive, so this news was hard to take. After many hours and numerous phone calls by my wife to SENAS (Special Educational Needs Advisory Service), we eventually had a place at a new, local nursery. Max moved, once again.

Although Max was still very dysregulated, the next academic year was a much better experience overall. A parental EHCP referral, visits from speech and language therapists, educational psychologists and occupational therapists gave us a glimmer of hope that

progress had been made. Max was given a place in a mainstream school for the following September, but in the first few weeks it felt like we were back to square one again. He was placed on a reduced timetable and although Max loved his 1:1, we had to call an early EHCP review to request that Max attend a special school. Thank goodness there was a place for him, because throughout the country the places are incredibly limited and the special schools are hideously underfunded. As I write this, things seem to be ticking along as best they can and we completely understand the journey ahead will never be plain sailing. I'm sure many readers of this book will have encountered similar issues or know families that have. There are potentially staff reading this that are stretched to breaking point to help children like Max, and are equally constrained by lack of funding and a system that refuses to listen. Fighting for your child may seem futile at times, but hopefully there will be a time ahead where children like Max are celebrated for all that they CAN do rather than penalised for everything that they find a struggle. I had to break from my usual silliness to share our family's experience, but it's an important message.

Normal service will be resumed for the rest of the book, I promise.

Adam, that was both heartfelt and sensible (I'm as shocked as you are, dear readers).

Now, the reason I get so narked about our education system is because I genuinely love working as part of it. Whether in class or delivering training to teachers and school staff across the country, I genuinely want to make the profession what it could and should be. I want schools to be thriving places that are completely focused upon the best outcomes for children, rather than businesses with the sole purpose of pleasing visiting Ofsted inspectors. Yep, I'm back to the 'Big O' again.

Here's the thing, I am not against the idea of an inspectorate. Of course we need to ensure, especially with issues such as safeguarding, that schools are maintaining the standards they should – and I know some schools are underperforming, some schools need help and support – but at this point, you will never convince me that Ofsted in its current form is a force for good in education. The best thing they could probably do right now is deep dive into a bin.

So, next is a quick explainer for any parents reading this that are not quite as familiar with what Ofsted do in our schools (teachers and school staff may want to skip the next paragraph if you are already far too well-versed on what happens when our 'critical friends' are paying a visit).

Ofsted is a regulatory and inspection body in England, responsible for inspecting a range of educational institutions, including state schools and some independent schools. It was established in 1992 with the aim of maintaining high educational standards. Ofsted inspections are intended to provide an independent assessment of the quality and standards of education in schools, with findings made available to the public. Now that sounds good on paper, but the reality is that Ofsted are by far the main reason for the current crisis in the recruitment and retention of teachers. Despite them having a framework to follow for their inspections, there are a lot of inspectors who don't follow it. I recognise there are some great inspectors who are really understanding, supportive and helpful, but there are clearly others who should be nowhere near a school. The stories I have been sent about bullying headteachers, heads who left their school after scandal upon scandal and who are now Ofsted inspectors, are worrying to say the least. Critics argue that Ofsted judgements can be highly subjective, leading to inconsistencies in ratings between schools. This inconsistency may stem from the differing interpretations of standards by inspectors, leading to variability in the outcomes of inspections. Such variability can undermine the credibility of the judgements, making it difficult for parents and educators to trust the ratings unequivocally.

The elephant in the room when talking about modern education in the last year involves Ofsted being in the news for the wrong reason. The pressure to perform well in Ofsted inspections can create a high-stress environment for teachers and staff. This pressure often translates into a narrow focus on meeting specific inspection criteria, sometimes at the expense of broader educational values or innovative teaching methods. Critics argue that this environment contributes to high levels of stress among educators, exacerbating teacher burnout and leading to a higher turnover rate within the profession. This desperation to chase the best grade has been brought into the spotlight recently after the tragic story of Ruth Perry.

Ruth was the headteacher of Caversham Primary School in Reading, and tragically took her own life in January 2023 following an Ofsted inspection that downgraded her school from 'Outstanding' to 'Inadequate', the lowest possible rating. Upon hearing the news I was shocked, but sadly not surprised. I know this hasn't been the first case where a headteacher has died after an inspection, but I felt empowered to strive to make sure it was the last. I think the worrying thing is that most people could understand how Ruth could get to that point. After sharing and discussing the news on my social media I was inundated by people telling their stories. One headteacher said after the first day of the inspection he left school at midnight, driving home knowing full well that he wasn't going to make it home, and it was only a phone call from his wife that changed his course of action. I had another leader talk about leaving a note for her family as she walked to a bridge, where, luckily, a Good Samaritan talked her down. A teacher who was pregnant said the stress of an inspection and the level of scrutiny from a cold, heartless inspector made her miscarry. Another threw themselves down the stairs in the hope of breaking her leg so she didn't have to go into school and face the inspectors. This is what the toxic culture of Ofsted is doing to people.

I created an anonymous online form where people could share their experiences of Ofsted and within four days it had had nearly 300 submissions. Very few were positive, and many reflected similar stories to ones I have just shared. You might be thinking, surely it can't be that bad? In my job I have to be checked and monitored, etc., but with Ofsted they are expecting to visit Lamborghini schools when we have the budget of a Vauxhall Nova. For the past four years they have made it clear that schools cannot use Covid as an excuse for students falling behind or poor behaviour, then Amanda Spielman, the head of Ofsted, announced she was leaving, saying Covid had made a huge impact.

The issue is with the grading system; those one- to two-word gradings carry so much weight and can literally cost you your job. If you happen to get an inspection that concludes the school is inadequate, if the school is a local authority-maintained school it is required to become an academy under the sponsorship of an academy trust. This is seen as a way to facilitate rapid improvement through new leadership and access to additional resources. But the reality is it means the SLT will be replaced, followed by the staff.

On top of that you have the impact on the local area. Having followed the inquest into Ruth's death, which concluded that the Ofsted inspection contributed to it, the part that got to me was the conversation she'd had with her GP. The GP said Ruth had never had any previous issues with her mental health and it was the inspection that caused it. He also said that 'she worried that local house prices would fall and that the whole community would be angry at her'. In what world should headteachers, with all the stress and pressure they are already having to go through, be worrying about the house prices in the local area? And we wonder why headteacher vacancies are nearly a fifth higher now than before the pandemic.

At the time of writing, there is a little hope surrounding Ofsted, although its new head, who has actually worked in a school (which makes a change), has certainly got his work cut out. Within a week of taking the job he did more to acknowledge the issues with Ofsted than his predecessor. The coroner's report from Ruth's death will force changes, and there have been recent calls from MPs for radical change including scrapping the one-word judgements. Only time will tell whether it happens, but if there is anything to learn from this, as a parent, it's to take an Ofsted inspection report with a pinch of salt.

I also wanted to recognise Ruth here. Ruth Perry was a beacon of dedication, passion and unwavering commitment to the world of education. Ruth's journey as a headteacher at Caversham Primary School was marked by an extraordinary devotion to her students' growth, well-being and academic excellence. Her legacy is not defined by the challenges of her final days but by the countless moments of inspiration, guidance and care that she offered to her school community. Ruth's story is a poignant reminder of the immense pressure that educators face and the profound impact they have on the lives of young learners. She championed the cause of education with grace and resilience, making a lasting difference in the hearts and minds of those she taught and worked with. As we remember Ruth, let us also reflect on the essential values she embodied: kindness, dedication and the relentless pursuit of creating a nurturing environment for every child. Her legacy urges us to advocate for a supportive and understanding system that recognises the human aspect of teaching, emphasising the need for compassion and support for educators who give so much of themselves. May Ruth Perry's memory continue to inspire a renewed dialogue on the well-being of teachers and the pivotal role they play in shaping our future. Let her dedication to her students and her profession be a guiding light for educational communities everywhere, reminding us of the strength, courage and love that lie at the heart of teaching.

One school, after receiving 'THE CALL', as it's affectionately known by school staff and governors, decided to send a message in response.

The head of the school made it clear that despite it being a legal requirement, the HM Inspectorate would not be welcome on site. Parents and school staff on social media praised the actions as a defiant gesture and standing up for what they feel is right. There was a beautiful moment that made national headlines where the entire school staff congregated at the gates to show solidarity. The assigned inspectors may have been wonderful humans and experienced practitioners, but on that day, it was essential that a stand was made. Sadly, it's incredibly hard to make gestures like that without consequences, but it shows that there is a desire for change.

Unfortunately, there's much more that needs changing. Getting angry about Ofsted is something I could do until the cows come home – and I regularly do it on my social media channels – but I just hope this tragedy will be a proper wake-up call for how schools are inspected, and, more importantly, supported in the future. I've plenty of answers to the questions as to what we do next, but we definitely need the people who are making the decisions to listen better.

Throughout this book and in our previous literary efforts, we've made light of some of the ridiculous behaviours and things that children say and do. Children are hilarious and some are bloody hard work, but at the end of the day, the overwhelming majority of the pupils we come into contact with or have the pleasure of meeting are absolute superstars.

There are some days when I'm teaching, and the first face I see as I walk into the classroom is a child that will go out of their way to make the world a better place. Children like them make it all worthwhile. Yes, the next face you see could be a child who is dead set on pushing as many of their teacher's buttons as possible, but if school staff are given the time and the resources to unpick his or her behaviour and understand the whole child, we might be able to better help them. It may take until break time to fully appreciate their presence, but they are just as deserving of a decent day in school... even if the first interaction with them is slightly rude or negative. Every child deserves to be able to achieve their best.

I've made a lot of comments over the years about how the education system in this country could be so much better than it has been for the last near-decade and a half.

In the next chapter I'll try to address how technology will be a key factor in hopefully making some of that a reality. For now, the biggest issue is the difference between talk and action with regards to improving personal well-being in schools. Speaking about improving people's well-being and doing something about it are often completely different things, though.

Earlier in this chapter, I put huge emphasis on the importance of sport in education, because I believe it is critical for empowering children to succeed in all areas and nothing would make me happier than to see things change for the better in that direction. Adam's surprisingly sensible take on SEND in schools and how it is hideously underfunded reflects the sad reality for so many families in this country as well. I hope there is some sort of change on the horizon, but I won't hold my breath just yet. Schools are filled with the most incredibly dedicated staff who just could do with the time to slow down and spend longer helping the children they work with to find their own ways in the world and be problem-solvers rather than statistics or exam robots.

Speaking of robots...

The Future starts Today

Apologies for the crap title of this chapter, but it was hard to think of something that wasn't a direct quote from a movie either set in the future or featuring time travel. The purpose of this chapter...

... is because Lee is addicted to talking about artificial intelligence (AI) and nobody will listen to him (apart from his mate, Dr Chips), so he thought he'd put all his thoughts in this book.

Well, yes and no. There are plenty of people interested in AI and it's going to seriously inform the next stage of our development as educators, so it's better to get on board now because the children we teach and our own children are going to be living it. The future really does start here. I mean, this book is about surviving the school year, and every year we somehow manage to survive. It's hard for teachers, hard for parents, and unless we give them a fighting chance, hardest for the children. If you were to have asked Leeroy Parkinson in 1998, when I was in my early secondary school years, if I believed that primary-aged children would be learning using a table-mat-sized touch-screen supercomputer that takes pictures, plays music and movies, and can video-call other such devices, I'd have asked what you'd been smoking. I'd only just got my head around *International Superstar Soccer Pro* on the first PlayStation.

As for predicting the future, we've already reached 2015, where Marty McFly time-travelled to in *Back to the Future Part II*. And yes, every time I think of this film I remain peeved that there are no real hoverboards. *Blade Runner*'s dystopian Los Angeles of 2019 had flying cars, but we're still waiting for those to become commercially available. The futuristic 1987 Arnold Schwarzenegger film *The Running Man* was set in 2019, and the worst reality show we have is *I'm a Celebrity*. Rather than chasing people around to murder them, we get Matt Hancock munching on kangaroo b*llocks.

My point is, we're already living in the future, according to the pop culture we grew up with, so what will the further future bring? When our children are the grown-ups we rely upon, we'll be the old farts saying that music these days isn't like the classics, you know, like Blink-182 and the Cheeky Girls. Chances are Mick Jagger and the Rolling Stones will still be touring, so watch out.

Where does teaching go in the next 20 years, what new initiatives will take education forward? Will teachers still be marking? Probably, because, despite the modern world moving on so much, schools are extraordinarily slow to catch up. Some would argue that this is a good thing, that it is one of the last aspects of life that reminds us of the good old days. But ultimately, our job as teachers is to educate, which includes education around technology. I truly believe that most of the issues we are facing with modern technology, such as social media, can best be addressed through education. My generation, and those who are older, have struggled; we've had to adapt quickly and therefore haven't had any education around using social media. But we need to make sure the next generation doesn't make the same mistakes we've made. I came across some troubling figures on Danny Nicholson's Whiteboard Blog about Ofcom's 2024 report into children's media use and attitudes. Of children aged between 5 and 7, 25 per cent own a smartphone, 38 per cent access social media platforms, around a third use social media unsupervised and half watch livestream content (which can contain a lot of dodgy stuff). And of children aged between 8 and 17, most use social media passively (scrolling/watching), but 3 in 10 are actively engaged (posting/commenting), while 4 in 10 are content creators and produce videos for platforms like TikTok and YouTube. And this last one isn't a surprise, but it's still worrying; only a third of parents know the correct minimum-age requirements for social media platforms. And now, we are about to enter a whole new world with the emerging AI technology that is coming along.

It has been said that we are about to go through the biggest industrial revolution of our lifetime. Now, if you are a similar age to myself, we've been through many technological advances, and often teachers will say to me, 'The problem is, with kids, they just know more than I do about technology.' While I don't necessarily agree with that, what I will say is that the one thing children don't have with technology is any sort of resilience. Now, that is not their fault, and we cannot blame them. They are the product of their environment, growing up in a world where technology works, whereas my generation is genuinely surprised when technology does work. The number of open gasps and 'ahs' I hear in my training when I show a simple tool, like how a 3D shape can unfold to show different aspects to people's faces, and teachers react as if that's the greatest thing they have ever seen. Now, I don't want this to become a comparison of generations, because I absolutely detest when that happens. But you know, I don't think kids realise the same struggles we went through growing up. Suddenly, we all had these mobile phones in our hands. Remember the first Nokia 3210 you had, and how you spent hours, days, weeks, trying to program a ringtone into the keypad so that it could go off on the bus and you could look so cool as those dulcet tones bashed out the latest Eminem song? Remember the struggles of just trying to get on the internet through dial-up and shouting to your mum downstairs to get off the phone to a friend so you could log on to MSN Messenger, hearing that screeching noise that still haunts our nightmares? Kids just don't know the struggle of trying to download an album on Napster or LimeWire without completely infecting their family PC with a virus. Remember the early days of social media? Remember when we used to poke each other? Do you remember that, or MySpace, where you actually had to code the site if you wanted a glittery title of what TV show you liked? But all of this is going to pale into insignificance compared with what's about to happen with AI.

I know that there is already apprehension among teachers in terms of AI. On my courses, I often get teachers saying things like, 'I'm not touching any of that AI stuff, and I don't want the robots to come and kill us all,' to which I reply, 'First of all, stop reading the *Daily Mail*, and secondly, the *Terminator* film is not based on historical fact.' Here's the thing: I can't sit here and say there won't be any negatives with artificial intelligence. There will be some incredible achievements, advancements and ways that will improve our lives, but there will also be some negatives. AI will not be the downfall of humanity, although how we choose to use it might. The robots aren't going to kill us, but there will be people who use artificial intelligence in negative ways. And I'm sure we're going to see this in the coming year, where we've got an election in the UK and also on the other side of the pond, with the opportunity people will take to create deep-fake AI videos of people saying certain things. But this is the point: we need to be educated. We need to be clued up to make sure we're navigating this new world in the right way. In the same way that people will argue that social media has been a fantastically positive tool to connect us as a society, while others say that it's been the worst thing that we've brought into our world, I suppose it depends on how we choose to use it. I think a lot of negativity comes from the fact that the majority of people using social media don't understand how it works, and so are highly susceptible to being manipulated and affected by those negative aspects of it.

So, what is AI, and how does it work? Artificial intelligence has been around for a long time. As a teacher who leads the subject of Computing in my school, one of the challenges is the constant risk of teaching a history of Computing. When I first started teaching, the subject was ICT (Information and Communication Technology), and we were all comfortable with that; it's what we learned in school. The problem with the old ICT curriculum was that it was far too focused on just simply using technology that most of us used in school, sort of 'death by Microsoft Office' – doing a spreadsheet, PowerPoint, and if you were lucky, a little bit of WordArt. Maybe you remember when you could get your title to curve in a semicircle in five different colours with a shadow?

Now, if you jump back to 10 years ago, there were nearly a million jobs going unfilled in this country because of a lack of digital skills. The workplace was crying out for software developers, programmers and coders. Just recently, I bumped into a parent of a student I used to teach, and asked, 'How is Oliver getting on?' His dad replied, 'Great, he's studying computer science at Manchester Uni.'

'Wow,' I replied.

'Yeah, he's getting paid £30k a year to do it!'

That's right, £30,000 a year to study. If you're reading this having been to uni yourself, please take a moment to imagine how different your university experience would have been with 30 grand a year. I raced back to school and started doing maths problems with my Year 4...

'Children, if it's three Jägerbombs for a tenner at the student union and I have £30,000, how many Jägerbombs can I get?'

My stepson is currently at uni studying business and he is likely to finish with over £60k's worth of debt. Oh, and the lad at Manchester has a job ready for him at the end, earning double what he was paid just for training.

That's where Michael Gove did possibly the one positive thing in his tenure, which was changing ICT to Computing and putting a much bigger focus on computer science and programming.

Holy crap, Lee! Did you just say nice things about Michael Gove?

Don't get used to it, Adam. On paper, this was the right thing to do. The reality, however, is that he didn't fund schools to get the hardware needed to actually teach an effective computing curriculum. Plus, he didn't invest in training for teachers. So, you ask most teachers, and they will say that Computing is the weakest area of the curriculum because we were never taught how to code or program. As a result, most teachers are just sort of winging it, going from the old IT curriculum – death by PowerPoint – to the new Computing curriculum, with 'death by Scratch', where teachers are scratching their heads and saying, 'Tell you what, why don't you make that cat dance or something?' Now, focusing on coding and programming was the right move. However, if we do not evolve our computing curriculum to embrace this emerging AI technology, by the time the children learning the current curriculum are of working age, AI is likely to perform most of the physical writing of the code. You can already get AI to do that now. Students having a thorough understanding of what the code can do and what problem the code is intended to solve will be incredibly important. However, the likelihood is that the physical writing of the code – the heavy lifting – will be done by AI.

So, how does AI work? When we think of a traditional computer, computers cannot think for themselves. What a computer does is follow a very clear algorithm, a set of instructions that it follows to carry out a certain task or job. AI works in a similar way; you are still coding, but you are essentially coding the AI to think in a similar way to how our brain thinks, by feeding it data. The more data you feed it, the more accurate it becomes in predicting the right result. It will never be 100 per cent accurate, but with enough data training, it can achieve 99.99 per cent accuracy. However, it's crucial to be aware that AI is only as good as the data it's trained on, so there are potential biases and examples of where AI can get things wrong based on bad data. For instance, there was a news article recently about some facial-recognition technology that couldn't accurately identify people of colour. Upon investigation, it was found that the data the AI was trained on was only from a certain demographic. So, you need to make sure that if you are creating your own AI, you are using a wide variety of data.

A simple task I've done with my class to teach how AI works through pattern recognition is to have them imagine they are artificial intelligence recognising whether an image depicts winter or summer. I start by showing lots of images of winter. These images act as data, and as the children analyse these images, they start to spot patterns. If I show you, the reader, lots of pictures of winter, you'll start picking up on patterns such as snow, bare trees, rain, darkness or people wearing coats and experiencing the cold, etc. The more images I show, the more confident you become in knowing whether something is set in winter. If I do the same thing with summer images, you will start noticing other patterns such as sunshine, bright-blue skies, leaves on the trees and people wearing shorts. Eventually, you will be able to predict whether an image is set in winter or summer based on all the data you have been trained on. This is a simple example of how AI works.

I've already started to build units within my Computing scheme of work to teach children about AI. I believe that by the time they leave primary school, they should know what AI is, recognise examples in their everyday lives, understand to an extent how it works, and further up the school, even have a go at creating their own machine-learning models.

Let's consider some ways in which you, the reader, interact with AI in your everyday lives. You might immediately think of devices like Alexa, Siri or Google Home, and other smart speakers, or features like AutoCorrect and facial recognition. You also encounter AI in your Apple or Google

Maps app when you input a route; if part of the route is red, it indicates there is a traffic jam, and it'll also predict how long that traffic jam will last based on data from people currently stuck in it. If you have a Netflix account, it uses data from what you're watching to then recommend and personalise your Netflix homepage. A significant area where AI plays a role is social media. Whether it's Twitter, Facebook, Instagram, TikTok or YouTube, when you log in to these platforms, you will see your 'For You' page or newsfeed full of content. AI is choosing the content you see based on the data of how you interact with the platform, what you've watched previously, what content you like and have commented on, but also data from people who are similar to you in terms of age, gender, location and demographic, etc.

And the question arises: what does social media want from you? Essentially, social media platforms want you to stay on their sites or apps for as long as possible. This is why they employ tools such as infinite scroll, ensuring you never reach the end of your newsfeed. The more time you spend on the platform, the more advertisements they can show you, and, consequently, the more money they make. You don't have to interact with those adverts, nor do you necessarily have to spend any money. Merely viewing them generates revenue for the platform. This highlights a key aspect of social media: you are not the customer; you are the product. Social media isn't free; you pay for it with your data. Once you understand this, you can start to navigate it with more awareness. You'll begin to grasp why you see certain pieces of content because the platform aims to keep you engaged. To achieve this, it often shows you content that validates your opinions and views on various issues.

This phenomenon leads us to spend hours in our little echo chambers, constantly being reassured that our perspectives are correct. This is one of the reasons why our society is now so polarised. Encountering someone with a differing opinion becomes challenging because we're so accustomed to being affirmed by the content on social media, never receiving a balanced view on any issue but rather a skewed one based on our beliefs and opinions.

I'll provide a simple example of this. I'm sure many of you have disagreed with someone from a different generation in your family over the Prince Harry and Meghan story. Personally, I'm very much Team Harry. He's around my age, and I believe if he doesn't want to be part of the royal family anymore, he should do whatever makes him happy. On the other hand, my mother-in-law, who is a bit older, is a staunch royalist and can't fathom why the couple would turn their back on what she sees as the greatest institution of our country. Now, guess who had my mother-in-law for Secret Santa this Christmas? Oh yes, she received a copy of Harry's book, along with a commemorative tea towel of their wedding. Our differing opinions are largely shaped by the content we are exposed to through our social media feeds.

There are both benefits and negatives associated with AI-powered algorithms on social media. A significant negative is that AI cannot evaluate the content it presents to us. It only has data on viewer engagement but lacks the capacity to discern whether content is truthful or potentially harmful. Taking the recent controversy surrounding Andrew Tate as an example, the platforms are largely at fault for not having mechanisms in place to monitor content. They relied solely on data indicating high engagement among boys aged 13 to 24 years old and, as a result, pushed this content to as many in that demographic as possible. Some of these young individuals weren't actively seeking it out; it simply appeared on their newsfeed. Engaging with such content signals to the platform that they approve of it, leading to more similar content being shown, and before long, they may find themselves entrenched in a way of thinking that can be misleading and dangerous.

However, understanding how these algorithms work can turn this into a positive. For me, my favourite CPD (Continuing Professional Development) platform over the past year has been TikTok. Now, you might wonder how, considering it's predominantly known for videos of people doing lip-syncs and dances. The key is to be in control of the AI algorithm rather than letting it control you. If I'm looking for new ideas to use in class, I actively search on TikTok for educational content, new websites for teachers, etc. This informs the algorithm about the type of content I want to see. Currently, I'm on a health kick, trying to exercise more and eat better to lose some weight before I leave my 30s. Consequently, my 'For You' page on TikTok is filled with useful teaching resources, some Manchester United content, but mainly recipes for low-calorie, high-protein meals.

It's crucial to be in control of the AI algorithm and not let it dictate your content consumption. This is also an important consideration if your children are starting to use social media. I must admit, I've recently allowed my children to have social media after holding off for as long as I could. However, I've set clear boundaries: they get one hour a day on TikTok, and at the end of each day, they hand over their devices to me for charging in my room. Before I go to bed, I check their watch history to monitor their activity. Additionally, I 'hack' the AI algorithm for them by searching for and engaging with content I deem appropriate, such as football skills videos, rugby tutorials, fun history facts suitable for 12-year-olds, or whatever topic they're studying in class, like *A Christmas Carol* by Charles Dickens. This strategy lets TikTok know the kind of content I want my children to see, leveraging the algorithm to our advantage.

There will also be numerous incredible advancements in the medical field due to artificial intelligence, along with discussions about us all having fully automated self-driving cars. The future, indeed, looks interesting. But for now, what can we do with the AI we currently have access to? As a teacher, I don't think there has been anything that has had such an immediate impact on reducing workload as this new strand of generative AI. As I've mentioned in this book, teachers find themselves in a dire situation, working an average of 57 hours a week. Last year, over 40,000 teachers left the profession, and that number doesn't include those who retired or took early retirement. Nearly 60 per cent of teachers are seriously considering leaving the profession, with workload being one of the main reasons. Two-thirds of staff cite workload as the primary reason for contemplating leaving their jobs. Seven out of ten teachers say their workloads are unacceptable, two-thirds report spending over half their time on non-teaching tasks, and a quarter of teachers spend more than three hours a week searching for resources online.

I'm not suggesting that AI will solve all of these issues. As I've already stated, significant structural changes regarding government and Ofsted are necessary. However, in such a desperate situation, anything that can help is worth exploring. Ideally, in a world where teachers were trusted and our education system wasn't broken, teachers wouldn't necessarily need to use AI for certain tasks. But if AI can write and handle paperwork as well as if I had done it myself, is it the best use of my time to do it manually? The type of AI I'm referring to here is this new strand of generative AI. Traditionally, AI focused mainly on pattern recognition, whereas generative AI, or what you might see referred to as large language models (LLMs), can actually create content.

To explain how this technology works, I use the analogy of asking AI to build a Lego structure. What the AI has access to are billions of Lego bricks, but these are not actual bricks; they are words and phrases from pretty much everything that has ever been published on the internet. This includes websites, web articles, news articles, PDFs, etc. up until the past year as the dataset. So, when you ask the AI to write something, it's picking up these 'bricks' (words or phrases) and deciding if they fit, discarding some, and replacing others until it builds what it considers to be the perfect answer, all at an incredible speed.

I'm often asked by teachers what the AI is trained on, and the answer is the internet. Another question is whether using this sort of AI technology is considered cheating, to which I reply, would you consider using Google cheating? What's really important, and something I constantly discuss in my training, is that using this technology as a teacher has two steps. The first step is to use the technology to create content, but equally, if not more important, is to then check and use your professional judgement to ensure what it creates is accurate and useful. You should always assume it's not entirely right; what it considers perfect will not always align with what we consider perfect. Most of the time, it's not far off, but it will always need tweaking, changing and adjusting. This is where we really need to consider intellectual integrity.

So, many of you are likely aware of ChatGPT from the company OpenAI, which has become the market leader in the large language model of generative AI. OpenAI has been on my radar for a number of years, but when they released ChatGPT in December 2022, things dramatically changed. It took Netflix a year to gain one million users, Instagram seven months, but ChatGPT achieved this in just five days. I've not seen anything else have such an immediate impact in disrupting so many different industries. I know many teachers are using ChatGPT and deriving great benefits from it. It's free, and if you haven't tried it yet, I encourage you to do so. However, for teachers, there are a couple of things to be mindful of. Firstly, the dataset for ChatGPT is vast, so teachers need to be very specific with their inputs to get the best outputs. Understanding how to effectively prompt it for content can be time-consuming. Additionally, there are GDPR (General Data Protection Regulation) concerns, since everything you input into ChatGPT is used for learning. It's not free in the traditional sense; we pay for it by contributing data.

Some councils and schools have banned it, but there are numerous beneficial ways it can be used. In fact, I've been so captivated by this AI that I helped build a platform that harnesses language-based AI specifically for teachers. In April 2023, TeachMateAI.com was launched. What sets TeachMateAI apart from ChatGPT is its full GDPR compliance; the AI does not retain any data, and all account data is stored in the UK. We've also trained the AI on more specific educational data and streamlined it for minimal input from teachers to get maximum output. Since its launch, it has helped save teachers over 10 hours a week each. With over 100 tools available, many focused on administrative tasks that otherwise detract from teaching, it offers significant assistance. For example, if you were to go on *Family Fortunes* and Gino D'Acampo said to you, we asked 100 teachers what's your favourite task to do as a teacher and you said write a risk assessment, a big cross would appear, but on TeachMateAI, the AI can take on the heavy lifting for that alongside other admin tasks.

The platform also aids in creating bespoke resources for lessons, generating comprehension tasks, model texts and other useful resources without hours of online searching. It's particularly beneficial for supporting children with SEND, adapting tasks, explaining concepts and offering ideas to make classrooms more inclusive. Upon its release, it assisted in writing over 120,000 reports. I did get quite a few negative messages on social media from parents who were outraged that teachers would use AI in this way, and how it completely detracts from the end-of-year written report. I didn't reply online because I have learned over the past 10 to 12 years that you cannot argue with anyone on the internet, but I was tempted to reply saying, if you think this is the first time a teacher has tried to cut corners in writing reports which they are expected to do in their own time and don't get paid any extra for, you are deluded. The chances are the report you are reading for your child was probably originally written for a student in 1998.

When teachers are NQTs (newly qualified teachers), when they don't know any better and because it is their first class that they go on such a journey with and who really mould them into the teacher they become, they spend weeks, months on those lengthy individualised reports. Then the year after, when they have to start from scratch, with so many other things going on, they do not have time for that, so they load up all their NQT reports and go, 'Right, Billy from my NQT class. Who is most like Billy this year?' and you just change the name. I can assure you no teacher in this country has ever done anything like that ;-). The feedback from teachers about using TeachMateAI to help with reports was that it not only saves time but also helped create the most personalised reports ever, because the teacher still identifies individual student strengths and areas for improvement, which the AI crafts into cohesive paragraphs.

This tool is poised to become incredibly useful for teachers, and while some have concerns about it de-skilling the profession, I believe it should be viewed as a tool to empower teachers to work smarter, not harder.

One question I am frequently asked is whether children should be using generative AI. As a primary school teacher, my view is that children at this stage don't necessarily need to use AI. They should first master the skills of writing, punctuation and grammar to understand how to write well. However, the conversation shifts when it comes to older students. I receive many inquiries from college tutors, sixth form teachers and university lecturers asking for advice on how to monitor the use of AI by their students. When asked about students using ChatGPT, my instinctive reaction is to say, 'I'm really jealous,' because I wish it had been around when I was at uni. It would've made my life so much easier. I remember doing a four-year BA degree in primary education and having to do a dissertation that would have no bearing on whether I could teach a group of children. I spent months writing 15,000 words on 'How interactive is an interactive whiteboard?' My answer can be summarised as 'not very', so if I had AI to help with some of that, it would've made my life a lot easier.

This brings us to the concept of intellectual integrity. AI can be a useful tool for checking and finding information, but it shouldn't simply replace the learning process. Teachers who know their students well should be able to discern if a child has used AI to write an essay, especially if there's a sudden, dramatic improvement in the quality of their work. This situation could spark a discussion about the best ways to assess student learning and whether emerging AI technology could signal the end of coursework. Although writing has never been my strong suit – indeed, I've dictated quite a bit of this – having good ideas and being able to present them effectively, whether through informative or humorous means, have always been my strength.

The question then becomes whether similar presentation tasks could be used to assess children's learning. It's likely that the government may double down on exams as the only fair reflection of a student's learning, but the future remains to be seen. The use of AI in education presents both challenges and opportunities, and it's crucial to navigate this landscape thoughtfully to ensure that students not only develop their academic skills but also maintain their intellectual integrity.

If you skipped this chapter because you just wanted to read fart jokes and stories about teachers making silly mistakes, I don't blame you. The world is an incredibly serious place and sometimes, it's the funny stuff that we need the most. Adam will definitely not have read this far!

Yes, I have! And anyway, how do I know this part of the book wasn't written by AI?

Well, you don't!

(Cue *X-Files* music)

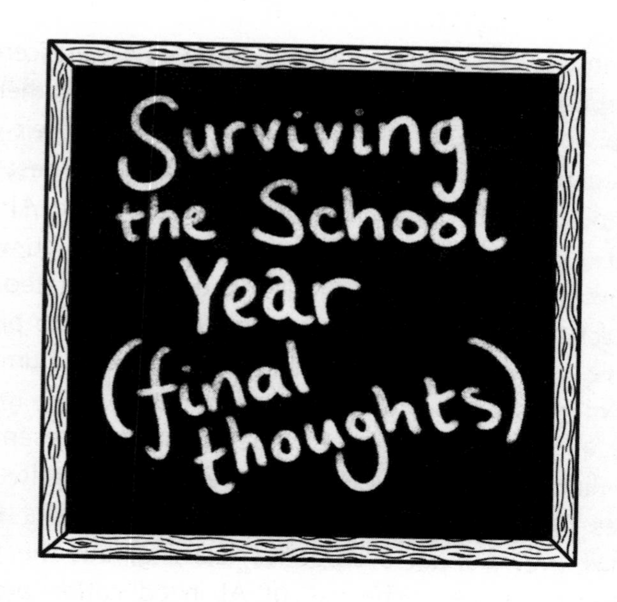

As the title of this book, *How to Survive the School Year*, suggests, the school year can be tough, really tough for some, and while plenty of the problems can be self-inflicted, it's easy to become overwhelmed when caring for primary children at home and at school.

Life is tricky for everyone, but whether you've got one child, two children, three children or 30 little darlings in a Year 2 class that struggle to sit still, having to be there for all their needs is challenging. I'm guessing you bought this book (or someone purchased it for you) because you either have children/grandchildren/nieces/nephews or you're a teacher/TA/school staff. Whatever your reason for being in possession of this book, even if you found it on a train and forgot to pass it on to lost property, you'll hopefully have read a few crazy tales, giggled at the shared experience of trying to plod through another school year and, most of all, realised that you're not on your own.

Whatever lies you see on Instagram, TikTok and Facebook about how perfect everyone else's life seems to be, as long as you're doing your best to bring up, teach or take good care of the small people you are responsible for, then you should give yourself credit for that. The swan analogy is a pretty good one, as while a swan looks flawless and graceful above the surface, gliding across the water as if it approached life without a care in the world, it's the legs paddling away furiously underneath the water that show the true experience of being a teacher or a parent in the modern world.

Keeping your head above water in such tricky circumstances IS ENOUGH. Your best IS good enough. It is all worth it, even if it doesn't feel like it sometimes. As we said at the start of this book, THIS IS NOT A PARENTING GUIDE. Adam and I are far from qualified to dish out parenting hacks or advice. The only advice is to feed them, clothe them, talk to them and teach them not to be knobheads.

Also, if they are young enough, watch plenty of *Hey Duggee*, as it's good for the soul.

If you're a teacher/TA (and or parent) reading this book, then hopefully you've spotted plenty in here that made you laugh and you realise that nobody is expecting you to do a perfect job. Well, I say nobody, just the SLT, Ofsted and particularly difficult parents. Also, watch out for the children that know far more about the adult world than they should at primary age, because they'll be judging the hell out of your every move! Other than that, you're sorted.

We've looked at plenty of funny things from inside and outside the classroom, lots of teacher fails, lots of parenting fails and, as always, remembered that primary-aged children continue to be the funniest accidental comedians in the world.

True that! I work with at least a hundred of them currently.

Half of what the current crop of parents and qualified teachers used to get up to in their youth hasn't been captured on camera phones, videos and the internet in general, and that's a huge relief. You might find an older, grainy clip of yourself from years gone by miming to 'Barbie Girl' or practising some backyard wrestling. There may be clips of you being a little sh*t at Auntie Doreen's birthday party that your family has never let you live down. Kids these days don't have that luxury, as their every smile, laugh, fart, sporting achievement, dance performance and meltdown in Tesco can easily be captured and shared with the world and their dog on social media. Equally, videos of their youth can be stored as evidence to be used at a later date or to help the police with their enquiries (Adam).

I'm starting to get worried!

Our young people need healthy adults, and that goes for mind, body and (if you believe in it) spirit. Modern parents and school staff seem to have WAY more in common with the younger generation than previous generations. Use that in a positive way.

Teachers and school staff will connect with their children in whatever way possible. Mr Hayden may be able to connect with his kids by sharing his love of Pokémon, Miss O'Grady is definitely still cool and her Year 6 class know it. The look on a child's face when they realise that their teacher shares similar interests is priceless.

A teacher can go from meticulously insisting that their class is lined up in silence to having a deep conversation with a child at break time about who is better, Ronaldo or Messi. They agree to disagree but that doesn't stop the child trying hard in the upcoming maths lesson. In fact, if little Dylan gets all of his long division questions right then the teacher will be willing to concede that his own answer of Zinedine Zidane may not be helping the discussion.

I've said it before and I'll say it again, teaching children is, was and should be the greatest job in the world. If you can strike a balance with the parents and children where there's a level of mutual respect and understanding, it's incredible. Memories of awesome times are made and the children will take them into their adult lives.

Sadly, it gets harder in the current climate and it's not completely untrue to say that home and school seem pitted against each other.

It works best when home and school work as a team, but I know that there are many parents and teachers that deliberately make everyone's lives difficult. Unfortunately, we can't round up all of these people and send them to the same school, so you just have to tread carefully and have minimal interaction with them where possible.

This book was named *How to Survive the School Year* because we understand that it often feels like we're all just trying to bumble through the week/month/term/year without causing too many problems. When many people hear the word 'survival', they often think of Bear Grylls, scouting/guiding or reality shows where people are stuck on an island with a penknife, a torch and half a packet of Polos. Survival is defined as:

noun

1. the state or fact of continuing to live or exist, typically in spite of an accident, ordeal, or difficult circumstances.

This is pretty much what we're all trying to do – accidents, ordeals or difficult circumstances permitting!

To quote the legendary musician, Prince:

> 'Dearly beloved, we are gathered here today to get through this thing called life!'

And that lyric, as most of you will be aware, is from the 1985 song 'Let's Go Crazy' that's on the *Purple Rain* soundtrack. We're not suggesting you all go crazy (figuratively or literally) but being able to get through life is the task at hand. Whatever you read, watch or hear on Facebook, Instagram, TikTok or Twitter/X from grifters that try to make out that everyone is too soft or sensitive these days, they may be suffering from a huge deficit of empathy. These people may make you wish that you could go around their house and go crazy, but perhaps don't do that. You could write them a strongly worded letter or email them with advice about being a kinder person, but the best way to deal with folks that exist to make other people miserable is to ignore them. Don't give them the satisfaction of them knowing they have got to you. BAMO, block and move on! If there are people in real life that you can't stand, just avoid them. You need to get through life in your own way and on your own terms.

Getting through is the key; succeed as much as you can but don't forget to look after yourself in the process. The young people (either at home or in the classroom) in your care need the healthiest version of you to help guide them through what is an increasingly hard yet equally exciting future. As we said at the start, we're not overly keen on giving advice in this book but here are a few tips you may wish to follow:

Dedicate time for yourself.
Open your mind to new ideas.
Give others your time when they need it most.

Take a step back to appreciate what is most important to you.
Use your time wisely and don't waste energy on being angry.
Relax and reenergise yourself.
Don't beat yourself up about things you can't control.
Smile!

Oh crap, I've just realised that the starting letters of each tip spell DOG TURDS. Well, there you go, final tip is to try not to step in **dog turds!**

Well done for surviving this book, and at whatever point of the school year you are reading it, I hope you're managing to keep your sh*t together. If you're struggling, reach out to someone that you trust or someone not involved with your situation. Budgets in the UK are tight for everything but there is help out there. Remember, the first step towards helping yourself can be the hardest. It may be that you feel trapped and need help getting back on your feet, you may be struggling financially with the cost of living, you may have some feelings of not being good enough and you might benefit from speaking to a professional. It also may be that you just need a night out with your mates where you can let your hair down and have a giggle.

We hope you've enjoyed reading our book about surviving the school year.

Now.... LET'S GO CRAZY!

Take care of yourselves, and each other.

Acknowledgements

From Lee

To Paul, our agent at Headway Talent, thank you for all your continued hard work and support. To Tim (@sadlerdoodles), thank you for all the brilliant work and support you have put in to this book. And, of course, to my brother from the same mother, Adam... 👍

None of this would be possible without my incredible other half, Claire. People often ask how I manage to do everything: teach, lead training, make videos, do the podcast, write and tour. The answer is my selfless wife Claire. She handles all the unseen tasks that keep the ship afloat. Her support and inspiration drive me to excel in everything I do, and I am forever grateful for her hard work, which often goes unnoticed.

To my beautiful children Callum, Harry, Charlie and Lily, being your dad is the best job in the world. You make me incredibly proud with your kindness, care, humour and beauty, even though you think I'm 'mid with no rizz'.

To my family and friends, thank you for all the support.

The success of the podcast, books and tour would not be possible without the most important piece of the puzzle... you guys. From the early days of blogging to the social media pages, teacher training, the podcast and tours, I am forever grateful for all your support. Nothing inspires me more nor continues to keep me motivated than reading your messages about how my ideas or funny insights have resonated and helped. I want to carry on helping, supporting and elevating the teaching profession to where it needs to be, and will always work hard to do so.

From Adam

To all my colleagues past and present, thank you for allowing me to do the job I love. To my friends, absolute legends, love you all. To my parents, your love and support has made me who I am and I'm forever grateful. To my wife Kim and children Isla and Max, everything I do, it's with you in mind, to make you proud. I would also like to take this opportunity to thank Lee; his hard work enabled the podcast to have a head start and he allowed me to share this wild journey with him – always appreciate you, brother!

From Tim

Thank you to my gorgeous and supportive wife Sarah (The Business Mum) and my two favourite dudes Michael and David.

Much love to my mum (Maggie), my dad (Paul) and my brother Gordon. My late sister Katie deserves a mention too.

To Lee, thank you so much for everything. Thanks for taking me with you on this amazing journey and helping me to achieve things beyond my wildest dreams. I will always be grateful.

Cheers, Adam, as well, you big monkey clown!